# MCAT®

## Critical Analysis and
## Reasoning Skills Workbook

2016 Edition

Jennifer Wooddell, Senior Editor and Question Writer

Gina Granter, M.A.
Alix Claps, M.A.

Edited for Production by
Judene Wright, M.S., M.A.Ed., National Content Director, MCAT Program, The Princeton Review

The Princeton Review would also like to thank all the writers and editors of previous editions for their contributions.

The MCAT is a registered trademark of the Association of American Medical Colleges, which does not sponsor or endorse this product.

The Princeton Review is not affiliated with Princeton University.

Copyright © 2014, 2011, 2010, 2009, 2008, 2007, 2005, 2001, 2000, 1999, 1998, 1997 by
TPR Education IP Holdings, LLC
All rights reserved.

2016 Edition

This manual is for the exclusive use of Princeton Review course students, and is not legal for resale.
PrincetonReview.com

# Contents

**Practice Passages** ............................................................ 1

**Practice Passages Solutions** ............................................. 47

**MCAT CARS Practice Tests**

**Practice Test 1** ................................................................ 101

    Answer Key ................................................................. 120

    Practice Test 1 Solutions ........................................... 125

**Practice Test 2** ................................................................ 141

    Answer Key ................................................................. 160

    Practice Test 2 Solutions ........................................... 165

**Practice Test 3** ................................................................ 183

    Answer Key ................................................................. 202

    Practice Test 3 Solutions ........................................... 207

**Practice Test 4** ................................................................ 225

    Answer Key ................................................................. 244

    Practice Test 4 Solutions ........................................... 249

# MCAT
# Critical Analysis and Reasoning Skills

# Practice Passages

## Passage 1 (Questions 1-7)

Often, the central problem in any business is that money is needed to make money. The following discusses the sale of equity, which is one response to this problem.

The sale of capital stock is a way to obtain money, through the sale of stock to individual investors beyond the scope of one's immediate acquaintances. Periods of high interest rates turn entrepreneurs to this equity market. This involves, of necessity, a dilution of ownership, and many owners are reluctant to take this step for that reason. Whether the owner is wise in declining to use outside equity financing depends upon the firm's long-range prospects. If there is an opportunity for substantial expansion on a continuing basis and if other sources are inadequate, the owner may decide logically to bring in other owners. Owning part of a larger business may be more profitable than owning all of a smaller business.

One way to sell capital stock is through private placement. This means that the firm's capital stock is sold to selected individuals, who are most likely to be the firm's employees, the owner's acquaintances, local residents, customers, and suppliers. Private sale of stock is difficult because the new firm is not known and has no ready market for its securities. However, the entrepreneur avoids many requirements of the securities law when a stock sale is restricted to a private placement.

However, some firms "go public" by making their stock available to the general public. These are typically the larger small-business firms. The reason often cited for a public sale is the need for additional working capital or, less frequently, for other capital needs. The personal financial objectives of owners may also enter into the reasoning behind the public sale of stock.

In undertaking the public sale of stock, the small firm subjects itself to greater public regulation. There are state regulations pertaining to the public sale of securities, and the Securities and Exchange Commission (SEC) also exercises surveillance over such offerings. The SEC is quite tolerant of small offerings, however, by permitting "Regulation A" offerings to be sold with minimum requirements for financial data and information.

Common stock may also be sold to underwriters, who guarantee the sale of securities. The compensation and fees paid to underwriters typically make the sale of securities in this manner expensive. The fees themselves may range from 10 percent to 30 percent, with 18 percent to 25 percent being typical. In addition, there are options and other fees that may run the actual costs higher. The reason for the high expense is, of course, the element of uncertainty and risk associated with public offerings of stock of small, relatively unknown firms.

Studies of public sale of stock by small firms reveal the fact that small companies frequently make financial arrangements that are not sound. Indeed, the lack of knowledge on the part of small-firm owners often leads to arrangements with brokers or securities dealers that are not in the best interest of the small firms.

The condition of the financial markets at any given time has a direct bearing on the prospects for the sale of capital stock. Entrepreneurs found the early years of the 1980s to be strong for new-venture stock sales. For example, George Ryan, founder and chairman of CADO Systems Corp., a microprocessor-computer manufacturer, said that going public with a stock sale was easy because "today's venture market is so hot that if you had a corner hot dog stand, you could take it public. There is a push to take companies public." Market conditions do change, however, and therefore must be studied carefully.

Adapted from *Small Business Management*, 6th ed.,
© 1983 South-Western Publishing Co.

1.  The passage implies that an owner who chooses not to sell capital stock despite the prospect of continued expansion is:

    A.  subject to increased regulation.
    B.  more conservative than might be necessary under the circumstances.
    C.  likely to lose control of the business.
    D.  sacrificing security for rapid growth.

2.  Based on information from the passage, what might prompt an owner to sell stock through a private placement offering?

    A.  Raising capital without diluting ownership
    B.  Raising capital without incurring debt
    C.  Raising capital with less interference from the SEC
    D.  Desiring the general public to become co-owners

3.  According to the passage, under what circumstances might owners decide to take their firms public?

    A.  When they have personal reasons for wanting to raise money
    B.  When an underwriter offers to guarantee the sale for an unusually low rate (e.g., 10 percent)
    C.  When they want the firm to grow rapidly
    D.  When the firm is very small (e.g., a hot dog stand)

4.  When a firm goes public through an underwriter, all of the following are true EXCEPT that:

    A.  the more money the firm raises in the sale, the more the underwriter profits.
    B.  if no one will buy stock in the new firm, the underwriter contributes the capital.
    C.  the high fees charged by underwriters may offset the costs they incur when a company fails.
    D.  the underwriter's profits are relatively low in the case of private placement offerings.

5.  Which one of the following about capital stock can be inferred from the passage?

    A.  A firm's employees can only buy private stock in that firm, not capital stock.
    B.  Those who have capital stock in a company own part of that company.
    C.  The lack of knowledge about capital stock of small-firm owners leads to many business bankruptcies.
    D.  The sale of capital stock is the most common way businesses generate capital.

6.  Which of the following best expresses the main idea of the passage?

    A.  The condition of financial markets influences the success of businesses.
    B.  The sale of equity is one way for businesses to raise money.
    C.  Relatively unknown firms can succeed through public offerings of stock.
    D.  The stock market is intrinsically related to the business world.

7.  Based on the passage, which one of the following statements most accurately describes SEC policy?

    A.  The SEC keeps a close eye on small firms because they frequently make financial arrangements that are not sound.
    B.  The SEC seeks to protect business owners from the risks of venture capitalism.
    C.  The SEC seeks to protect the public from the risks of venture capitalism.
    D.  The SEC limits the fees underwriters can charge.

## Passage 2 (Questions 1-6)

In *Prometheus Bound* Aeschylus writes:

> …At first
> Senseless as beasts I gave men sense,
> possessed them of mind…
> In the beginning, seeing, they saw amiss,
> and hearing, heard not, but like phantoms huddled
> In dreams, the perplexed story of their days
> Confounded.

Prometheus is in a fit of righteous indignation. He has introduced civilization to a befuddled and superstitious mankind, and for his pains Zeus has chained him to a rock and set a vulture to pluck at his liver. In the passage following the above quotation, Prometheus describes the principal gifts, other than fire, that he has bestowed on mankind. They are, in order: astronomy; mathematics; writing; the domestication of animals; the invention of chariots, sailing ships and medicine; and the discovery of divination by dreams and other methods. The final gift strikes the modern ear as odd. Along with the account in Genesis of the exile from Eden, *Prometheus Bound* seems to be one of the major works in Western literature that presents a viable allegory of the evolution of man—although in this case concentrating much more on the "evolver" than on the evolved. "Prometheus" is Greek for "foresight," that quality claimed to reside in the frontal lobes of the neocortex; and foresight and anxiety are both present in Aeschylus' character portrait.

What is the connection between dreams and the evolution of man? Aeschylus is perhaps saying that our prehuman ancestors lived their waking lives in a state akin to our dreaming lives; and that one of the principal benefits of the development of human intelligence is our ability to understand the true nature and import of dreams.

There are, it seems, three principal states of mind in human beings: waking, sleeping, and dreaming. An electroencephalograph, which detects brain waves, records quite distinct patterns of electrical activity in the brain during these three states. Brain waves represent very small currents and voltages produced by the electrical circuitry of the brain. Typical strengths of such brain-wave signals are measured in microvolts. Typical frequencies are between 1 and about 20 hertz (or cycles per second)—less than the familiar 60 cycles per second frequency of alternating currents in electrical outlets in North America.

But what is sleep good for? There is no doubt that if we stay up too long the body generates neurochemicals that literally force us to go to sleep. Sleep-deprived animals generate such molecules in their cerebrospinal fluid, and the cerebrospinal fluid of sleep-deprived animals induces sleep when injected into other animals who are perfectly wide awake. There must, then, be a very powerful reason for sleep.

The conventional answer of physiology and folk medicine alike is that sleep has a restorative effect; it is an opportunity for the body to perform mental and physical housekeeping away from the needs of daily living. But the actual evidence for this view, apart from its common-sense plausibility, seems to be sparse. Furthermore, there are some worrisome aspects about the contention. For example, an animal is exceptionally vulnerable when sleeping. Granted that most animals sleep in nests, caves, holes in trees or logs or otherwise recessed or camouflaged locations. Even so, their helplessness while asleep remains high. Our nocturnal vulnerability is very evident; the Greeks recognized Morpheus and Thanatos, the gods of sleep and death, as brothers.

Adapted from C. Sagan, *The Dragons of Eden—Speculations on the Evolution of Human Intelligence*, © 1977 Ballantine Books.

1. In the passage, the author is primarily concerned with doing which one of the following?

   A. Describing classical and modern understandings of the function of sleeping and dreaming
   B. Advocating a modern technological understanding of sleeping
   C. Describing the three principal states of mind
   D. Summarizing the controversy over the connection between dreams and the evolution of man

2. In what way does the passage imply that *Prometheus Bound* and Genesis differ?

   A. The latter focuses more on humankind than does the former.
   B. While one is literary, the other is only religious.
   C. *Prometheus Bound* is more literal.
   D. They come from different regions, cultures, and historical periods.

3. It can be inferred from the passage that the author would most likely agree with which one of the following regarding the idea that sleep has a "restorative" effect?

   A. Vulnerability of animals during sleep supports this idea.
   B. Physiological evidence has finally corroborated this idea.
   C. This idea is contradicted by the actual evidence.
   D. This idea is intuitively correct.

4. The purpose served by the excerpt from *Prometheus Bound* at the beginning of the passage is to:

   A. elaborate on the author's main point about dreams.
   B. compare less intelligent animals to humans.
   C. introduce a mythological view about the development of humans.
   D. dispute a commonly held view about the creation of humans.

5. How does the author suggest in the passage text that sleep and death are similar?

   I. By pointing out that the Greeks saw it that way
   II. By noting that the experience of sleep is like death
   III. By suggesting that we may be easily killed while asleep

   A. I only
   B. II only
   C. I and II only
   D. I and III only

6. The author uses electroencephalographic evidence to:

   A. compare the rate of thought with the speed of other electrical phenomena.
   B. demonstrate that dreaming is distinct from both sleep and waking.
   C. show that brain activity does not require much energy.
   D. put Aeschylus' statements in terms "the modern ear" can understand.

## Passage 3 (Questions 1-7)

In [philosophic] contemplation…we start from the not-Self, and through its greatness the boundaries of Self are enlarged; through the infinity of the universe the mind which contemplates it achieves some share in infinity.

For this reason greatness of soul is not fostered by those philosophies which assimilate the universe to Man. Knowledge is a form of union of Self and not-Self; like all union, it is impaired by dominion, and therefore by any attempt to force the universe into conformity with what we find in ourselves. There is a widespread philosophical tendency towards the view which tells us that Man is the measure of all things, that truth is manmade, that space and time and the world of universals are properties of the mind, and that if there be anything not created by the mind, it is unknowable and of no account for us. This view, if our previous discussions were correct, is untrue; but in addition to being untrue, it has the effect of robbing philosophic contemplation of all that gives it value, since it fetters contemplation to Self. What it calls knowledge is not a union with the not-Self, but a set of prejudices, habits, and desires, making an impenetrable veil between us and the world beyond. The man who finds pleasure in such a theory of knowledge is like the man who never leaves the domestic circle for fear his word might not be law.

The true philosophic contemplation, on the contrary, finds its satisfaction in every enlargement of the not-Self, in everything that magnifies the objects contemplated, and thereby the subject contemplating. Everything, in contemplation, that is personal or private, everything that depends upon habit, self-interest, or desire, distorts the object, and hence impairs the union which the intellect seeks. By thus making a barrier between subject and object, such personal and private things become a prison to the intellect. The free intellect will see as God might see, without a here and now, without hopes and fears, without the trammels of customary beliefs and traditional prejudices, calmly, dispassionately, in the sole and exclusive desire of knowledge—knowledge as impersonal, as purely contemplative, as it is possible for man to attain. Hence also the free intellect will value more the abstract and universal knowledge into which the accidents of private history do not enter, than the knowledge brought by the senses, and dependent, as such knowledge must be, upon an exclusive and personal point of view and a body whose sense-organs distort as much as they reveal.

The mind which has become accustomed to the freedom and impartiality of philosophic contemplation will preserve something of the same freedom and impartiality in the world of action and emotion. It will view its purposes and desires as parts of the whole, with the absence of insistence that results from seeing them as infinitesimal fragments in a world of which all the rest is unaffected by any one man's deeds. The impartiality which, in contemplation, is the unalloyed desire for truth, is the very same quality of mind which, in action, is justice, and in emotion is that universal love which can be given to all, and not only to those who are judged useful or admirable. Thus contemplation enlarges not only the objects of our thoughts, but also the objects of our actions and our affections: it makes us citizens of the universe, not only of one walled city at war with all the rest. In this citizenship of the universe consists man's true freedom, and his liberation from the thralldom of narrow hopes and fears.

Adapted from B. Russell, *The Problems of Philosophy*, © 1986 Oxford University Press, Inc.

1.  According to the passage, from which of the following points should philosophic speculation originate?

    A.  The Self
    B.  Contemplation on the Self
    C.  Contemplation on the universe
    D.  The not-Self

2.  The author implies that philosophies themselves are inclined to:

    A.  reveal the truth about the universe.
    B.  be worth studying.
    C.  be egocentric.
    D.  put our personal experiences of the world into overly abstract terms.

3.  Which one of the following topics related to the value of philosophic contemplation is NOT addressed in the passage?

    A.  Enriching one's imagination
    B.  Expanding one's conception of the world beyond one's self
    C.  Diminishing the influences which close the mind to speculation
    D.  Enlarging one's perspective on the human race

4.  The author mentions "the man who never leaves the domestic circle" (paragraph 2) in order to:

    A.  criticize people who break the law.
    B.  draw an analogy between such a man and a philosopher who claims that the external world is a product of the human mind.
    C.  describe true philosophic contemplation.
    D.  explain the nature of the not-Self.

5.  The "not-Self" probably refers to:

    A.  cognizance of the realm outside the Self.
    B.  a state of non-self-centeredness.
    C.  the unconscious.
    D.  the world external to an individual.

6.  It is reasonable to conclude that the author of this passage would refute the claim that:

    A.  the universe is neither hostile nor indifferent.
    B.  the individual experience is unique and isolated.
    C.  one person can effect change in the world.
    D.  the mind is rendered great through philosophic meditation.

7.  In the passage, which one of the following is asserted about the "free intellect" (paragraph 3)?

    A.  It values sensual knowledge.
    B.  It views the world as a means to its own end.
    C.  It escapes temporality.
    D.  It is trammeled by abstract knowledge.

_____

## Passage 4 (Questions 1-7)

The first official association of the Food and Drug Administration [FDA] with a cyclamate product came in January 1950, when Abbott Laboratories filed a new drug application [NDA] for Sucaryl Sodium (a cyclamate product). Abbott's new drug tablets were "intended for use in foods and beverages by diabetics and by others who must restrict their intake of sugar," according to the Abbott drug application. It was the original intention of Abbott to use the product as a drug. For strictly food use, a new drug application would not have been necessary. Dr. A. J. Lehman of the FDA reviewed the Abbott Laboratories test data supplied with the application and dismissed it as useless. The application, he said, was "an illustration of how an experiment should not be conducted." The numbers of test animals were too small, control groups were discontinued too early in the experiments, not enough autopsies were performed, and the report itself was vague.

On the basis of its own data, Abbott's request to market cyclamates would have been rejected, but the FDA took the unusual position of approving the request on the basis of two-year feeding studies that it had conducted in its own laboratories. Dr. Lehman's report concluded: "If we had not studied this compound I would be quite reluctant to permit its use even for drug use, not to mention as an artificial sweetener for foods. It should be pointed out to Abbott that the evidence to support their case is not contained in this NDA; and that it is on the basis of our own work that recommendations are being made to permit this application to become effective."

It is important to note that, when the pressure on cyclamates came to a head in October 1969, almost twenty years later, a review of the FDA data relied on by Dr. Lehman revealed "a highly suspicious frequency of lung tumors...(which) assumed significant back-up importance." In addition, of the less than one hundred rats tested by the FDA, six had rare ovarian, kidney, skin, or uterine tumors that would ordinarily occur about once in ten thousand cases—making this more than six hundred times the normal occurrence. The appearance of malignant tumors had been clearly noted in the 1950 FDA laboratory sheets on which the conclusions of safety were based. Combining these suggestions of cancer with the shoddiness of Abbott's test should have clearly indicated that more tests of cyclamates were needed before allowing them to be marketed. But the FDA demanded no further tests. This was the first of many danger signals about cyclamates that the FDA ignored.

The next warning about cyclamates came to the FDA officially from the Food Nutrition Board of the National Academy of Sciences—National Research Council (NAS-NRC) in 1954. The FDA took no action to restrict the use of cyclamates at that time. The warning was repeated in 1955, 1962, and in modified form in 1968. In a special communication to the Food and Drug Administration in November, 1954, the Food Nutrition Board said, "The priority of public welfare over all other considerations precludes, therefore, the uncontrolled distribution of foodstuffs containing cyclamate."

Adapted from J. S. Turner, *The Chemical Feast, The Center for the Study of Responsive Law*, © 1970 Grossman Publishers.

1. From the information in the passage, it can be inferred that the author would support which of the following agendas if another drug company had a new product to test?

   I. The company should be allowed to proceed with very little governmental interference in order to be able to market the product as soon as possible to those who need it.
   II. The product should be subject to very careful testing by the company that is producing and marketing it.
   III. After rigorous testing by the company producing the product, it should be allowed on the market with only minor inspection by the FDA, since that agency is inept.

   A. I only
   B. II only
   C. III only
   D. II and III only

2. Based on the information in the passage, it is safe to make all of the following assumptions EXCEPT that:

   A. the FDA will approve chemicals more readily as drugs than as foods.
   B. substances that are intended for use in foods are sometimes not scrutinized closely enough.
   C. the FDA has influence on the marketing of both foods and drugs.
   D. the NDA is usually an administrative and political formality.

3. According to the passage, what was the intended use of cyclamates?

   A. To cure diabetes
   B. To promote weight loss
   C. To make food taste sweet
   D. To treat cancer

4. It can be inferred from the passage that the FDA:

   A. usually does not approve a new drug until it has been tested in FDA laboratories.
   B. usually bases new drug approval on data presented in an NDA.
   C. uses the NDA only as a way to call attention to a new drug.
   D. does not require NDAs for food additives intended for treatment of disease.

5. The author of the passage would most likely agree that the responsibility for the continued presence of cyclamates on the market rests largely with:

   A. the NAS-NRC.
   B. Abbott Laboratories.
   C. the FDA.
   D. consumers of the drug.

6. Why does the author mention the "shoddiness of Abbott's test" in paragraph 3?

   A. To cast doubt on the safety of cyclamates
   B. Because the test indicated cyclamates to be dangerous
   C. To highlight the FDA's superior study
   D. Because it suggested that some part of the application process had been dishonest

7. It is reasonable to infer from the passage that which one of the following correctly characterizes the FDA and the NAS-NRC?

   A. Both are regulatory agencies concerned with public health.
   B. Both employ scientists whose ostensible concern is public health.
   C. Both are primarily research organizations.
   D. Neither has the power to ban chemicals; they can only recommend.

## Passage 5 (Questions 1-5)

In the United States the per capita costs of schooling have risen almost as fast as the cost of medical treatment. But increased treatment by both doctors and teachers has shown steadily declining results. Medical expenses concentrated on those above forty-five have doubled several times over a period of forty years with a resulting 3 percent increase in life expectancy in men. The increase in educational expenditures has produced even stranger results; otherwise President Nixon could not have been moved this spring to promise that every child shall soon have the "Right to Read" before leaving school.

In the United States it would take $80 billion per year to provide what educators regard as equal treatment for all in grammar and high school. This is well over twice the $36 billion now being spent. Independent cost projections prepared at HEW and at the University of Florida indicate that by 1974 the comparable figures will be $107 billion as against the $45 billion now projected, and these figures wholly omit the enormous costs of what is called "higher education," for which demand is growing even faster. The United States, which spent nearly $80 billion in 1969 for "defense," including its deployment in Vietnam, is obviously too poor to provide equal schooling. The President's Committee for the Study of School Finance should ask not how to support or how to trim such increasing costs, but how they can be avoided.

Equal obligatory schooling must be recognized as at least economically unfeasible. In Latin America the amount of public money spent on each graduate student is between 350 and 1,500 times the amount spent on the median citizen (that is, the citizen who holds the middle ground between the poorest and the richest). In the United States the discrepancy is smaller, but the discrimination is keener. The richest parents, some 10 percent, can afford private education for their children and help them to benefit from foundation grants. But in addition they obtain ten times the per capita amount of public funds if this is compared with the per capita expenditure made on the children of the 10 percent who are poorest. The principal reasons for this are that rich children stay longer in school, that a year in a university is disproportionately more expensive than a year in high school, and that most private universities depend—at least indirectly—on tax-derived finances.

Obligatory schooling inevitably polarizes a society; it also grades the nations of the world according to an international caste system. Countries are rated like castes whose educational dignity is determined by the average years of schooling of its citizens, a rating which is closely related to per capita gross national product, and much more painful.

Adapted from I. Illich, *Deschooling Society*, © 1971 Harper & Row.

1.  The central thesis of the passage is that:

    A.  obligatory education does not and cannot provide equal education.
    B.  the educational shortcomings of the United States, in contrast to those of Latin America, are merely the result of poor allocation of available resources.
    C.  both education and medical care are severely underfunded.
    D.  defense spending is sapping funds which would be better spent on education.

2.  With which of the following solutions to the problems presented by obligatory education would the author most likely agree?

    A.  Education should not be obligatory for those who cannot afford to pay for it.
    B.  Education should not be obligatory at all.
    C.  More money should be dedicated to education for the poorest citizens.
    D.  Countries should cooperate to establish common minimal educational standards.

3.  According to the passage, education in the United States is like health care in all of the following ways EXCEPT:

    A.  it has reached a point of diminishing returns where increased spending no longer results in significant advances.
    B.  the benefits it confers are surprisingly small.
    C.  it is always unfairly distributed between rich and poor.
    D.  the amount of money being spent on older consumers of these services is increasing.

4.  According to the passage, what is the main reason for discrimination in the distribution of public funds for education in the United States?

    A.  Children of wealthy parents can attend private schools.
    B.  Children of richer parents can obtain foundation grants more easily.
    C.  Children of wealthy parents tend to be smarter.
    D.  Children of wealthy parents are more likely to attend college.

5.  The author discusses public spending on students in Latin America and the United States in order to suggest that:

    A.  equal education is possible in the United States but not in Latin America.
    B.  educational inequality is more discriminatory in the United States than in Latin America.
    C.  educational spending is more efficient in the United States.
    D.  obligatory schooling inevitably leads to a caste system.

## Passage 6 (Questions 1-7)

As Xenophanes recognized as long ago as the sixth century before Christ, whether or not God made man in His own image, it is certain that man makes gods in his. The gods of Greek mythology first appear in the writings of Homer and Hesiod, and, from the character and actions of these picturesque and, for the most part, friendly beings, we get some idea of the men who made them and brought them to Greece.

But ritual is more fundamental than mythology, and the study of Greek ritual during recent years has shown that, beneath the belief or skepticism with which the Olympians were regarded lay an older magic, with traditional rites for the promotion of fertility by the celebration of the annual cycle of life and death, and the propitiation of unfriendly ghosts, gods, or demons. Some such survivals were doubtless widespread and, prolonged into classical times, probably made the substance of Eleusinian and Orphic mysteries. Against this dark and dangerous background arose Olympic mythology on the one hand and early philosophy and science on the other.

In later classical times the need of a creed higher than the Olympian was felt, and Aeschylus, Sophocles, and Plato finally evolved from the pleasant but crude polytheism the idea of a single, supreme, and righteous Zeus. But the decay of Olympus led to a revival of old and the invasion of new magic cults among the people, while some philosophers were looking to a vision of the uniformity of nature under divine and universal law.

The first school of thought to assume that the universe is natural and explicable by rational inquiry was that of the Ionian nature-philosophers of Asia Minor. One of the earliest known to us is Thales of Miletus (*c.* 580 B.C.), merchant, statesman, engineer, mathematician and astronomer. Thales is said to have visited Egypt, and from the empirical rules for land-surveying there in vogue, to have originated the science of deductive geometry. He pictured the Earth as a flat disc, floating on water, instead of resting on a limitless solid bottom, and propounded the idea of a cycle from air, earth, and water through the bodies of plants and animals to air, earth, and water again.

Anaximander (*ob.* 545) recognized that the heavens revolve round the pole star, and inferred that the visible dome of the sky is half a complete sphere, with the Earth at its center, the Sun passing underground at night. Worlds arise from the primordial stuff of chaos by natural causes, such as those that are still at work. The first animals came from sea slime, and men from the bellies of fish. Primary matter is eternal, but all things made from it are doomed to destruction.

Some men, such as Empedocles of Sicily, held that there were four elements, earth, water, air and—still more tenuous—fire. By combinations of the four, the various types of matter were made. Empedocles proved the corporeal nature of air by showing that water can enter a vessel only as air escapes.

The Ionian philosophy was brought to Athens by Anaxagoras of Smyrna about 460 B.C. Anaxagoras added to its mechanical bent by the belief that the heavenly bodies are of the same nature as the Earth: the Sun being not the god Helios but a burning stone.

The Ionians also made advances in practical arts, inventing or importing the potter's wheel, the level, the lathe, the set square and the style or gnomon, used as a sundial to tell the time and to determine when the Sun's altitude at noon was greatest.

Adapted from Sir W. C. Dampier, *A Shorter History of Science*, © 1957 Meridian Books.

1. The author of the passage would most likely agree that:

   A. Ionian philosophers were inconsistent to think the Earth was a flat disc both floating on water and resting on a limitless solid bottom.
   B. primary matter is doomed to destruction.
   C. despite the Ionian philosophers' occasional errors, they deserve credit for being the first to attempt to explain the world rationally.
   D. it was more commonplace in ancient times to give religious explanations of natural phenomena than it was to give scientific ones.

2. The passage implies that ritual underlying early Greek mythology was characterized by:

   A. ritual dancing.
   B. early signs of rationalism.
   C. threatening deities.
   D. monotheistic impulses.

3. Ionian philosophy can be described with each of the following terms EXCEPT:

   A. atomistic (matter has a finite number of indivisible essential forms that are variously combined to create reality).
   B. empirical (matter is essentially physical and can be characterized through observation and experiment).
   C. geocentric (the earth is at the center of the universe).
   D. idealistic (the only reality that exists is that constituted by our own mind and consciousness).

4. According to the passage, deductive geometry had its origins in:

   A. abstract theories which were later confirmed by observation.
   B. empirical rules for land surveying.
   C. mythical accounts of the origins of the universe.
   D. observations of the movements of stars and planets and of the nature of matter.

5. According to the passage, which of the following events was most responsible for the emergence of new magic cults in classical times?

   A. The shift away from monotheism towards polytheism
   B. The emergence of Eleusinian and Orphic mysteries
   C. The decay of Olympus
   D. The growing popularity of alchemy

6. Which of the following, if true, would most *weaken* the author's claim that the ancient Greek idea of Zeus was an evolution away from polytheism?

   A. The vast majority of Ionian philosophers never believed in Zeus.
   B. The magic cults that were revived were monotheistic.
   C. The idea of Zeus also caused the common people to obey the laws of ancient Greece.
   D. Sophocles envisioned the persona of Zeus as a single body which enclosed a variety of personalities similar in their behaviors to the former Olympian gods.

7. Which of the following, if true, would most strengthen the author's claim that ancient Greek ritual was more fundamental than Greek mythology?

   A. Ancient Greeks who were inwardly skeptical of the mythological gods never revealed their doubts out of fear of reprisal.
   B. The oldest evidence of ancient Greek society is a vase picturing a fertility rite and such rites were performed annually well into the middle ages.
   C. Ionian philosophers rejected all forms of ritual as well as the mythical gods.
   D. In the ancient Greek city of Athens one could be exiled for failing to worship Zeus.

---

## Passage 7 (Questions 1-7)

The Aristotelian worldview was the single most important source and support for the pre-Copernican tradition of astronomical practice. But Aristotle's day is not our day, and a real mental transposition is therefore necessary in approaching his writings, particularly those dealing with physics and cosmology. Failure to make this transposition has resulted in some strained and distorted explanations of the endurance of Aristotelian physics in antiquity and during the Middle Ages.

We are, for example, often told that it is only because medieval scientists preferred the authority of the written word, preferably ancient, to the authority of their own eyes that they could continue to accept Aristotle's absurd dictum that heavy bodies fall faster than light ones. Modern science, on this prevalent interpretation, began when Galileo rejected texts in favor of experiments and observed that two bodies of unequal weight, released from the top of the tower of Pisa, struck the ground simultaneously. Today, every schoolboy knows that heavy bodies and light bodies fall together.

But the schoolboy is wrong and so is this story. In the everyday world, as Aristotle saw, heavy bodies do fall faster than light ones. That is the primitive perception. Galileo's law is more useful to science than is Aristotle's, not because it represents experience more perfectly, but because it goes behind the superficial regularity disclosed by the senses to a more essential, but hidden, aspect of motion. To verify Galileo's law by observation demands special equipment; the unaided senses will not yield or confirm it. Galileo himself got the law not from observation, at least not from new observation, but from a chain of logical arguments.... Probably he did not perform the experiment at the tower of Pisa. That was performed by one of his critics, and the result supported Aristotle. The heavy body did hit the ground first.

The popular story of Galileo's refutation of Aristotle is largely a myth, motivated by a failure of historical perspective. We like to forget that many of the concepts in which we believe were painfully drummed into us in our youth. We too easily take them as natural and indubitable products of our own unaided perceptions, dismissing concepts different from our own as errors, rooted in ignorance or stupidity and perpetuated by blind obedience to authority. Our own education stands between us and the past.

Part of the authority of Aristotle's writings derives from the brilliance of his own original ideas, and part derives from their immense range and logical coherence, which are as impressive today as ever. But the primary source of Aristotle's authority lies in a third aspect of his thought, one which it is more difficult for the modern mind to recapture. Aristotle was able to express in an abstract and consistent manner many spontaneous perceptions of the universe that had existed for centuries before he gave them a logical verbal rationale. In many cases these are just the perceptions that, since the seventeenth century, elementary scientific education has increasingly banished from the adult Western mind.

Today the view of nature held by most sophisticated adults shows few important parallels to Aristotle's, but the opinions of children, and of many non-Western peoples do parallel his with surprising frequency. Aristotle's substantive ideas about nature show important residues of earlier and more elementary perceptions of the universe. Unless alert to those residues we will surely miss the force of important segments of Aristotelian doctrine.

Adapted from T. S. Kuhn, *The Copernican Revolution,*
© 1957 The President and Fellows of Harvard College.

1. The passage implies that medieval scholars accepted Aristotle's conceptions of physics and astronomy because:

   A. Aristotle knew more than they did.
   B. they accepted ancient authority, especially written.
   C. they did not have the instruments to test Aristotle's propositions.
   D. their observations accorded with Aristotle's.

2. According to the passage, the significance of Galileo's discovery for modern science lies in the fact that:

   A. he developed better instrumentation for measuring motion.
   B. he confirmed scientifically what had only been observed before.
   C. he showed that observation may not accurately disclose physical laws.
   D. he showed that Aristotle was wrong.

3. "Primitive perception" (paragraph 3) is perception which is:

   A. wrong.
   B. characteristic of children.
   C. unaided by instruments.
   D. distorted by primitive instrumentation.

4. The "failure of historical perspective" (paragraph 4) that causes us to misunderstand how ideas are accepted or rejected is caused by:

   A. the failures of our educational system.
   B. the confusion between what we have learned and what we have observed for ourselves.
   C. inaccuracies in the historical record.
   D. ignorance and stupidity.

5. One of the main precepts of ancient cosmology was that the Earth was flat. It can be inferred from the passage that the endurance of that belief was based on:

   A. common-sense experience.
   B. the refusal of people of that time to accept abstract scientific explanations.
   C. the authority of ancient religious writings.
   D. the beliefs of children and tribal peoples.

6. According to the passage, what were the reasons for Aristotle's enormous authority?

   I. The brilliance of his ideas
   II. The appeal of his ideas to children and uneducated minds
   III. The fact that he explained the common experience of the world in an abstract way

   A. I only
   B. I and II only
   C. I and III only
   D. II and III only

7. What does the passage imply about the nature of human beliefs?

   A. We believe only what our senses show us.
   B. We tend to accept what we were taught to believe.
   C. We tend to believe what we want to believe.
   D. We see the world as logically coherent.

## Passage 8 (Questions 1–7)

From Romania to Germany, from Tallinn to Belgrade, a major historical process—the death of communism—is taking place. The German Democratic Republic does not exist anymore as a separate state. And the former GDR will serve as the first measure of the price a post-Communist society has to pay for entering the normal European orbit. In Yugoslavia we will see whether the federation can survive without communism, and whether the nations of Yugoslavia will want to exist as a federation. (On a larger scale, we will witness the same process in the Soviet Union.)

One thing seems common to all these countries: dictatorship has been defeated and freedom has won, yet the victory of freedom has not yet meant the triumph of democracy. Democracy is something more than freedom. Democracy is freedom institutionalized, freedom submitted to the limits of the law, freedom functioning as an object of compromise between the major political forces on the scene.

We have freedom, but we still have not achieved the democratic order. That is why this freedom is so fragile. In the years of democratic opposition to communism, we supposed that the easiest thing would be to introduce changes in the economy. In fact, we thought that the march from a planned economy to a market economy would take place within the framework of the *nomenklatura* system, and that the market within the Communist state would explode the totalitarian structures. Only then would the time come to build the institutions of a civil society; and only at the end, with the completion of the market economy and the civil society, would the time of great political transformations finally arrive.

The opposite happened. First came the big political change, the great shock, which either broke the monopoly and the principle itself of Communist Party rule or simply pushed the Communists out of power. Then came the creation of civil society, whose institutions were created in great pain, and which had trouble negotiating the empty space of freedom. And only then, as the third moment of change, the final task was undertaken: that of transforming the totalitarian economy into a normal economy where different forms of ownership and different economic actors will live one next to the other.

Today we are in a typical moment of transition. No one can say where we are headed. The people of the democratic opposition have the feeling that we won. We taste the sweetness of our victory the same way the Communists, only yesterday our prison guards, taste the bitterness of their defeat. And yet, even as we are conscious of our victory, we feel that we are, in a strange way, losing. In Bulgaria the Communists have won the parliamentary elections and will govern the country, without losing their social legitimacy. In Romania, the National Salvation Front, largely dominated by people from the old Communist *nomenklatura*, has won. In other countries democratic institutions seem shaky, and the political horizon is cloudy. The masquerade goes on: dozens of groups and parties are created, each announces similar slogans, each accuses its adversaries of all possible sins, and each declares itself representative of the national interest. Personal disputes are more important than disputes over values. Arguments over labels are fiercer than arguments over ideas.

Adapted from A. Michnik, *The Two Faces of Eastern Europe*, © 1990 A. Michnik.

1. Which of the following best expresses the main idea of the passage?

   A. Communism will never completely vanish from the Earth.
   B. Democracy is the highest good that any Eastern European country can ever hope to achieve.
   C. Market economies do not always behave as we might predict.
   D. Although many formerly Communist countries are now "free," this does not necessarily mean that they have a democracy.

2. It was originally thought that the order of events in the transformation of society would be represented by which of the following?

   A. The totalitarian structure would collapse, leaving in its wake a social structure whose task would be to change the state-controlled economy into a free market.
   B. The transformation of the economy would destroy totalitarianism, after which a different social and political structure would be born.
   C. The people would freely elect political representatives who would then transform the economy, which would then undermine the totalitarian structure.
   D. The change to a democratic state would necessarily undermine totalitarianism, after which a new economy would be created.

3. Which of the following best represents the relationship between freedom and democracy, as it is described by the author?

   A. A country can have freedom without having democracy.
   B. If a country has freedom, it necessarily has democracy.
   C. A country can have democracy without having freedom.
   D. A country can never have democracy if it has limited freedom.

4. Which of the following best describes the author's attitude toward what has taken place in Communist society?

   A. He is relieved that at last the democratic order has surfaced.
   B. He sees the value of returning to the old order.
   C. He is disappointed with the nature of the democracy that has emerged but nevertheless pleased with the victory of freedom.
   D. He is confident that a free economy will ultimately provide the basis for a true democracy.

5. When the author mentions "the same process" (paragraph 1), it can be inferred from the passage that he is most likely referring to:

   A. the gradual shift away from authoritarian politics.
   B. the potential disintegration of the Soviet Union.
   C. the possible breakdown in the general distribution systems in the Soviet Republic.
   D. the expected sale of state-owned farms to private enterprise.

6. Which of the following does the author imply has contributed to the difficulties involved in creating a new democratic order in Yugoslavia?

   I. The people who existed under a totalitarian structure did not have the experience of "negotiating the empty space of freedom."
   II. Mistaking the order in which political, economic, and social restructuring would occur
   III. Changes in the economy were more difficult than anticipated.

   A. II only
   B. I and III only
   C. II and III only
   D. I, II, and III

7. It can be inferred from the passage that the democratic opposition feels that it is "in a strange way, losing" (paragraph 5) because:

   A. some of the old governments are still unwilling to give in to freedoms at the individual level.
   B. the new governments are not strong enough to exist as a single federation.
   C. newly elected officials have ties to old political parties.
   D. no new parties have been created to fill the vacuum created by the victory of freedom.

## Passage 9 (Questions 1-6)

"The study of the causes of poverty," Alfred Marshall observed at the turn of the century, "is the study of the causes of the degradation of a large part of mankind." He spoke of contemporary England as well as of the world beyond. A vast number of people both in town and country, he noted, had insufficient food, clothing, and house-room; they were: "Overworked and undertaught, weary and careworn, without quiet and without leisure." The chance of their succor, he concluded, gave to economic studies "their chief and their highest interest."

No contemporary economist would be likely to make such an observation about the United States. Conventional economic discourse makes obeisance to the continued existence of some poverty. "We must remember that we still have a great many poor people." In the nineteen-sixties, poverty promised, for a time, to become a subject of serious political concern. Then war came and the concern evaporated or was displaced. For economists of conventional mood, the reminders that the poor still exist are a useful way of allaying uneasiness about the relevance of conventional economic goals. For some people, wants must be synthesized. Hence, the importance of the goods to them is not per se very high. So much may be conceded. But others are far closer to physical need. And hence we must not be cavalier about the urgency of providing them with the most for the least. The sales tax may have merit for the opulent, but it still bears heavily on the poor. The poor get jobs more easily when the economy is expanding. Thus, poverty survives in economic discourse partly as a buttress to the conventional economic wisdom.

The privation of which Marshall spoke was, a half-century ago, the common lot at least of all who worked without special skill. As a general affliction, it was ended by increased output which, however imperfectly it may have been distributed, nevertheless accrued in substantial amount to those who worked for a living. The result was to reduce poverty from the problem of a majority to that of a minority. It ceased to be a general case and became a special case. It is this which has put the problem of poverty into its peculiar modern form.

For poverty does survive. In part, it is a physical matter; those afflicted have such limited and insufficient food, such poor clothing, such crowded, cold and dirty shelter that life is painful as well as comparatively brief. But just as it is far too tempting to say that, in matters of living standards, everything is relative, so it is wrong to rest everything on absolutes. People are poverty-stricken when their income, even if adequate for survival, falls radically behind that of the community. Then they cannot have what the larger community regards as the minimum necessary for decency; and they cannot wholly escape, therefore, the judgment of the larger community that they are indecent. They are degraded for, in the literal sense, they live outside the grades or categories which the community regards as acceptable.

Adapted from J. K. Galbraith, *The Position of Poverty*, © 1984 J. K. Galbraith.

1. Which one of the following best expresses the main idea of the passage?

   A. Contemporary economists can draw on the past to develop radical strategies for eliminating poverty.
   B. Poverty-stricken people are degraded because the community does not find them acceptable.
   C. Contemporary economists, unlike economists of the past, count on the continued existence of poverty, despite its deleterious effects.
   D. The problem of poverty has been reduced from a problem of the many to a problem of the few.

2. In the context of economics at the turn of the century, the phrase "their chief and their highest interest" (paragraph 1) most directly implies that:

   A. the value of economic studies lies entirely in its ability to improve people's lives.
   B. the primary goal of economic studies should be improving the lot of a vast number of people.
   C. economic studies should be concerned chiefly with high interest rates as a cause of poverty.
   D. the chief and highest interest of all humanity should be the study of economics.

3. According to the passage, how has the problem of poverty changed since the turn of the 20th century?

   A. The gap between the richest and poorest people has widened.
   B. It shifted from a problem of the masses to an affliction of a select few.
   C. Sales tax has become more of a burden on the impoverished.
   D. The poor can now rely on social welfare programs.

4. The passage indicates that the "peculiar form" of modern poverty is characterized by:

   A. the concentration of poverty among specific racial groups.
   B. a large proportion of the population no longer having shelter.
   C. people who may have the necessities but whose income is far below community standards of decency.
   D. a significant unemployment problem despite a continually expanding economy.

5. The passage suggests that which of the following most likely displaced the concern for poverty in the 1960s?

   A. A steadily decreasing unemployment rate
   B. An increase in racial tensions
   C. Military conflict
   D. Environmental concerns

6. Which of the following, if true, most *weakens* the author's point that the poor are now those whose income falls "radically behind that of the community" (paragraph 4)?

   A. Definitions of poverty vary from person to person.
   B. Socioeconomic factors often dictate an area in which a person lives.
   C. When one's standard of living is markedly lower than that of the general community, one's self esteem plummets making the individual feel poor.
   D. Poverty is defined by one's capacity to provide adequate food and shelter.

## Passage 10 (Questions 1-5)

Meanings are stored in long-term memory. What is required is a loop between long-term memory and the earlier stages of information processing. That loop is shown in Figure 1:

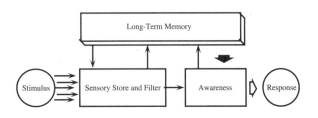

**Figure 1**

Such a feedback loop allows for the sensory store to sort its contents by drawing on the vast repertoire of experience, on the meanings and understandings built up over a life span, stored in long-term memory. The judgment "salient" or "irrelevant" can be made only on the basis of the knowledge in long-term memory. With access to the mind's lifelong store of experience, preferences, and goals, the filter can sift through the mass of impressions that assail it at each successive moment, and immediately tune in or out what matters.

Indeed, contemporary theorists now assume that information passing through the sensory store is subjected to scrutiny and filtered on the basis of its meaning and relevance. "Essentially," sums up Matthew Erdelyi, a cognitive psychologist, "long-term memory itself becomes the filter, deciding what to block from short-term storage (and therefore awareness), thereby determining indirectly what to accept for eventual storage in long-term memory itself."

There are compelling reasons for this arrangement in the design of the mind. The region of consciousness would be far too cluttered were it not reached by a vastly reduced information flow. The more thoroughly information in sensory storage can be sorted out, the more efficiently the next way station—awareness—can operate. If too much gets through, awareness is swamped.... It is of critical import that this filter operate at a peak, in order to save us from continuous distraction by a mass of irrelevant information. If the filter were much less thorough we might literally be driven to distraction by distractions, as happens in schizophrenia.

The idea that information passes through an intelligent filter led to what has become the prevailing view of how information flows through the mind. The most commonly pictured flow chart was proposed by Donald Norman in 1968; Figure 1 is a simplified version of his model. In this model what enters through the senses gets a thorough, automatic scan by long-term memory—specifically by "semantic" memory, the repository of meanings and knowledge about the world. For example, every bundle of sounds automatically is directed to an "address" in semantic memory that yields its meaning. If you hear the word "grunt," semantic memory recognizes its meaning; if you hear a grunt, semantic memory also recognizes that that sound is not a word.

All this filtering goes on out of awareness. What gets through to awareness is what messages have pertinence to whatever mental activity is current. If you are looking for restaurants, you will notice signs for them and not for gas stations; if you are skimming through the newspaper, you will notice those items that you care about. What gets through enters awareness, and only what is useful occupies that mental space.

Adapted from D. Goleman, *Vital Lies, Simple Truths: The Psychology of Self Deception,* © 1989 D. Goleman.

1. The model of the mind described in this passage implies that our perceptions of reality are:

   A. objective once we have learned how to be aware of the contents of long-term memory.
   B. undistorted perceptions of the sensations of the moment combined with distorted memories of past events.
   C. always influenced by our past experiences and needs of the moment.
   D. significantly cluttered by memories of past experiences.

2. It can be inferred from the passage that which of the following would be LEAST likely to be stored in semantic memory?

   A. The years in which the US Civil War was fought
   B. The title of a piece of classical music
   C. The skills necessary for driving a car
   D. The ability to distinguish between a doorbell and a ringing telephone

3. Which of the following assertions is NOT supported within the passage by example or analogy?

   A. "The judgment 'salient' or 'irrelevant' can be made only on the basis of the knowledge in long-term memory" (paragraph 2).
   B. "What gets through to awareness is what messages have pertinence to whatever mental activity is current" (paragraph 6).
   C. "It is of critical import that this filter operate at a peak, in order to save us from continuous distraction" (paragraph 4).
   D. "In this model what enters through the senses gets a thorough automatic scan by long-term memory…" (paragraph 5).

4. Based on the information presented in the passage, the flow chart is most likely provided as which of the following?

   A. An actual schematic of the physical organization of the brain
   B. An approximation of the way in which the brain is physically organized
   C. A misrepresentation of what we now know about the brain and the function of long-term memory
   D. A graphic model that allows theorists to communicate about postulated functions of the brain

5. According to contemporary theorists such as Matthew Erdelyi, the model of the mind graphically presented in Figure 1 may be partially misleading. Based on the information in the passage, what would most likely be a more accurate graphical representation of this model in contemporary terms?

   A. The box representing "Long-Term Memory" should be either identical with or superimposed over the box representing "Sensory Store and Filter."
   B. A box representing "Long-Term Memory/Filter" should be placed before a box representing "Sensory Store."
   C. The box representing "Long-Term Memory" should be placed after the box representing "Sensory Store and Filter."
   D. The box representing "Awareness" should be before the box representing "Sensory Store and Filter."

## Passage 11 (Questions 1-6)

The premise with which the multiculturalists begin is unexceptional: that it is important to recognize and to celebrate the wide range of cultures that cohabit the United States. In what sounds like an inflection of traditional American pluralism, the multiculturalists argue that we must recognize difference, that difference is legitimate; in its kindlier versions, multiculturalism represents the discovery on the part of minority groups that they can play a part in molding the larger culture even as they are molded by it. And on the campus, multiculturalism, defined more locally as the need to recognize cultural variations among students, has tried with some success to talk about how a racially and ethnically diverse student body can enrich everyone's education.

Phillip Green, a political scientist at Smith and a thoughtful proponent of multiculturalism, notes that for a significant portion of the students, particularly minority students, the politics of identity is all-consuming. "Students," he says, "are unhappy with the thin gruel of rationalism. They require a therapeutic curriculum to overcome not straightforward racism but ignorant stereotyping."

But multiculturalism's hard-liners, who seem to make up the majority of the movement, damn as racism any attempt to draw the myriad of American groups into a common American culture. For these multiculturalists, differences are absolute, irreducible, intractable—occasions not for understanding but for separations. The multiculturalist, it turns out, is not especially interested in the great American hyphen, in the syncretistic (and therefore naturally tolerant) identities that allow Americans to belong to more than a single culture, to be both particularists and universalists.

This time-honored American mixture of assimilation and traditional allegiance is denounced as a danger to racial and gender authenticity. This is an extraordinary reversal of the traditional liberal commitment to a "truth" that transcends parochialisms. In the new race/class/gender dispensation (class being the least important of the three), universality is replaced by, among other things, feminist science, Nubian numerals (as part of an Afrocentric science), and what Marilyn Frankenstein of the University of Massachusetts—Boston describes as "ethno-mathematics," in which the cultural basis of counting comes to the fore.

The multiculturalists insist on seeing all perspectives as tainted by the perceiver's particular point of view. Impartial knowledge, they argue, is not possible, because ideas are simply the expression of individual identity, or of the unspoken but inescapable assumptions that are inscribed in a culture or a language. The problem with this warmed-over Nietzscheanism is that it threatens to leave no ground for anybody to stand on. And so the multiculturalists make a leap, necessary for their own intellectual survival, and proceed to argue that there are some categories, such as race and gender, that do in fact embody an unmistakable knowledge of oppression. Victims are at least epistemologically lucky. Objectivity is a mask for oppression. And so an appalled former 1960s radical complained to me that self-proclaimed witches were teaching classes on witchcraft. "They're not teaching students how to think," she said, "they're telling them what to believe."

Adapted from F. Siegel, *The Cult of Multiculturalism,*
© 1991 F. Siegel.

1. Based on the information in the passage, which of the following ideas would the majority of multiculturalists NOT believe?

   A. We should recognize and celebrate the significant differences among the many cultures in the United States.
   B. No ethnic group is inherently more intelligent than another.
   C. There is a cultural basis to both mathematical and scientific theory.
   D. Objectivity will help us to avoid the stereotyping that leads to racism.

2. According to the passage, the traditional liberal position is based on a belief that:

   A. tolerance of difference is crucially important to American culture.
   B. despite cultural differences, all peoples hold some beliefs in common.
   C. members of ethnic minorities deserve some dispensation for the hardships they have endured.
   D. expressions of individual identity must not take second place to the common good.

3. The author states that in a "kindlier version" of multiculturalism, minorities discover "that they can play a part in molding the larger culture even as they are molded by it" (paragraph 1). Assuming that no new immigrants were introduced into existing American culture for many centuries to come, which of the following would be a likely outcome of this "kindlier version" of multiculturalism?

   A. At some time in the future, there may be one culture with no observable ethnic differences.
   B. Eventually the dominant culture would overwhelm the minority cultures, who would lose their ethnic identities.
   C. A multiplicity of ethnic cultural groups would remain, yet specific characteristics of each of those groups would change.
   D. The same ethnic groups would remain, and they would preserve their ethnic heritage intact.

4. Which one of the following legislative proposals would a hard-line multiculturalist most likely oppose?

   A. The re-establishment of university dormitories that would admit only women
   B. An attempt to eliminate instructions in Spanish on official documents in California
   C. Guarantees for proportional representation of ethnic groups on city councils
   D. Legislation that would allow an interpreter to speak for an immigrant at a citizenship hearing

5. Considering the subject of the passage, which of the following is the most likely meaning of "the politics of identity" (paragraph 2)?

   A. The attempt to discover individual identities through political action
   B. The political agenda that aspires to create a new pride of identity for Americans
   C. The current obsession for therapy groups that help individuals discover their inner selves
   D. The trend among minority students to discover their identities in relation to their ethnic groups

6. Which of the following best describes the attitude of the writer toward multiculturalism?

   A. Entirely disapproving of its fundamental beliefs
   B. Somewhat critical yet open-minded
   C. Eager to set it back on the correct track
   D. Scholarly and detached

---

## Passage 12 (Questions 1-6)

Resemblance does not make things so much alike as difference makes them unlike. Nature has committed herself to make nothing other that was not different. Therefore I do not much like the opinion of the man who thought by the multitude of laws to curb the authority of judges by cutting up their meat for them. He was not aware that there is as much liberty and latitude in the interpretation of laws as in the making of them. And those people fool themselves who think they can lessen and stop our disputes by recalling us to the express words of the Bible. For our mind finds the field no less spacious in examining the meaning of others than in putting forth its own, as if there were less animosity and tartness in commenting than in inventing.

We see how much he was mistaken. For we have in France more laws than all the rest of the world together, and more than would be necessary to rule all the worlds of Epicurus, *as formerly we suffered from crimes, so now we suffer from laws*; and yet we have left so much to the opinions and decisions of our judges that there never was such a powerful and licentious freedom. What have our legislators gained by selecting a hundred thousand particular cases and acts and applying to them a hundred thousand laws? This number bears no proportion to the infinite diversity of human actions. The multiplication of our invented cases will never equal the variety of the real cases. Add to them a hundred times as many more: it still will not happen that out of future events there will be found any which will encounter one, in the many thousands of selected and recorded events, that will fit and match it so exactly that there will not remain some circumstances and difference which will require a different consideration in judgment. There is little relation between our actions, which are in perpetual mutation, and fixed and immutable laws. The most desirable laws are those that are most rare, most simple and general; and I even believe that it would be better to have none at all than to have them in such numbers as we have.

Nature always gives us better laws than those we give ourselves. Witness the picture of the Golden Age of the poets and the state in which we see nations live who have no other laws. Here are some who for the sole judges of their quarrels take the first passerby who is traveling through their mountains. And these others on market-day elect one from among themselves who decides all their suits on the spot. What danger would there be if the wisest should settle ours in this way, according to the circumstances and at sight, without being bound by past case and future precedent? For every foot its own shoe. King Ferdinand, when he sent colonists to the Indies, wisely provided that no students of law should be taken there, for fear that lawsuits might abound in that new world, since it is by nature a science generating altercation and division, judging, with Plato, that lawyers and doctors are a bad provision for a country.

Adapted from M. de Montaigne, *Essays: On Experience,* © 1958 Stanford University Press.

1.  The main point of the passage is that:

    A.  laws were unnecessary in earlier times.
    B.  lawyers are unscrupulous.
    C.  laws should be based on similarity, not difference.
    D.  France has too many laws.


2.  Which of the following can most reasonably be concluded regarding the multiplicity of laws in France?

    A.  One useful way to make laws fit complex circumstances is to invent as many laws as there are possible situations.
    B.  Lawyers are inclined to make new laws continuously in order to make themselves indispensable to the culture.
    C.  All things are more unlike than they are alike, so no law has any relation to any other law.
    D.  One cannot restrict the liberty of judges simply by multiplying the number of laws.


3.  The author refers to the man who thought he would curb the authority of judges "by cutting up their meat for them" (paragraph 1). In this phrase, this man intended:

    A.  that judges should have the lawyers argue cases such that decisions could be made without any necessity of judicial interpretation.
    B.  to multiply the number of laws so that judges would never have to make decisions on their own.
    C.  to simplify legal procedure by breaking it into smaller steps.
    D.  to pre-process issues and information so less sophisticated judges could be selected to serve in judicial capacities.


4.  The author suggests that nature provides better laws than does humanity. He supports this assertion with which of the following?

    A.  The observation that it is possible for a culture to exist without an extensive legal system
    B.  Observations of simple and general laws in rural French culture
    C.  A romantic belief in the wisdom of humanity that emerges in natural settings
    D.  His belief that God created all things, including nature


5.  The passage suggests which of the following about the connection between law and human behavior?

    A.  Laws are clearly designed to counteract the worst effects of human behavior.
    B.  The rigidity of immutable laws is not easily applied to the erratic tendencies of human behavior.
    C.  Human behavior is natural, but laws are unnatural.
    D.  It is rare that laws are as simple as most human behavior.


6.  The author's tone in the second paragraph regarding the judicial system in France can be characterized as:

    A.  concerned and frustrated.
    B.  confused.
    C.  derisive and amused.
    D.  apathetic.

## Passage 13 (Questions 1-6)

The Mexican theater in the Southwest before World War II is characterized by flexibility and adaptability to the varying tastes and economic conditions of the communities. An actor like Leonardo Garcia Astol, for example, while initiated into serious drama and melodrama in his father's Compania Azteca, had to conform, as time went on, to doing vaudeville sketches, creating the beloved character of a comic tramp, and later, by working in radio drama and television in Spanish. Indeed, actors trained in the classical tradition or in the lyric tradition of *zarzuela* found themselves doing variety acts and vaudeville during the twenties, and especially, during the Depression. When vaudeville became popular, a number of Mexican performers were able to cross over into the Anglo-American circuits with their song and dance, and some performed actively in Canada. The Chautauqua circuit, for example, contracted Los Hermanos Llera, singers, for 125 performances across the United States (*La Prensa*, December 10, 1925). Acting and singing star Nelly Fernandez had many successful tours with other Mexican performers throughout the United States and Canada, in part through the Pantages circuit, earning $1,000 per month during the Depression (La Opinion, August 8, 1933). *El Heraldo de Mexico* in Los Angeles on June 6, 1925, advertised the Nelly Fernandez-Rafael Diaz company in a Los Angeles show entitled *A Night in Mexico* at the Pantages Vaudeville Theater there, clearly catering to an English-language audience in the most populous Mexican city of the United States.

The two cities with the largest Mexican populations, Los Angeles and San Antonio, naturally became theatrical centers, the former also feeding on the important film industry in Hollywood. In fact, Los Angeles became a manpower pool for Hispanic theater. Actors, directors, technicians, and musicians from throughout the Southwest, New York, and the whole Spanish-speaking world were drawn here looking for employment. Naturally, Los Angeles became the center for the recruitment of talent in the formation of theatrical companies to perform either locally or on tour through the Southwest. Both Los Angeles and San Antonio went through a period of intense expansion and building of new theatrical facilities in the late teens and early twenties. Los Angeles was able to support five major Hispanic theater houses with programs that changed daily. The theaters were Teatro Hidalgo, Teatro Zendejas, and Teatro Principal. Four other theaters—Princess, California, California International, and Estela—were also important, and at least fifteen others housed professional companies on a more irregular basis between 1915 and 1935.

The documentary record of the first decade of the century is extremely broken and mainly shows performances in cabarets and clubs. It is in the second decade that a full-fledged theatrical movement is really in evidence, starting with the Teatro Hidalgo on September 10, 1911, and its performance of the *zarzuela El puñao de rosas*. The Hidalgo, owned and operated by a local business, Mayo and Company, was the longest lived Hispanic theater, having hosted live performances well into 1934, when the documentary record again becomes obscure. Until 1919, the Hidalgo was probably the only permanent theater house serving the Hispanic community, while other stages, like Lyceum Hall, Cabaret Sanroman, and the Empress Theater, were still being leased to touring companies that were not performing at the Hidalgo.

Adapted from N. Kanellos, *A History of Hispanic Theatre in the United States: Origins to 1940,* © 1990 N. Kanellos.

1. The passage suggests that Mexican actors of the 1920s and 1930s were most successful if they:

   A. had mastered a variety of performing styles.
   B. could perform in English as well as Spanish.
   C. had talents that enabled them to work in vaudeville.
   D. crossed over from the stage into radio and television.

2. According to the passage, what happened to the theater during the Depression?

   A. Theater did not change, though the rest of society was deeply affected.
   B. The amount of theatrical activity was affected more than the nature of theatrical activity.
   C. Drama became even more serious.
   D. Changes in the theater during the Depression were of an artistic nature.

3. Which of the following would the author most likely agree is an accurate description of Los Angeles as a cultural center?

   A. Los Angeles natives became a greater source of manpower for Hispanic than for other ethnic theater.
   B. There was a great demand for theater there because it was the largest city in the United States.
   C. Hispanic theater was expanded by the economy there.
   D. Most dramatic activity in Los Angeles was Hispanic.

4. We can infer from the passage that theatrical activity after the Depression was characterized by:

   A. the preference of lighter entertainment over serious drama.
   B. a renaissance of classical and lyrical drama.
   C. the emergence of a new generation of actors who adapted to the public's changing tastes.
   D. the passage does not provide enough information to make an inference.

5. Based on information in the passage, how might the author believe the Depression influenced the assimilation of Hispanics into American culture?

   A. The Depression worsened ethnic tensions for Hispanics.
   B. The Depression contributed to ethnic integration.
   C. Hispanics were isolated from mainstream culture during the Depression.
   D. While the Anglo-dominated Hollywood film industry flourished, Hispanic theater struggled to survive.

6. Based on the passage, which of the following is true of the Hidalgo theater?

   A. It was probably the only Hispanic theater in Los Angeles in 1918.
   B. It closed around 1934.
   C. It housed touring companies only when temporary theaters designed for such groups were full.
   D. Whether it operated after 1934 is not known.

———————————————————

## Passage 14 (Questions 1-6)

Traditionally, [film] theorists have focused attention on two areas of inquiry: the work of art, and the artist. Those who have stressed the work of art have explored the inner dynamics of movies. These theorists can also be divided into realists and expressionists. The principal spokesman for the theory of Expressionism was Rudolf Arnheim.

Most theories of Realism emphasize the documentary aspect of film art. Movies are evaluated primarily in terms of how accurately they reflect external reality. Perhaps the most comprehensive theory of Realism was put forth by Siegfried Kracauer in his book *Theory of Film: the Redemption of Physical Reality*. Kracauer doesn't ignore expressionistic movies. He acknowledges the existence of a "formative tendency" which he traces back to the early experiments of Méliès. In general, however, he considers expressionistic movies as aberrations of the central aesthetic of cinema. The basic premise of Kracauer's aesthetic is that film is essentially an extension of photography and shares with it a "marked affinity" for recording the visible world around us. Unlike other art forms, photography and cinema tend to leave the raw materials of reality more or less intact. There is a minimum of "interference" on the artist's part, for film is not an art of creativity so much as an art of "being there."

Kracauer is hostile toward movies that demonstrate a "formative tendency," that is, distortions and manipulations that violate these natural affinities. Historical films and fantasies he regards as tending to move away from the basic concerns of the medium. Thus, he approves of certain elements in the early semi-documentary films of Eisenstein, which use non-professional players, authentic locations, and natural lighting. But Kracauer condemns Eisenstein's editing practices which distort the time–space continuum of reality. Furthermore, he disapproves of films that are propagandistic, for they impose an ideology or a single doctrine over the natural copiousness of reality.

Kracauer also dismisses most literary and dramatic adaptations because he believes that literature is ultimately concerned with "interior realities," what people are thinking and feeling. Adaptations from novels are permissible only when the narrative elements lend themselves to a realistic presentation. The fiction of Émile Zola, with its emphasis on slice-of-life occurrences, would be admissible in the cinema; the novels of Jane Austen, with their exquisitely filigreed plots, would not.

However, Kracauer underestimates the flexibility of an audience's response to nonrealistic movies. It's also true that we're often aware of the contrivances in historical movies and fantasies, but usually when the cinematic techniques are clumsy and heavy-handed. On the other hand, there are many movies that seem saturated in the details of a remote period. Many scenes from *Birth of a Nation* look as authentic as the Civil War photographs of Mathew Brady. Even fantasy films like *King Kong* and *Fantastic Voyage* are startlingly realistic. They present us with a self-contained "universe" which we are able to enter by temporarily forgetting the outside world of reality.

Adapted from L. D. Giannetti, *Understanding Movies*, © 1976 Prentice-Hall.

1. Which of the following best summarizes the primary purpose of the author of this passage?

   A. To compare Arnheim and Kracauer's contrasting approaches to film criticism
   B. To describe and critique Kracauer's theory of cinematic realism
   C. To discuss theories of art and the extent to which they are applicable to film criticism
   D. To point out a flaw in Kracauer's estimation of the audience's reaction to nonrealistic movies

2. With which of the following statements would Kracauer be most likely to agree?

   A. "The angle from which an object is photographed can often serve as a useful authorial commentary on the subject matter."
   B. "Like other artists, the film director selects certain expressive details from the chaotic plenitude of physical reality."
   C. "Film is best suited to recording events and objects…'nature caught in the act'."
   D. "The very act of photographing an object involves profound disturbances of that object as it is perceived in reality."

3. Which of the following if true would most undermine the author's description of the various schools of thought regarding cinema?

   A. Realist filmmakers normally refuse to portray historical political figures in such a way as to create sympathy for those figures' causes.
   B. Expressionist films often distort space and time in order to show the true emotional states of the characters.
   C. Some realist films are based on novels written by authors who are not from the filmmaker's own nation or culture.
   D. A majority of realist movies are filmed with the use of lamps and reflectors in order to eliminate distracting shadows.

4. Which of the following statements is most strongly supported by the passage?

   A. Kracauer based his cinematic theory in part on his ideas about how audiences react to films.
   B. Rudolf Arnheim advocated an artist-centered approach to film.
   C. All Realist theorists prioritize the documentary aspect of the art of film.
   D. Kracauer accepts some expressionistic movies, in particular those of Méliès, as valid experiments in the context of the historical development of filmmaking.

5. Of the following novels, which would Kracauer find to be most acceptable for adaptation by a filmmaker, according to the information provided in the passage?

   A. A story of a woman who, through insanity, crosses the boundary line into surreality
   B. A work of social realism that portrays the shocking conditions in Chicago meat-processing plants
   C. A study of how the human mind and body react to war
   D. A study of the intertwining daily lives of three women, using fragmentation of plot lines to display the real disjunctures in their life experiences

6. Which of the following statements best captures the author's criticism of Kracauer's theoretical approach?

   A. It is overly restrictive to accept as legitimate only films that accurately capture physical reality.
   B. Film theorists should focus more on the artist than on the work itself.
   C. Even films that portray experiences distant from our daily reality can convince us for the moment that we are viewing a depiction of real events.
   D. Cinema has more in common with other art forms than admitted by Kracauer, and thus more "interference" on the part of the film director is justified.

## Passage 15 (Questions 1-6)

Births to teenage mothers who are grossly unprepared to raise their children to live acceptable, tolerable, self-sufficient lives are the result of three failures. The families and environments of a great many teenage mothers furnish an example of promiscuity and early motherhood that girls emulate. Public schools, society's first chance to intervene in deficient upbringings, teach too little, too late. Family planning clinics, society's last chance to intervene, have too little money to attend to teenage pregnancy cases properly and are severely restrained by what many consider misguided federal regulations that prohibit dissemination of information about abortion.

The overwhelming majority of births that will result in unproductive or criminal careers occur to teenage girls from impoverished families. All too frequently, those girls are themselves the daughters of girls from such families. Without money, and with their parents' example, the girls turn to sex as a primary recreation. It is as though daughters born to teenage girls are carriers of a disease called teenage pregnancy, and the sons of teenage mothers exhibit a disease called anti-social or criminal behavior.

A national investigation of public school education attests to the grave deficiencies in school programs and call for a different approach. Thousands of teachers told Alan Guttmacher Institute researchers that they felt sex education was inadequate and conducted too late. Students, they indicated, were shortchanged in several ways: schools devote an average of only six or seven hours per year to instruction on sexual topics. Less than two of those hours are spent on contraception. Information on reproductive subjects, which students desperately need during the onset of puberty, in the 7th and 8th grades, is not taught until high school.

Family planning clinics need more money and more independence. Clinic visits for sexually transmissible diseases (STDs) have increased by 80% since 1984. It is estimated that $2 million of state and federal money is spent on family planning each year in New York State. Since 1987, clinics have had to draw on pregnancy-prevention resources to start departments for dealing with the human immunodeficiency virus (HIV) without any new appropriation of funds. The cost of Pap tests has more than doubled, adding some $1 million to the financial squeeze and leaving even less money for contraceptive education and pregnancy counseling services. Clinics in some areas are having such difficulty coping with these problems that waiting times for appointments occasionally reach five weeks.

Data show that girls from more affluent homes are as sexually active as the girls described above. The pregnancy rate for such girls is, however, shockingly lower. Furthermore, the more affluent girls who become pregnant have little need for family planning clinics. They are able, through their friends and families, to learn about and obtain abortions virtually whenever they want to end their pregnancies. Since many of these girls attend private schools, the sex education program is richer, provided at an earlier age, and in the control of their parents instead of in the hands of bureaucrats and politicians.

(*Note*: This passage was written in 1991.)

1. Based on the information in the passage, with which of the following statements would the author LEAST likely agree?

   A. Society should work to improve educational and medical programs designed to prevent teenage pregnancy.
   B. Girls from affluent families are less sexually active than are girls from impoverished families.
   C. In many cases, childbearing could reasonably be postponed for many years.
   D. Teenagers should be discouraged from having casual sex.

2. Using the information in the passage one can readily conclude that:

   I. affluent families are more likely to discourage their children from having abortions.
   II. affluent parents are more likely to support substantive sexual education programs than are bureaucrats and politicians.
   III. the difference in the birth rates is not attributable to different levels of sexual activity.

   A. II only
   B. III only
   C. I and II only
   D. II and III only

3. Biological fertility among women normally begins in the early teenage years. The author suggests that this creates specific difficulties for teenagers because:

   A. teens are most likely to act in a sexually irresponsible manner.
   B. caring for a baby is most difficult during its first year of life.
   C. biologically mature women have an interest in sex but not in education.
   D. many teenagers can bear children but cannot care responsibly for them.

4. It can be inferred from the passage that the Guttmacher study was significant primarily because it:

   A. discussed the best age to become sexually active.
   B. compared the sex education received by affluent girls with that received by non-affluent girls.
   C. outlined the inadequacy of sex education provided through family planning clinics.
   D. highlighted the inadequacies of sex education currently available.

5. The main thesis of the passage is that:

   A. teenage pregnancy is a serious problem and demands greater availability of education and medical resources.
   B. the relationship of family background to teen pregnancy is a predictor of future sexual activity.
   C. responsible sexual activity cannot be achieved through seven hours of instruction a year.
   D. school boards should have greater powers than bureaucrats and politicians.

6. The passage suggests that undesirable sexual activity is sexual activity that directly results in:

   A. increased welfare rolls.
   B. pregnant teens setting a bad example for their peers in public schools.
   C. birth to unmarried mothers.
   D. pregnancy of girls not yet able to be responsible parents.

## Passage 16 (Questions 1-6)

The traditional salute to the American flag describes America as "one nation, indivisible," but America is divided in a hundred ways and its divisions seem always to be at odds with one another. Americans are diverse in their ancestry, their heritage, their habits, their tastes, and their values. Nothing and no one is "typically American." Americans quarter within their ranks the farmers of the Midwest, the songwriters of Tennessee, the taxi drivers of Manhattan, the miners of Pennsylvania, and the medical researchers of Massachusetts. These distinct and diverse national elements frequently produce national disharmony.

From its very beginning the name United States was more important for the word "state" than the word "united." In the new-born nation the individual states closely guarded their separateness, fighting off the persistent growth and encroachment of the federal government. On a regular basis the United States Supreme Court must still decide whether the federal government may or may not, in relation to some matter or other, impose its will on the states. We are a nation of bickering factions.

In terms of natural resources the United States has certain vital deficiencies, consuming, for example, more than half the world rubber crop and growing none; using a huge proportion of the world's raw silk without cultivating any silkworms of which to speak. The country is virtually devoid of tin or platinum; it has precious little manganese, quicksilver, tungsten, or nickel. Its political structure is based on freedom and independence, but America is far from independent of the outside world.

And when we mention the "American economy," of what do we speak? The regions of the nation differ vastly in their economic capacities, since the republic embodies countless units, each with its own economy, based upon its own sources of wealth, dominated by self-interest, and in competition with every other unit. If the political boundaries of our states coincided with the economic boundaries, then the area now known as the US would be far less potent, far less rich than it is. New England would be struggling for food, and in the Northwest an automobile would be as rare as it is in underdeveloped countries that have difficulty accumulating foreign exchange.

Yet, from all of this paradox, diversity and disparity, there has emerged a nation of no small wealth and influence. That the nation by its own standards has problems is certain. But for nearly a century the United States has been called the greatest nation on earth. The source of its greatness is to some extent difficult to identify because America is different from other nations in so many ways. No nation combines America's particular diversity of ethnicity, with its expansive land mass, its variety of natural resources, and its British colonial history. Nonetheless it is fair to say that America's greatness probably stems primarily from the interaction and cooperation of its diverse components. It is commerce between and among the states and the people that fulfills the American destiny.

Adapted from A. Bloom, *The Closing of the American Mind,*
© 1987 Simon & Schuster.

1. According to the passage, the United States:

   A. produces many diverse and vital goods.
   B. is rapidly becoming independent of the outside world.
   C. is severely lacking in natural resources.
   D. fails to produce, on its own, all of the commodities it consumes.

2. The author's description of the relationship between the individual states and the federal government indicates that:

   A. individual state governments must be careful to guard against federal encroachment.
   B. state governments tend to resist expansion of federal authority.
   C. separation of state and federal governments guarantees growth.
   D. the US Supreme Court prevents the federal government from interfering in state matters.

3. Information presented in the passage suggests that the profound differences among Americans have provided the United States with:

   A. internal tensions, international prestige, and economic prosperity.
   B. excellent and diverse cuisines.
   C. an economy whose boundaries are consistent with political realities.
   D. citizens who can now be considered "typically" American.

4. Which of the following questions can best be answered by statements made or implied in the passage?

   A. What are the prospects that Americans will, in the future, decrease their consumption of raw silk and rubber?
   B. Which of America's immigrant groups has had the greatest positive influence on American culture?
   C. Why did the American government endorse a flag salute that refers to "one nation, indivisible"?
   D. Is there likely to be a negative economic effect from future increases in trade and communication among America's various sections and factions?

5. According to the passage, the American economy is characterized by:

   I. local diversity.
   II. competition among different geographic units.
   III. regional inabilities to produce needed commodities.

   A. I only
   B. II only
   C. I and III only
   D. I, II, and III

6. The author states that it is difficult to identify the precise source of America's greatness because:

   I. America has a unique combination of features.
   II. America does not interact significantly with other nations.
   III. America is a highly homogenous society.

   A. I only
   B. I and II only
   C. II and III only
   D. I, II, and III

## Passage 17 (Questions 1-6)

There are two basic kinds of correct or valid argument: deductive and inductive. The essential property of a *deductively valid argument* is this: If its premises are true, then its conclusion must be true also. To put it another way, if the premises of a deductively valid argument are true, then its conclusion cannot be false. On the other hand, the premises of an *inductively valid argument* do not guarantee the truth of its conclusion, although it does make the conclusion probable.

We have here a fundamental difference between deductive and inductive reasoning: The conclusion of a deductively valid argument is just as certain as its premises, while the conclusion of an inductively valid argument is less certain than its premises. Inductive conclusions have that extra element of doubt (however slight) because they make claims not already made by their premises.

Perhaps the basic idea behind valid induction is that of pattern or resemblance. For example, we want our conception of the future, our idea about what this or that will be like, to fit a pattern we glean from what this or that was like in the past. We feel justified in expecting the pattern of the future to match the pattern of the past.

Different deductive arguments have different structures. This form is traditionally called *Modus Ponens*:

*Form:*   1.  If *A* then *B*.
          2.  *A*.
              therefore
          3.  *B*.

Now, here is another commonly used and intuitively valid deductive form, called *Modus Tollens*:

*Form:*   1.  If *A* then *B*.
          2.  Not *B*.
              therefore
          3.  Not *A*.

Here is the argument form called *Disjunctive Syllogism*:

*Form:*   1.  *A* or *B*.
          2.  Not *A*.
              therefore
          3.  *B*.

And here is the valid argument form called *Hypothetical Syllogism*:

*Form:*   1.  If *A* then *B*.
          2.  If *B* then *C*.
              therefore
          3.  If *A* then *C*.

Any argument that doesn't have a deductively valid form is said to be *deductively invalid*. The number of deductively invalid argument forms is legion, but a few are so common they've been given names. Here are two: The form called *Fallacy of Denying the Antecedent*,

*Form:*   1.  If *A* then *B*.
          2.  Not *A*.
              therefore
          3.  Not *B*.

and the *Fallacy of Asserting the Consequent*,

*Form:*   1.  If *A* then *B*.
          2.  *B*.
              therefore
          3.  *A*.

We can think of induction, or patterning, as a principle of reasoning that moves from evidence about some members of a class to a conclusion about all members of that class. What is called *induction by enumeration* is the simplest form of induction. In induction by enumeration, we infer from the fact that all *A*s observed so far are *B*s to the conclusion that all *A*s whatsoever are *B*s.

While there are several different theories about how to determine the probability of the conclusion of a particular induction by enumeration, almost all agree on one point: In addition to sheer size, the quality of a sample is important. We want a sample to be representative of the population it was drawn from.

When we reason inductively, we are often looking for explanations or causes. But finding a statistical connection does not always mean that we can claim a causal connection. This is true even if the statistical connection is 100 percent.

Adapted from H. Kahane, *Logic and Contemporary Rhetoric: The Use of Reason in Everyday Life* (4th. ed.), © 1984 Wadsworth.

1.  Which of the following statements best represents a main difference between deductive and inductive logic, as the two methods of reasoning are described in the passage?

    A.  In deductive logic, we move from the general to the specific, while in inductive logic we move from the specific to the general.
    B.  Deductive conclusions are already contained within their premises, while inductive conclusions are not.
    C.  In inductive, unlike in deductive reasoning, the truth of the premises is sufficient to prove the truth of the conclusion.
    D.  In deduction, the truth of the premises affirms the truth of the conclusion drawn on the basis of them. In induction, the truth of the conclusion, if demonstrated, affirms the truth of the premises.

2.  In paragraph 8, the author discusses ways in which claims may be deductively invalid. Which of the following arguments, by those standards would NOT be judged to be deductively valid?

    A.  "Any politician who promises to solve all the problems of society is untrustworthy. Politician Smith makes only limited promises, and so we can believe what she has to say."
    B.  "If we don't solve the problem of poverty in our nation, social unrest will result. Social unrest leads to economic instability, therefore continued poverty weakens our economy."
    C.  "If plants are provided with sufficient sunshine, they will grow rapidly. This ficus tree gets plenty of sunlight, therefore it will get bigger soon."
    D.  "Regimes are either democratic or totalitarian. This state, given the absence of a legitimate legislative body, cannot be called democratic. Therefore, it must be totalitarian."

3.  When an argument is inductive, that argument:

    A.  is necessarily less conclusive than an argument that attempts to use deductive logic.
    B.  is based on probability, such that the likelihood that its premises are all true is no greater than the likelihood of the truth of its conclusion.
    C.  seeks to find or identify causes or explanations.
    D.  when valid, is likely to be based on evaluation of a representative sample of a population.

4.  Suppose a medical researcher investigating the incidence of Crohn's disease were to discover that all those suffering from the disease were also infected with a microorganism called MAP. The researcher argues that this evidence proves a causal relationship between MAP and Crohn's disease. Based on the information provided in the argument, which of the following can be most legitimately concluded?

    A.  This argument, given the large sample size, is inductively valid. Thus, there is a clear causal relationship between MAP and Crohn's disease.
    B.  While compelling, this argument is in the final analysis inductively invalid: we can never assert causality with 100 percent certainty.
    C.  Given the representativeness of the sample, this argument is deductively valid. Thus, there is a high probability that the conclusion drawn by the researcher is true.
    D.  Because the research evaluated all of those with the disease, it could be valid. Thus it gives strong yet not conclusive evidence for the validity of the researcher's claims.

5.  Consider the following argument: "If one is to be considered a decent human being, then one must come to the aid of others in their time of need. Otto risked his own life to rescue a child from a burning building. Thus we should honor and celebrate Otto as a truly decent man." This argument exemplifies which of the following?

    A.  Fallacy of denying the antecedent
    B.  Modus Ponens
    C.  Fallacy of asserting the consequent
    D.  Inductive reasoning

6.  As it is used in the passage, "fallacy of denying the antecedent" most likely exists when:

    A.  an argument claims that A causes B, and yet the supposed cause A can be shown to exist without the supposed effect B.
    B.  evidence that A always leads to B is taken as proof that the absence of A indicates the absence of B.
    C.  one argues inductively that because something has never been true in the past, it will never be true in the future.
    D.  a claim is asserted as deductively valid without proof of the truth of all of its premises.

## Passage 18 (Questions 1-6)

The 1960s were critical years for the Kel Ahaggar, a Tuareg population located in Algeria. The socialist policies of a newly independent Algerian government led to their slave- and *Harratin*-cultivated gardens being taken from them. The northern caravans were slowly replaced by mechanized transport, while the onset of a series of drought years brought pastoralism—the mainstay of their subsistence economy—to its knees.

For many Kel Ahaggar the difficult and painful transition from semi-nomadic pastoralism to a more sedentary lifestyle was ameliorated by the development of tourism. By the late 1980s, however, this lifeline had been effectively curtailed, first by the Tuareg uprisings in Niger and Mali, then, since 1992, by the Algerian crisis.

Most Tuareg, suffering this loss of income from tourism, were forced to abandon their tents and semi-nomadic lifestyle and settle in villages and small cultivation centers. The socioeconomic strategy of the Algerian government has been to encourage and contribute financially to this process, in order to compensate for the loss of tourist income and thus ensure the political stability of the region. Although a revolt by Algeria's Tuareg has always been most unlikely, it is not something that the Algerian government discounts. The policy has done much to allay the Tuareg antagonism to the Algerian government that characterized the early years of Algerian national independence. At the same time, it has also facilitated a marked increase in Islamization and Algerianization among the Tuareg.

A worrying aspect of the increase in Islamization on a society that was overwhelmingly monogamous is its impact on women who, fearing that their husbands may take additional wives, are inclined to demonstrate their "youth" and "fertility" by accelerating pregnancies. Whereas traditional Tuareg society spaced births in accordance with prevailing ecological conditions, women are now tending to give birth on an almost annual basis with serious health, demographic, and socioeconomic implications.

The decline in the status of women is being compounded by two other factors: the declining significance of the matriline and sedentarization. Traditional Kel Ahaggar society was predominantly matrilineal. Group membership, access to political rights, and office, and land rights were transmitted through the matriline. With political power now subsumed within the state and traditional land rights abolished, the relevancy of the matriline has become marginal. Not surprisingly, it appears that this transformation of such a fundamental social and cultural construct is already being reflected in changes in marital strategies and patterns.

Sedentarization is also having a perverse effect on the roles and position of women. In their traditional nomadic state, with men away raiding, on caravans or other business, the domestic domain, including the tending of goat herds, education of children, etc., was the preserve of women. The transition from tent to village is thus being associated with a marked diminution of the domestic responsibilities and authority of women.

Adapted from J. Keenan, "The Father's Friend—Returning to the Tuareg as an 'elder'," in *Anthropology Today*, Vol. 16 #4, © Aug 2000.

1. Which of the following can be inferred to be a difference between the Kel Ahaggar and other Tuareg groups, based only on the passage?

   A. The Tuareg of Mali and Niger have revolted against their respective governments, while the relationship between the Kel Ahaggar and the Algerian state has been largely cooperative.
   B. Because of the higher level of instability in their regions, Tuareg communities outside of Algeria were never able to develop a significant tourist trade.
   C. The Tuareg of Algeria were forced to find economic alternatives to their traditional way of life because of political and environmental changes; those outside of Algeria, not subject to the same stresses, were more able to maintain a life of semi-nomadic pastoralism.
   D. The Algerian Tuareg, unlike Tuareg in other countries, have never rebelled against the state.

2. Suppose it were demonstrated that the development of tourism 1) brought the Tuareg into contact with people from other cultures with very different social structures and gender relationships and 2) caused the men to stay closer to the base encampment for longer periods of time. What impact would these findings have on the author's argument as it is presented in the passage?

   A. It would prove that the development, not the failure of tourism was the true cause of sedentarization.
   B. It would support the author's claim that the Algerian state's socioeconomic strategy helped maintain political stability.
   C. It would indicate a possible alternative causal explanation for changes in the roles and status of women.
   D. It would support the author's claim that the Algerian government's socioeconomic strategy had a significant effect on traditional Tuareg culture.

3. Based solely on information presented in the passage, it can be inferred that the Kel Ahaggar's physical environment:

   A. is for the most part arid desert, unable to support agriculture.
   B. limits the size of the nomadic population that can be easily sustained within it.
   C. is characterized largely by mountainous regions.
   D. is attractive to tourists because of its beauty.

4. Which of the following claims, if shown to be true, would most strengthen the author's explanation of why the status of Tuareg women changed?

   A. Sedentary cultures tend to have higher birth rates, since sustained agriculture can support a larger population than can nomadism or semi-nomadism.
   B. In nomadic cultures, political power within the community tends to be held by and transmitted through those with the most contact with outsiders, given the need to trade and maintain peaceful relations with a wide variety of other communities.
   C. Political power in the modern state is invariably patriarchal, founded on male control over the means of production.
   D. Transitions to socialism often bring increased benefits to women in societies where they had previously been relegated to the sociopolitical margins.

5. As used in the passage, the word "matrilineal" (paragraph 5) most likely refers to:

   A. a system in which political leaders are predominantly women.
   B. a social system inconsistent with the basic principles of Islam.
   C. a social structure in which only female heads of households may own land.
   D. a social system within which a son's land rights would be transferred to him through his mother.

6. According to the author, which of the following was true of tourism in Algeria during the late 1980s and/or early 1990s?

   A. It was sponsored and supported by the Algerian government.
   B. It was discouraged by reports of banditry in the region.
   C. It was affected by social and political turmoil in other nations.
   D. It initially thrived, but was eventually handicapped by the shift to a less nomadic lifestyle.

## Passage 19 (Questions 1-6)

Until the turn of the last century, the only sorts of art produced by ancient Africans that had enjoyed any display or recognition were those that seemed to represent classic Greek sculptural ideals, long revered by European art collectors. Such pieces, perhaps, should be called "African art." On the other hand, what might be named "Black art" has only been appreciated for the last ninety years or so, but is today a crucial component of world art in general. Credit for that happy fact goes to several collectors and scholars who, at the end of the nineteenth and beginning of the twentieth centuries, recognized that the ancient African artist had devised striking structures that expressed deep visions of spirituality.

Black art is compelling for its emotional power and for the straightforward nature of its form. It bespeaks a reverent spirituality—a fact that can escape no serious observer of Black sculpture. Black sculpture sets forth in a curious and intensely engaging harmony the seemingly diverse forces of stillness and rest on the one hand with power and energy on the other. Sculpted figures that seem to have little relation to that which we see in nature somehow manage to achieve a higher truth.

Black art as now appreciated, attracts that part of our psyche that seems to be sure in the existence, and indeed to hunger for an understanding, of the forces which govern all things somewhere from beyond, from within, or perhaps from beneath. The closer and the more probing his inspection, the more is the observer impressed by the ingenuity, and even the audacity of the premises and principles on which Black art is fashioned.

Furthermore, study indicates that the African artist had to work within the constraints of relatively crude tooling techniques and technologies. This finding makes the nature of Black art all the more intriguing. Black art exudes powerful feeling, yet its creation evidently required immense patience, calculation, and planning. The Black artist was required to, and was able to, exercise extraordinary technical care and caution; and at the same time give vent to powerful passions.

Such considerations naturally make one eager to know more of the peoples who evidenced such artistic devotion. One wishes to understand the cultural spirit that generated their commitment; and, most importantly, one yearns to understand why the artists created their works—what they wished to express, and to whom. An appreciation of Black art, therefore, cannot truly be complete in the absence of a competent study of African culture.

It must be acknowledged that when Black art was first brought to light there was a certain unbridled enthusiasm that failed to distinguish among degrees of quality. But that phenomenon is common to the discovery of new art forms. With time, more mature and discriminating patterns of appreciation ultimately take hold, and that has been the case with Black art.

1. Which of the following represents a reason that Black art was not appreciated until relatively recent times?

   A. Africans did not produce art of recognizable quality until the beginning of the twentieth century.
   B. Until the twentieth century scholars and collectors tended to be guided by standards that pertained to ancient Greek sculpture.
   C. Black art is too spiritual in its nature to have commanded the reverence of earlier scholars.
   D. The difference between African art and Black art was insufficiently striking to collectors of the nineteenth century.

2. The author indicates that Black art appeals to which of the following human attributes?

   A. A tendency to ignore that which is real in nature and to prefer that which promotes harmony
   B. A wish to escape from the conflict between peace and power
   C. A longing to achieve greater respect for spirituality
   D. A fundamental belief that unseen phenomena control the universe

3. According to the author's view, one who pursues a study of African culture will likely be:

   A. at least partly prepared to appreciate Black art.
   B. fascinated by the artistic motives of Black sculptors.
   C. confused by "African art."
   D. confused by the meanings and messages of Black art.

4. Suppose it were discovered that the Black artists discussed by the author had far more advanced tools and technologies than is indicated in the passage. Which of the author's assertions would be most *weakened* by such a discovery?

   A. Black artists had the ability to combine extreme technical care with passionate expression.
   B. Black art combines a sense of stillness with a sense of energy.
   C. Black art attempts to put the observer in touch with a truth higher than the nature we see.
   D. Black art is an important component of world art today.

5. Given the statements made by the author, if a previously unappreciated form of art were suddenly given wide attention, the public would most likely:

   A. be slow to admire the art because there would be no basis on which to judge its value.
   B. want to know whether the works on display conformed to classic conceptions of art.
   C. fail at first to distinguish between those works that reflected quality and those that did not.
   D. show particular enthusiasm for the technique behind the works of art but not for the meaning of the art itself.

6. The passage mentions all of the following about Black art EXCEPT its:

   A. emotional power.
   B. lack of technical competency.
   C. straightforward nature.
   D. achievement of a higher truth.

_____

## Passage 20 (Questions 1-6)

The art teacher can permit, allow for, or provide opportunity for aesthetic/creative experience by:

- offering many varied occasions for children's sensory play, experiment, and growth at their own pace;
- accepting and welcoming their responses, feelings, interests, and plans;
- valuing children's variations and offbeat departures rather than insisting on conformity to norms or predetermined goals;
- keeping the program flexible for learning.

The child needs psychological "elbow room" if he is to assert himself in free, independent action rather than move only as a result of pressures outside himself. To be useful to the child, such psychological room must have some definition and known boundaries, for who would venture to leap into the air if he could not assume that some kind of ground would be down there to land upon?

What constitutes "enough room" for aesthetic/creative growth will vary with each child, from the one who finds freedom for his sensing and imagining within the formality of a fire drill to another who, in a phase of rebellion, may be looking only for reasons why he cannot move, no matter what the setting. A child's feeling of freedom for movement is built up gradually out of a long series of small ventures and tests. The teacher, who wants each child to have the highest possible quality of experiencing, will be alert to signs from him that he has enough freedom and is at work on his own.

Sometimes teachers themselves, bowed down by outside pressures and limitations, become paralyzed and unable to take positive action with existing possibilities. Their narrowing expectations will reduce open planning and tolerance of variation unless they too can begin to feel some freedom of movement in teaching and learning.

In classroom practice the two most critical factors in facilitating the aesthetic/creative experience are the allocation of time to such experiences and the facilitation of choice in selecting among various aesthetic and creative learning activities.

Although "art-time" is sometimes "Color while the others are finishing their reading," or perhaps "She doesn't come till Thursday," most schools schedule regular periods for work with a variety of art materials; these periods can be important permitting factors for children's learning. But there also need to be possibilities for building learning-with-feeling out of all of the children's lively interests, whenever they occur. A teacher who has learned to value aesthetic/creative experience will always want more than humdrum learning for his children, in an art period or in any other period.

© TPR Education IP Holdings, LLC

1.  One can reasonably infer that the author describes time as a critical factor in permitting aesthetic/creative experience in order to show that:

    A.  without sufficient time devoted to aesthetic/creative experiences, creativity in children cannot flourish.
    B.  flexibility is more important than strict routines.
    C.  children taught within a time limit are highly progressive and creative.
    D.  proper classroom stimulation produces highly creative and aesthetic children.

2.  Of the following conclusions, which is most consistent with information contained in the passage?

    A.  Occasional art instruction should produce a first-rate artist.
    B.  Art classes should always be scheduled spontaneously.
    C.  Children should be forced to create.
    D.  Educators should devote more resources to activities that permit creativity.

3.  The analogy relating to a leap into the air suggests that:

    A.  leaping into the air is safe if there is ground below and psychological room is always safe.
    B.  leaping into the air is always safe and psychological room is safe if there are limits.
    C.  leaping into the air is safe if there is ground below and psychological room is safe if there are limits.
    D.  leaping into the air is always safe and psychological room is always safe.

4.  The techniques listed at the beginning of the passage are significant because they:

    A.  specify the proper amount of "elbow room" that teachers should give to children.
    B.  provide general guidelines for teachers who wish to promote the aesthetic/creative experience.
    C.  are solely concerned with providing psychological freedom to children.
    D.  discredit time and choice as factors that develop aesthetic/creative facilities.

5.  The central thesis of the passage is that:

    A.  through proper techniques art teachers can promote aesthetic/creative growth for children.
    B.  the connection between time and choice has not been fully defined.
    C.  creativity cannot be achieved through one approach.
    D.  flexible schedules can compensate for uncreative children.

6.  The passage indicates that the elements most important to the creative/aesthetic experience are:

    A.  learning and feeling.
    B.  time and choice.
    C.  understanding and motivation.
    D.  innovation and tolerance.

## Passage 21 (Questions 1-5)

At the end of the nineteenth century, photography had been known in one or the other of its forms for sixty years. For a long time photographers were laughed at good-naturedly and were one of the stock subjects for jokes and caricatures. Slowly, as the community itself began to take photographs with hand cameras, there was no joke left because the photographer was everybody. The photograph and its attendant processes took over at one and the same time two very different utilitarian functions of the graphic processes. One of these was the reporting of news. The other was the recording of works of art of all kinds. Where the requirements of the first of these functions could be and still were on occasion fulfilled by the old techniques, the other had been taken over irretrievably by photography.

Up to that time very few people had been aware of the difference between pictorial expression and pictorial communication of statements of fact. The profound difference between creating something and making a statement about the quality and character of something had not been perceived. The men who did these things were all classified as artists and the public accepted them all as such, even if it did distinguish between those it regarded as good and as poor artists. The difference between the two groups of artists was generally considered to be merely a matter of their comparative skill. But photography and its processes quietly stepped in and by taking over one of the two fields for its own made the distinction that the world had failed to see. The ground was cut from under the feet not only of the humble workaday factual illustrators but also of people like the etcher Jacquemart who had gained a worldwide reputation for his ability to render the textures and sheens of precious objects such as porcelains, glass, and metal work. When it was discovered that the photographic processes did all of that infinitely more accurately than Jacquemart could, it was also realized that Jacquemart had been merely a reporter of works of art and not a maker of them, no matter how extraordinary his technical skill.

At first the public had talked a great deal about what it called photographic distortion—which only meant that the camera had not been taught, as human beings had been, to disregard perspective in most of its seeing. But the world, as it became acclimated, or, to use the psychologists's word, conditioned, to photographic images, gradually ceased to talk about photographic distortion. Thus by conditioning its audience, the photograph became the norm for the appearance of everything. It was not long before men began to think photographically, and thus to see for themselves things that previously it had taken the photograph to reveal to their astonished and protesting eyes. Just as nature had once imitated art, now it began to imitate the picture made by the camera. Willy nilly many of the painters began to follow suit.

The results overall, I believe, have been a permanent gain, if in no other way than that the empty verisimilitude, the particular reportorial formlessness and the lack of design which marked so much of nineteenth and early twentieth-century work of the defter and slicker kinds, has tended to find its level on insurance calendars rather than on the walls of public buildings and museums.

Adapted from S. Sontag, *On Photography.* © 2001 by Picador.

1.  The primary purpose of the passage is to:

    A.  explain how photography, although at first not taken seriously, eventually gained public acceptance as a legitimate art form.
    B.  describe how, because of photography, a distinction came to be made between creative artistic work and the factual depiction of objects.
    C.  explain how photography on one hand allows us to better portray and communicate the character of things, and yet on the other has led to the unfortunate devaluation of the work of highly skilled artists.
    D.  describe how photography has affected in a positive way how the public perceives and evaluates both pictorial representations of reality and reality itself.

2.  Alfred Stieglitz, a well-respected modern photographer, wrote that "the ability to make a truly artistic photograph . . . is the result of an artistic instinct coupled with years of labor." Based only on passage information, the author of the passage would most likely:

    A.  agree that this may be true, given that a skilled photograph is not necessarily an artistic photograph.
    B.  be skeptical of the statement because the technical aspects of photography can be quickly mastered by the average person.
    C.  accept the statement as a natural continuation of the author's own analysis of art and photography.
    D.  have no opinion, as the passage does not discuss qualities of artistry.

3.  The author's discussion of the relationship between the depiction and the perception of nature suggests that:

    A.  art's fundamental goal is to represent the essence of nature, which rarely corresponds to the obvious appearance of natural forms.
    B.  viewing representations of nature can change how we perceive nature itself, which then affects how we represent it.
    C.  theoretical discussions of the character of nature and natural objects can change how we perceive and so how we represent nature.
    D.  the creation of an artistic representation of nature will always be more highly valued than representations of objects that represent nature.

4.  "Photographic distortion" (paragraph 3) most likely refers to:

    A.  the ways in which photographers manipulate images.
    B.  a quality that always distinguishes photographs from paintings.
    C.  something that results from the fact that the camera, unlike the human brain, does not interpret what it "sees."
    D.  the inferior images produced by cameras in the early stages of development of photographic technology.

5.  With which of the following statements about Jacquemart would the author be most likely to agree?

    I.   He was once seen as a good artist on the basis of his great skill in etching.
    II.  His work was eventually devalued only because his etchings did not show the qualities of precious objects as well as a photograph could.
    III. He gained a worldwide reputation as an illustrator.

    A.  I only
    B.  II only
    C.  I and II only
    D.  I and III only

---

## Passage 22 (Questions 1-7)

News of the French Revolution came in 1789 to a Portugal that was struggling to return to the traditional order of the Middle Ages after the violent and scandalous attempt of the Marquès de Pombal in the 1760s to bring Portugal abreast, in culture and law, with the France of Louis XV and the Spain of Charles III. In both [Spain and Portugal], the agents of the Inquisition now loomed like lions at a palace gate to repel or stamp out any such words or thoughts that might question the traditional institutions of Church and monarchy.

At the bottom of the social scale stood other guardians of the past: the simple, mostly unlettered commoners—peasants, craftsmen, tradesmen, soldiers—who were fondly habituated to their transmitted faith, comforted by its legends, awed by its miracles, thrilled by its ritual. At the top were the feudal barons, models of manners and owners of the soil; a timid, feebleminded Queen Maria Francisca, and her son John, regent (1799) and then (1816-26) king; all dependably protective of the Church as the indispensable support of private morals, social order, and absolute, divine-right monarchy.

Amid these diverse sentinels of tradition lurked a small minority—students, Freemasons, scientists, poets, businessmen, a few officials, even a noble or two—who were irked by the despotism of the past, furtively flirted with philosophy, and dreamed of representative government, free trade, free assembly, free press, and free thought.

Upon that timid minority, those shocked commoners, those startled dignitaries and Inquisitors, the news of the French Revolution, however dulled by delay, came as an exhilarating or terrifying revelation. When Louis XVI was deposed by a Paris uprising (1792), Queen Maria felt her throne tremble. In 1793, infuriated by the execution of Louis XVI, the Portuguese government joined Spain in a holy war against France, and sent a squadron to join the British fleet in the Mediterranean. Soon Spain negotiated a separate peace (1795); Portugal asked for a like accommodation, but France refused, alleging that Portugal was in effect a colony and ally of England.

Certain economic factors led to this refusal, and to an eventual alliance of Spain and France against England and Portugal. Behind the military and political situation of Portugal lay the precarious structure of its economic life. As with Spain, the nation's wealth depended on the importation of precious metals from its colonies. No middle class existed to develop natural resources with progressive agriculture and technological industry. When command of the seas passed to England, the supply of gold became subject to evading the British Navy or making terms with the British government. While Portugal chose to make terms,

Spain chose to fight against England, and almost exhausted her resources to build a navy. When that navy, reluctantly merged with the French, was defeated at Trafalgar in 1805, Spain became dependent upon revolutionary France, which was now under the rule of Napoleon. Portugal, to avoid absorption by France and Spain, became dependent upon England.

Next, in an attempt to isolate and weaken England, Napoleon persuaded the Spanish government to join with France in invading Portugal. The Portuguese royal family fled in an English vessel to Brazil. On November 30, 1807, Junot, a general under Napoleon's command, led a French–Spanish army, almost unresisted, into Lisbon, the Portuguese capital. Liberal leaders in Portugal flocked to the new government, hoping that Napoleon would annex their country and give it representative institutions. Junot and Napoleon humored these men, secretly laughed at them, announced (February 1, 1808) "that the House of Braganza has ceased to reign," and Napoleon more and more behaved like a king.

Adapted from W. and A. Durant, *The Age of Napoleon: A History of European Civilization from 1789 to 1815.* © 1975 Simon & Schuster.

1.  The author states that Napoleon "more and more behaved like a king" (final paragraph) most likely in order to:

    A.  indicate that Napoleon usurped the throne of Portugal and claimed the divine rights of a monarch.
    B.  suggest that monarchist and other traditional political orders often restrict individual freedoms such as the right to free speech and assembly.
    C.  indicate that the Portuguese liberals' hopes for a representative government were not to be realized under Napoleon's rule.
    D.  suggest that Napoleon subverted Junot's goal of instituting a representative government in Portugal.

2. Based on information provided in the passage, which of the following played a direct or indirect role in Napoleon's invasion of Portugal?

   I. Portugal's economic dependence on industrial imports from England
   II. A weak middle class which was unable to effectively mediate between lower-class demands for political representation and the nobility's support for the divine rights of the monarch
   III. The absence of advanced industrial or highly developed agricultural sectors in Portugal

   A. II only
   B. III only
   C. I and III only
   D. II and III only

3. Which of the following can be inferred from the author's discussion of the Inquisition?

   A. The Inquisition was created in Portugal and Spain as a result of the threat posed to the monarchical order by the French revolution.
   B. Agents of the Inquisition played a role in the restoration of King John to the Portuguese throne in 1816.
   C. The beliefs and goals that drove the Inquisition were inconsistent with the ideas of the Marquès de Pombal.
   D. The agents of the Inquisition successfully prevented any new political and philosophical tenets from influencing the Portuguese population in the late 18th century.

4. Which of the following assertions made in the passage is NOT supported by example, explanation, or analogy?

   A. The economic system of Portugal was precarious in the late 18th century.
   B. Most of those at the bottom of the Portuguese social scale supported the traditional political order.
   C. Portugal harbored a minority who dreamed of a new representative government.
   D. The Portuguese feudal barons were models of manners inherited from the past.

5. Some historians claim that a primary cause of the French Revolution was an overburdened fiscal system and the French monarchy's resulting need for new and higher taxes. This sparked protests and led to widespread demands for profound political reforms. This information would most support which of the following assumptions made by the author in this passage?

   A. Traditional political orders which deny political representation to large sections of the population are inherently weak, and so are vulnerable to attack from internal dissidents or external enemies.
   B. The economy of a nation can be a determining factor in its political and/or military position.
   C. The lack of a strong middle class can delay the development of industrialization, and leave a state dangerously dependent on colonial resources.
   D. High taxes needed by the Portuguese monarchy to build its naval forces played a role in the weakness of the Portuguese state in the late 18th and early 19th centuries, and contributed to the success of Napoleon's invasion.

6. Which of the following most accurately describes alliances or concerted actions that existed or occurred at some time between 1789 and 1808, as described in the passage?

   A. Portugal formed a military alliance with Brazil, and Spain cooperated with France.
   B. Spain acted in concert with France, and Portugal cooperated with Spain.
   C. Portugal allied with Britain, and Spain allied with Brazil.
   D. Portugal cooperated with Britain, and Charles III formed a military alliance with Louis XV.

7. With which of the following statements would the author be most likely to agree?

   A. Political independence is necessary for economic independence.
   B. Portugal's reliance on its agricultural sector impeded the development of domestic industry and manufacturing.
   C. A small but well organized liberal minority within Portugal, hoping for greater representation and individual liberties, facilitated Napoleon's invasion of its own nation.
   D. The Portuguese monarchy placed restrictions on trade before the coming of the French Revolution.

# MCAT
Critical Analysis and
Reasoning Skills

Practice Passages
Solutions

## Passage 1

This is a Now passage.

**Main Points:**

P1: Sale of equity one way to get money to make money
P2: It may be more profitable to be part owner of a big business than sole owner of a small one
P3: One way to sell capital stock is private sale to individuals
P4: Another way is public sale to general public
P5: Public sale subject to more regulation
P6: Stock may also be sold to underwriters-expensive
P7: Small companies often make mistakes in public sales
P8: Condition of financial market affects sale prospects

**Bottom Line:** Businesses can earn capital by selling stock, and there are many factors that determine how they may do so.

| | | |
|---|---|---|
| 1. | B | This is an Inference question. |
| | A: | No. Greater regulation comes as a result of selling stock, not of not selling it. |
| | **B:** | **Yes. The passage states that "the owner may decide logically to bring in other owners" (paragraph 2), which means that the owner might be wise to sell stock in this situation.** |
| | C: | No. By not selling stock, the owner retains control because there is no "dilution of ownership" (paragraph 2). |
| | D: | No. The passage indicates just the opposite: selling stock is one way of financing expansion and growth of a business (paragraph 2). The owner may be sacrificing a measure of security for growth if she did sell stock. |

| | | |
|---|---|---|
| 2. | C | This is an Inference question. |
| | A: | No. The passage implies that any sale of stock "involves, of necessity, a dilution of ownership" (paragraph 2). |
| | B: | No. Any sale of stock (unlike borrowing) is a way of raising capital without incurring debt. Thus, sale through a private placement offering is not special in this respect. |
| | **C:** | **Yes. The "entrepreneur avoids many requirements of the securities law" (paragraph 3), although presumably not all of them.** |
| | D: | No. A private placement is offered to "selected individuals" (paragraph 3), not the general public. |

3.  A   This is a Retrieval question.
    **A:**   **Yes. The passage states that "the personal financial objectives of owners may also enter into the reasoning behind the public sale of stock" (paragraph 4).**
    B:   No. An unusually low rate may affect the decision whether or not to use an underwriter (see paragraph 6), but the passage gives no indication that underwriters' rates drive the initial decision of whether or not to go public in the first place.
    C:   No. "Going public" involves public sale of stock (paragraph 4). The passage does not indicate that public sale (as opposed to private placement) is more likely to facilitate rapid growth. There is less support for this answer than we have for choice A.
    D:   No. On the contrary, the passage suggests that it is "typically the larger small-business firms" that go public (paragraph 4). The example of the hot dog stand is an exaggeration that shows how easy it was for practically anyone to go public in the growth-oriented 1980s (paragraph 8).

4.  D   This is an Inference/EXCEPT question.
    A:   No. This is true because the underwriters' fees are a percentage of the firm's profits (paragraph 6).
    B:   No. This is also true. The underwriter guarantees the sale of securities (paragraph 6); therefore, when the securities (stock) don't sell, the underwriter sustains a loss but the firm still receives the money. While this is not directly stated in the passage, it is implied. Therefore it is better supported than choice D, which directly contradicts the passage.
    C:   No. This is also true as an inference from the statement that "The reason for the high expense is, of course, the element of uncertainty and risk associated with public offerings of stock of small, relatively unknown firms" (paragraph 6).
    **D:**   **Yes. This statement is false. The passage makes clear that underwriters are involved only in public offerings, not in private placements; paragraphs 4–8 all discuss public sale.**

5.  B   This is an Inference question.
    A:   No. Private placement is a way of selling capital stock. As far as this passage goes, we do not even know if there is such a thing as "private stock." The passage also clearly states that employees can buy capital stock (paragraph 3).
    **B:**   **Yes. Paragraph 2 discusses how the sale of capital stock dilutes ownership and how the original owner, after selling capital stock, owns less of her business.**
    C:   No. This choice is too extreme. Paragraph 7 indicates that their financial arrangements are frequently "unsound" or often "not in the best interest of the small firms," but we do not know that it leads to bankruptcy.
    D:   No. We are not given any information about what is the most common way businesses generate capital. Sale of equity is described in paragraph 1 as one way, but no mention is made of the most common way.

6.    B        This is a Main Idea question.

        A:      No. This choice is too narrow. It can be inferred from paragraph 8, but it leaves out most of the major themes of the passage.

        **B:**      **Yes. This is stated in the first paragraph; the rest of the passage explains the ways in which sale of equity may help raise money, and the specific issues involved in such a sale.**

        C:      No. This choice is too narrow to be the main idea. Furthermore, the author does not indicate that relatively unknown firms, in particular, can succeed in "going public."

        D:      No. This choice is too vague and general to capture the main idea of the passage, which is specifically about the sale of capital stock.

7.    C        This is an Inference question.

        A:      No. This choice takes a part of the passage (paragraph 7) out of context. The author makes no connection between SEC regulation on one hand, and whether or not small businesses make the best possible decisions on the other hand.

        B:      No. The SEC protects the public, not the owners (paragraph 5).

        **C:**      **Yes. The SEC seeks to regulate firms in order to protect investors and the public from fraudulent offerings. This is implied by the statement "In undertaking the public sale of stock, the firm subjects itself to greater public regulation" (paragraph 5) and from the fact that the SEC is discussed in the context of public sale of stock.**

        D:      No. Underwriters are discussed in the sixth paragraph, and there is no mention of the SEC there.

# Passage 2

This is a Later passage.

**Main Points:**

P1:  Dreams and confusion
P2:  Prometheus's gifts to mankind
P3:  Ability to understand dreams is benefit of human intelligence
P4:  Three distinct states of human brain activity
P5:  There must be a powerful reason for sleep
P6:  There is little evidence to support reason for sleep; sleep leaves us vulnerable

**Bottom Line:** We have long wondered about dreams, but sleep and dreams not fully understood.

1.    A        This is a Primary Purpose question.

        **A:**      **Yes. The first paragraph (the quote) and the second paragraph introduce the classical idea of dreams as a gift. The third paragraph refers to classical thought (Aeschylus) on dreams and human evolution. The final three paragraphs discuss modern research and ideas on sleep and dreaming. Therefore, this choice includes all aspects of the passage without being too general.**

        B:      No. The author describes both ancient and modern ideas about sleep and dreaming, and suggests that we still do not fully understand the function of sleep (paragraph 6). Thus, the author is not advocating any one point of view, including a modern or technological view.

        C:      No. This statement is too narrow: it relates only to paragraph 4.

        D:      No. The passage provides no evidence of a controversy. If anything, the author seems to think the classical and modern understandings of sleep and dreams are complementary.

2.  A       This is an Inference question.
    **A:**   **Yes. The phrase "although in this case concentrating much more on the 'evolver' than on the evolved" (paragraph 2) implies that *Prometheus Bound* concentrates on Prometheus's story, whereas Genesis focuses on the story of humanity. We know that Prometheus himself is not human (the "evolved"), as he has "introduced civilization to a befuddled and superstitious mankind" (paragraph 2). The passage describes him in the role of "evolver."**
    B:       No. Both works are referred to as "major works in Western literature" (paragraph 2). This option is Out of Scope; it is an Outside Knowledge Attractor.
    C:       No. According to the passage, both are works of literature that present "viable allegories" or symbolic stories (paragraph 2), not literal fact.
    D:       No. Both works are referred to simply as "works in Western literature" (paragraph 2). Historical, cultural, and geographical differences are not mentioned. This option is Out of Scope; it is an Outside Knowledge Attractor.

3.  D       This is an Inference question.
    A:       No. Paragraph 6 indicates that vulnerability during sleep is one of the "worrisome aspects about the contention" that sleep has a restorative effect, not support for it.
    B:       No. We know that the actual evidence "seems to be sparse" (paragraph 6), so in this indeterminate state there can be no *final* corroboration.
    C:       No. There is nothing to indicate that the worrisome aspects of the sleep-as-restoration hypothesis act to contradict that hypothesis, and sparse evidence is not contradictory evidence--it is a lack of evidence.
    **D:**   **Yes. The passage states that "the actual evidence for this view, apart from its common-sense plausibility, seems to be sparse" (paragraph 6). This shows that the idea in question is scientifically unsupported (but not proven false or contradicted by the evidence), and that the author thinks the idea is intuitively attractive (as indicated by the phrase "common sense plausibility").**

4.  C       This is a Structure question.
    A:       No. Something that begins the passage cannot be an elaboration; an elaboration would continue a theme or idea already introduced.
    B:       No. People are only described as being "as beasts" prior to Prometheus' gifts, and no sustained comparison occurs in the first two sentences of the excerpt.
    **C:**   **Yes. The author's first paragraph shows us that the excerpt was used to introduce one "viable allegory [symbolic story] of the evolution of man."**
    D:       No. Neither the author nor the excerpt dispute or disagree with a contrasting point of view.

5. **D** This is an Inference/Roman numeral question.

    **I:** **True. The sentence, "Our nocturnal vulnerability is very evident; the Greeks recognized Morpheus and Thanatos, the gods of sleep and death, as brothers" (paragraph 6) supports the author's suggestion that sleep and death are similar.**

    **II:** False. Even though we may think of the sleep/death experiences as similar in some ways (as in observing a sleeping person from afar), the author makes no mention of this fact to support his argument. This choice represents outside knowledge or personal opinion.

    **III:** **True. The author says animals are "exceptionally vulnerable" (paragraph 6) and applies this to humans as well. This suggests that sleep may lead to death in some situations.**

6. **B** This is a Structure question.

    **A:** No. The author does indeed make this comparison (paragraph 4), but this is not his purpose in raising the evidence of electroencephalography.

    **B:** **Yes. This is shown especially well in paragraph 4.**

    **C:** No. The brain's energy requirements are not mentioned in the passage. This answer choice is Out of Scope.

    **D:** No. There is no direct connection between Aeschylus's story and electroencephalographic evidence that waking, sleeping, and dreaming are three distinct states. These two parts of the passage have related yet distinct themes. This is a decoy Attractor.

## Passage 3

This is a Later/Killer passage.

**Main Points:**

P1: Self's boundaries are enlarged by thoughts of infinity
P2: Man is not measure of all things: limited view
P3: Free intellect values not-Self
P4: Man's true freedom is in seeing self as part of larger whole

**Bottom Line:** Intellectual freedom requires us to think outside ourselves and contemplate the infinite.

1. **D** This is a Retrieval question.

    **A:** No. This choice contradicts the main theme of the passage, which is that we must look outside of ourselves.

    **B:** No. This choice has the same problem as choice A. The author argues the opposite: "The true philosophic contemplation, on the contrary, finds its satisfaction in every enlargement of the Not-Self" (paragraph 3).

    **C:** No. While the "not-Self" is in fact the universe, philosophic speculation would be the equivalent of contemplation. Thus the choice states that philosophic speculation should begin with contemplation of contemplation. Compare this directly with choice D.

    **D:** **Yes. The author states in the first sentence of the first paragraph that philosophic contemplation begins from the not-Self: "we start from the not-Self."**

2.　C　This is an Inference question.
　　A:　No. Philosophies that see "Man as the measure of all things" cut us off from knowledge and understanding of the "world beyond" (paragraph 2). According to the author, this is a "widespread philosophical tendency"; that is, what philosophies are inclined to do.
　　B:　No. The author does not encourage us to study different philosophies, but instead describes the nature of true philosophic contemplation.
　　**C:　Yes. "Egocentric" can mean self-involved, as in seeing oneself as the center of all things. In paragraph 2 the author describes what he calls "those philosophies which assimilate the universe to Man"; that is, which tend to describe the universe in a way that corresponds to the human experience of it.**
　　D:　No. True philosophic contemplation will "value more the abstract and universal knowledge into which the accidents of private history do not enter" (paragraph 3). Abstraction is portrayed positively, not negatively by the author. However, most philosophy tends to see man as "the measure of all things," and so to imprison us in an overly personal and private view of the world (paragraphs 2 and 3). Therefore, philosophies tend to do just the opposite of this answer choice.

3.　A　This is an Inference/NOT question.
　　**A:　Yes. The author does not explicitly address the imagination's enrichment in this passage.**
　　B:　No. The author explores this answer choice in almost every sentence of the passage. Transforming an egocentric perspective to a more outward-looking point of view is one of the passage's more important ideas.
　　C:　No. The author refers to this answer choice in the last paragraph. In "true" contemplation, one's "prejudices, habits, and desires" (paragraph 2) distorting real philosophic inquiry are among the "accidents of private history" (paragraph 3) that are left behind (paragraph 4).
　　D:　No. The author alludes to this result of "true" philosophic pondering, especially in paragraph 4.

4.　B　This is a Structure question.
　　A:　No. The author is using the word "law" figuratively in paragraph 2 to express a notion of certainty.
　　**B:　Yes. The whole sentence (in paragraph 2) says, "The man who finds pleasure in such a theory of knowledge is like the man...." That theory of knowledge is one that claims everything knowable is created by the mind.**
　　C:　No. The author talks about true philosophic contemplation in the next paragraph.
　　D:　No. The author has already implicitly explained the nature of the not-Self and this "man" is instead like one who never contemplated the not-Self.

5.  D       This is an Inference question.
    A:      No. A simple *awareness* of life outside one's Self (or oneself) does not define the "not-Self."
    B:      No. A state of non self-centeredness might be necessary for a true appreciation of the not-Self, but it does not by itself constitute the not-Self.
    C:      No. There is no textual basis for this answer choice. The unconscious could still be part of the Self.
    **D:      Yes. The relationship between the Self and the not-Self is set up in the first two paragraphs. Key clues include the words "the infinity of the universe" and "the world beyond." All the author means by "not-Self" is anything that is not you, which would be everything in the universe outside of you.**

6.  B       This is an Inference question.
    A:      No. The author would probably agree with this assertion. Paragraphs 1 and 4 suggest that the universe is a good and edifying place.
    **B:      Yes. The author does not promote this essentially existential claim; see particularly paragraph 4 in which human experiences are described as "parts of the whole."**
    C:      No. The author would not refute this answer choice. In paragraph 4 he implies that the world can be affected "by any one man's deeds."
    D:      No. The author argues this point—introduced in paragraph 1—throughout most of the essay.

7.  C       This is an Inference question.
    A:      No. In paragraph 3, the author states that the free intellect will value abstract knowledge more than sense-based knowledge.
    B:      No. The author depicts (especially in the last paragraph) the free intellect as more altruistic than this answer choice implies.
    **C:      Yes. In paragraph 3 the author points to the free intellect's flight from temporality by seeing "without a here and now."**
    D:      No. To trammel means "to confine or hinder." As stated in the explanation for choice A, the free intellect favors abstract knowledge and, hence, is not entrapped by it (paragraph 3).

## Passage 4

This is a Now passage.

**Main Points:**

P1: FDA saw Abbott cyclamate tests as useless
P2: But approved based own own studies
P3: FDA should have called for more testing
P4: Further evidence of danger but no FDA action

**Bottom Line:** The FDA should not have approved cyclamates.

1.  B     This is an Inference/Roman numeral question.
    - I:   False. The whole passage emphasizes that governmental interference is crucial, since a company is often too eager to put a product on the market.
    - **II:**   **True. The author clearly is critical of a company, such as Abbott Laboratories, that creates a vague, shoddy report about a new product. Careful testing by the company should be a requirement.**
    - III:   False. Although the author criticizes the FDA for its lack of action on cyclamates, there is no evidence that the writer would want companies seeking to have a product placed on the market to avoid the FDA altogether. Actually, it is more likely that the author would feel that some government intervention is absolutely crucial.

2.  D     This is an Inference/EXCEPT question.
    Note: The credited response will be inconsistent with, or not supported by, the passage.
    - A:   No. Lehman asserts that he would be reluctant to permit cyclamates "even for drug use, not to mention as an artificial sweetener for foods" (paragraph 2).
    - B:   No. The whole scenario indicates questionable levels of scrutiny by the FDA where determining acceptable levels of toxicity in daily food intake is concerned.
    - C:   No. This is well supported by the passage's description of events, the eventual appearance of cyclamates on consumer shelves, and their slow disappearance despite warnings issued to the FDA.
    - **D:**   **Yes. The passage suggests that the approval of Abbott's inadequate NDA was unusual and only possible because the FDA had conducted its own study (paragraph 2). Hence the usual route of approval depends on an NDA.**

3.  C     This is a Retrieval question.
    - A:   No. Cyclamates do not cure diabetes; they are merely a tool in its treatment (paragraph 1).
    - B:   No. This may be true of artificial sweeteners, but cyclamates were "intended for use in foods and beverages by diabetics and others who must restrict their intake of sugar" (paragraph 1). These lines imply that cyclamates were designed for those who, for medical reasons, must not eat sugar. Do not use outside knowledge to infer that the "others" refers to overweight persons; obesity is never mentioned in the passage.
    - **C:**   **Yes. Cyclamates were proposed as substitutes for sugar (paragraph 1).**
    - D:   No. If anything, cyclamates cause cancer (paragraph 3).

4.  B     This is an Inference question.

    A:     No. Approving cyclamates based on its own research is an "unusual position" (paragraph 2) for the FDA to take.

    **B:     Yes. Lehman's approval for cyclamates' use is not based on support "contained in this NDA" (paragraph 2); the passage portrays this approval as a departure from standard procedure.**

    C:     No. Note the word "only." The NDA is described as a normally essential part of the process of approving a new drug (paragraphs 1 and 2).

    D:     No. The passage suggests the opposite. Cyclamates are a food additive intended to help diabetics manage their disease (paragraph 1), and the FDA would normally have required an NDA in order to approve the use of cyclamates (paragraph 2).

5.  C     This is an Inference question.

    A:     No. The NAS-NRC provided warnings about the dangers of cyclamates (paragraph 4). The author does not suggest that this organization had the capacity or duty to further act on that warning; that responsibility lay with the FDA.

    B:     No. Abbott Laboratories had the approval of the supposed watchdog, so its marketing of cyclamates is understandable.

    **C:     Yes. The author discusses the FDA's various failures to act on information indicating the dangers of cyclamates, information that included results from the FDA's own studies (see paragraph 3). Therefore we can infer that the author would place the most blame on the FDA, given that it had the power and the duty to keep dangerous drugs off the market.**

    D:     No. The author places no blame or responsibility on the consumers themselves. It was the FDA that had the duty to protect the public welfare, given that it had both access to information not available to the public and the ability to keep dangerous drugs off the market.

6.  A     This is a Structure question.

    **A:     Yes. The author mentions the shoddiness of the test as part of his argument against cyclamates. The author claims that when the supposed support for cyclamates was found to be questionable, more testing was clearly indicated (paragraph 3).**

    B:     No. Abbott's test itself was merely shoddy; it was the FDA tests that showed that cyclamates could be dangerous (paragraph 3).

    C:     No. The shoddiness of the test serves to help bring down cyclamates, not build up the FDA.

    D:     No. There is no implication of dishonesty, only incompetence.

7.  B        This is an Inference question.
    A:       No. The NAS-NRC is a research organization that cannot ban chemicals and has no regulatory role. This follows from the fact that it must take its urgent recommendations to the FDA and cannot act on them itself (paragraph 4).
    **B:      Yes. Both the FDA and the NAS-NRC employ scientists whose job it is to monitor the safety of foods and drugs that are intended to be marketed for public consumption.**
    C:       No. The passage suggests that the FDA made an unusual move in basing its recommendations on its own research (paragraph 2), thus implying that research is not the FDA's *primary* function.
    D:       No. As a regulatory agency, the FDA can ban drugs. The beginning of the second paragraph makes it clear that the FDA had the power to ban or to approve cyclamates.

# Passage 5

This is a Now passage.

**Main Points:**

P1:   Despite increased cost of schooling, results have declined
P2:   Government spends about half what required to have equal education
P3:   Equal obligatory schooling is not economically feasible, and rich benefit more
P4:   Obligatory schooling has negative results

**Bottom Line:** Obligatory schooling, instead of equalizing students, polarizes society.

1.  A        This is a Main Point question.
    **A:      Yes. Choice A aptly summarizes the passage, without going beyond it. See especially the opening to paragraph 3, "Equal obligatory schooling must be recognized as at least economically unfeasible." In other words, regardless of any other failings, it cannot succeed economically.**
    B:       No. Both Latin America and the United States allocate resources unequally to education. Also, Latin America is mentioned only in passing (paragraph 3), so this is not the central thesis. Be careful not to confuse evidence (here, about Latin America) with the author's larger claims being supported by that evidence. claims
    C:       No. The author implies that increasing educational funding is irrelevant. In fact, the sentence "The President's Committee for the Study of School Finance should ask not how to support or how to trim such increasing costs, but how they can be avoided" (paragraph 2) implies that he thinks that an increase in funding would be counterproductive. Additionally, the mention of medical expenses makes this a Decoy Attractor. While medical expenses are mentioned as a means of comparison (that is, presented as evidence), they are not central to the author's claim.
    D:       No. This is implied by the sentence "The United States, which spent nearly eighty billion dollars in 1969 for 'defense' including its deployment in Vietnam, is obviously too poor to provide equal schooling" (paragraph 2), but the author does not expand on this point. Therefore, it is too narrow to be the central thesis.

2.  B    This is an Inference question.
    A:   No. Nothing in the passage suggests that the author would advocate a solution that would polarize society even more. In fact, paragraph 3 suggests he thinks that the rich already get more than their fair share.
    **B:   Yes. The author does not merely imply that obligatory education has some shortcomings; he suggests that it is fundamentally flawed. This is made clear by the opening to paragraph 3 and by the closing paragraph, where he states that obligatory education polarizes society and sets up a caste system. Therefore, out of these four choices, this is the statement with which the author would be most likely to agree.**
    C:   No. The author makes it clear in paragraph 2 that he is interested in avoiding costs.
    D:   No. The author does not discuss international cooperation, or the importance of international standards. Furthermore, in the final paragraph he indicates that he disapproves of the current "international caste system" which judges countries on the basis of number of years of education (which is much like the idea of common standards).

3.  C    This is a Retrieval/EXCEPT question.
         Note: The credited response will be the choice that does NOT describe how education is similar to health care.
    A:   No. The first paragraph suggests that more money is being spent on both health care and education and that the results have not met expectations.
    B:   No. Such a reading is suggested by the "3 percent increase in life expectancy in men" (paragraph 1) and by the implied inability of some schoolchildren to read despite increased spending on education.
    **C:   Yes. The passage does not state or imply that health care is unfairly distributed between rich and poor (although we may personally believe that it is so, and thus we may have been tempted to "read" this implication into the passage). Remember to watch out for absolute words such as "always."**
    D:   No. The passage states that "Medical expenses concentrated on those above forty-five have doubled several times" (paragraph 1) and that both the demand for and the costs of higher education are growing faster than the demand for and costs of elementary and high school education (first three sentences of paragraph 2). Keep in mind that "older is a relative term, so while the author does not talk explicitly about age in his discussion of education, the differentiation between early and higher education is enough here to support this answer choice.

4.  D    This is a Retrieval question.
    A:   No. Although this statement is true according to the passage (paragraph 3), it is not given as the main reason for discrimination in the distribution of public funds.
    B:   No. As with choice A, this is supported by the passage (paragraph 3), but is not the answer to this particular question.
    C:   No. The passage suggests a connection between wealth and access to education, not wealth and intelligence.
    **D:   Yes. Paragraph 3 states: "The principal reasons for [the fact that the children of rich parents obtain ten times more public funding than the children of poor parents] are that rich children stay longer in school, that a year in a university is...more expensive than a year in high school, and that most private universities depend...on tax-derived finances." a Retrieval or Inference question stem uses words like "main reason" in the stem, be sure to look for synonyms, in this case "principal reasons," in the text.**

5.  B       This is a Structure question.
    A:      No. That author argues that the rich receive better schooling and more public funds in the US and therefore, discrimination is worse here (paragraph 3).
    **B:      Yes. In paragraph 3 the author states: "In the United States the discrepancy is smaller but the discrimination is keener." The author then goes on to explain how much better off the children of the rich are, compared to the children of the poor.**
    C:      No. Nothing in the passage suggests this; if anything, given the lack of return on money spent, educational spending in the US is inefficient.
    D:      No. The international caste system is not mentioned until paragraph 4, and the author does not connect it to his comparison of the US and Latin America.

## Passage 6

This is a Now passage.

**Main Points:**

P1:  Nature of Greek gods indicates nature of Greeks
P2:  Older darker ritual magic beneath myths
P3:  Philosophers developed monotheism in form of Zeus
P4:  Ionians: universe is natural, explainable
P5:  Anaximander theorized Earth-Sun relationship and origins of life
P6:  Empedocles argued  4 elements of matter
P7:  Anaxagoras on the sun
P8:  Ionians made practical, not just theoretical, advances

**Bottom Line:** Olympian myths gave way to Ionian philosophers' explanation of universe through reason.

1.  C       This is an Inference question.
    A:      No. The belief that the Earth is a flat disc floating in water is attributed to Thales (paragraph 4), not to all Ionian philosophers. Furthermore, by stating that Thales "pictured the Earth as a flat disc, floating on water, instead of resting on a limitless flat bottom (paragraph 4) the author suggests that thinkers *preceding* the Ionians held this belief. In sum, no one is described as holding both of those beliefs at the same time.
    B:      No. This choice takes words out of context. While Anaximander believed the opposite ("Primary matter is eternal, but all things made from it are doomed to destruction" (paragraph 5)), you have no indication that the author disagrees with Anaximander on this issue.
    **C:      Yes. That they were first is stated in paragraph 4, and that they made errors is evidenced throughout.**
    D:      No. We are given no information about what was more or less commonplace in ancient times. Also, keep in mind that the Ionian philosophers lived in ancient times, and they are described as having a rational (that is, scientific) rather than religious approach to understanding the universe.

2.   C   This is an Inference question.

   A:   No. The passage refers to "an older magic, with traditional rites for the promotion of fertility by the celebration of the annual cycle of life and death" (paragraph 2), but does not mention dancing. Be careful not to use outside knowledge.

   B:   No. Nothing in the description indicates that the world of early mythology was rational. It is the Ionian philosophers (not early Greek mythologists) who are described as interested in "rational inquiry" (paragraph 4).

   C:   **Yes. The early "ghosts, gods, or demons" (paragraph 2) appear to be threatening, since they are "unfriendly" and must be "propitiated" or appeased.**

   D:   No. Early Greek mythology incorporated multiple gods (paragraph 1) and is described by the author as polytheistic. Monotheism is the practice of worshipping a single god: this was true of later (classical) Greek mythology (paragraph 3).

3.   D   This is an Inference question.
      Note: The credited response will be the choice that does NOT describe Ionian philosophy.

   A:   No. This term does describe Ionian philosophy. The passage says that "Primary matter is eternal, but all things made from it are doomed to destruction" (paragraph 5) and "there were four elements, earth, water, air and—still more tenuous—fire. By combinations of the four, the various types of matter were made" (paragraph 6).

   B:   No. This term also fits (see quotations above, as well as Empedocles's investigations into the corporeal nature of air in paragraph 6).

   C:   No. This term applies, since Anaximander inferred that "the visible dome of the sky is half a complete sphere, with the Earth at its center, the Sun passing underground at night" (paragraph 5).

   D:   **Yes. This term cannot apply; it contradicts the terms in choices A–C, which all describe views that assume reality is not simply defined by human perception or consciousness.**

4.   B   This is a Retrieval question.

   A:   No. *Deductive* geometry had its roots in "empirical rules for land surveying" (paragraph 4), not in abstract theories. Furthermore, the passage does not mention later confirmation through observation.

   B:   **Yes. Thales originated it from the Egyptian rules for land-surveying (paragraph 4).**

   C:   No. Thales posited ideas that we may now see as mythical views of the universe (paragraph 4), but the author does not suggest that deductive geometry arose from those views. Thales' belief that the Earth is a flat disc floating is not directly connected by the author to deductive geometry.

   D:   No. The passage clearly states that Thales originated deductive geometry from "the empirical rules for land-surveying" (paragraph 4).

5.    C      This is a Retrieval question.
      A:     No. This is inconsistent with paragraph 3 where that author discusses the shift towards monotheism.
      B:     No. The mysteries are mentioned in the second paragraph and have nothing to do with the emergence of the cults.
      **C:     Yes. In paragraph 3, the author explicitly states that the decay of Olympus led to both the revival of old cults and the emergence of new ones.**
      D:     No. This is Out of Scope. Alchemy is never mentioned in the passage.

6.    D      This is a Weaken question.
      A:     No. The Ionian philosophers do not necessarily represent all ancient Greeks or what may be happening to ancient Greek religious culture.
      B:     No. If anything, this answer choice strengthens his argument.
      C:     No. People obeying laws because of Zeus indicates an evolution away from belief in many gods.
      **D:     Yes. This statement, if true, indicates that the idea of Zeus as "single, supreme, and righteous" (paragraph 3) could coexist with a belief in multiple gods. Now the gods express themselves through Zeus, but they still exist as distinct and identifiable personalities.**

7.    B      This is a Strengthen question.
      A:     No. This would show the importance of mythology and would more likely weaken the author's claim.
      **B:     Yes. If rituals such as fertility rites not only preceded the appearance of Olympian mythology (paragraph 2), but persisted long after the mythology disappeared, it would strengthen the author's claim that ritual was more fundamental.**
      C:     No. It tells us nothing about which is more fundamental if they rejected both.
      D:     No. This would show the importance of mythology and would more likely weaken the author's claim.

## Passage 7
This is a Later passage.

### Main Points:

P1:  Aristotle's worldview important but have to understand context or will misinterpret
P2:  Example of distorted explanation: authority of written word
P3:  But wrong—really due to everyday perception
P4:  Education leads us astray
P5:  Main source of Aristotle's authority: expressed everyday perception
P6:  Aristotle's ideas show us something about pre-scientific perception

**Bottom Line:** Even though Aristotle's view of nature is inconsistent with modern science, its resonance with basic experiential perception means we must acknowledge its importance.

1.  D       This is an Inference question.
    A:      No. The author does not compare Aristotle to medieval scholars on the basis of overall level or amount of knowledge. Be careful not to use Outside Knowledge (see Out of Scope Attractors in the Review) or opinion.
    B:      No. The author suggests in the first sentence of paragraph 2 that this is what we have learned to believe in school and that it is a misconception. This is a Words out of Context (Decoy) Attractor because it takes text directly from the passage but ignores context: the last sentence of paragraph 1 combined with the "for example" in the first sentence of paragraph 2 further establishes this information as incorrect according to the author.
    C:      No. Although the author does suggest that confirmation of Galileo's conclusions requires special equipment, he does not imply that Galileo had such equipment, or that medical scholars lacked it; therefore it is not lack of equipment that caused medieval scholars to agree with Aristotle. This is a Not the Issue (Out of Scope) Attractor.
    **D:**      **Yes. The passage suggests that everyday observation does agree with Aristotle's conclusions and that experiments performed by Galileo's opponent confirmed that heavy bodies fall first (see paragraph 3).**

2.  C       This is a Retrieval question.
    A:      No. The author suggests that Galileo arrived at his conclusions through a "chain of logical arguments" (paragraph 3) rather than through observation; the significance of his discovery had nothing to do with better instrumentation.
    B:      No. On the contrary, his calculations went against prior observations. This is an "opposite" Attractor.
    **C:**      **Yes. The author claims that Galileo's discovery was significant "because it goes behind the superficial regularity disclosed by the senses to a more essential, but hidden, aspect of motion" (paragraph 3).**
    D:      No. The author indicates that in a way, Aristotle was right; that is, his ideas accurately reflect everyday experience (paragraph 3). The author states that "Galileo's law is more useful to science than Aristotle's not because it represents experience more perfectly," but because it represents a deeper, hidden reality (paragraph 3).

3.  C     This is an Inference question.
    A:    No. Primitive perception is in fact correct insofar as it describes the way things appear in the world. The author states that in the observation of falling bodies from the tower of Pisa, the heavier object hit the ground first (paragraph 3). This is a Negation (Decoy) Attractor.
    B:    No. Although the author does state that the beliefs of "primitive" people and children accord with Aristotle's (see last paragraph), the sense of the expression "primitive perception" does not derive from the same understanding of the word "primitive." This is a Words out of Context (Decoy) Attractor.
    **C:    Yes. It is what everyone sees in "the everyday world" (paragraph 3). It is sensory perception; that is, perception unaided by instruments.**
    D:    No. Primitive perception is precisely perception without any instruments. This is a Reversal/Negation (Decoy) Attractor.

4.  B     This is an Inference question.
    A:    No. Though the "failure" may in part be brought about by what we have been taught, the problem is not with the educational *system*.
    **B:    Yes. The author states that "we too easily take them [the ideas we learned in school] as natural and indubitable products of our own unaided perceptions," (paragraph 4), and therefore we are unable to see the world as people who do not have our own educational background see it.**
    C:    No. The author does not suggest that the historical record is itself factually inaccurate. The problem lies in our own failures to understand and interpret that record correctly, and to understand why we have the beliefs that we hold today.
    D:    No. "Ignorance or stupidity" (paragraph 4) is what we attribute to medieval scholars because of our "failure of historical perspective." This is a Words Out of Context (Decoy) Attractor.

5.  A     This is a New Information question.
    **A:    Yes. The main idea of the passage concerns Aristotle's enduring authority and its basis in his expression of a common-sense experience of the world in a coherent system. Common-sense experience does indeed tell us that the earth is flat.**
    B:    No. This choice is too extreme. Even though Galileo's theories involved greater abstraction than Aristotle's, the author does not suggest that ancient peoples rejected all abstract ideas.
    C:    No. There is nothing in the passage about religious writings. This is an "Out of Scope" Attractor.
    D:    No. Nothing in the passage connects the beliefs of children (in particular) or of tribal peoples to the ideas of ancient cosmology; while they share a common-sense world view, the author never suggests a causal link between beliefs of children and precepts of cosmology.

6.  C     This is a Retrieval/Roman numeral question.
    I:    **True. See paragraph 5. "Part" of Aristotle's authority derived from the "brilliance" and originality "of his own...ideas."**
    II:   False. His views "parallel" those of children because they explain common experience of the world, unaided by instruments and undistorted by education. Nowhere, however, does the passage suggest that his views "appeal" to children and uneducated people. Be careful not to fall for Decoy Attractors; carefully reread aspects of the passage that appear to resonate with the question.
    III:  **True. Aristotle was "able to express in an abstract and consistent manner many spontaneous perceptions of the universe that had existed for centuries" (paragraph 5).**


7.  B     This is an Inference question.
    A:    No. Galileo's law, which we accept as valid, came not from what he saw but from logical argument. In fact, it cannot be confirmed by our unaided senses (paragraph 3). We **do** believe things to be true that contradict the evidence provided by our senses, thus the word "only" in this choice is too extreme. Remember that extreme words are often a marker of an Attractor unless the passage employs them or if you are dealing with a "most Strengthen" or "most Weaken" question.
    B:    **Yes, that is why the author says that "our own education stands between us and the past" (paragraph 4).**
    C:    No. The passage does not suggest that we have a personal psychological motivation to believe certain things.
    D:    No. Aristotle's writings are described as logically coherent in paragraph 5, but that is the only discussion in the passage of logical coherence. It is not applied to how people generally view the world.

## Passage 8

This is a Now passage.

**Main Points:**

P1: Death of Communism occurring
P2: Freedom does not necessarily mean democracy
P3: Expected order or transformation
P4: But, political transformation preceded rather than followed achievement of civil society
P5: Future uncertain

**Bottom Line:** Despite the end of Communism, formerly communist countries do not have a democracy.

1.  D       This is a Main Idea question.
    A:      No. While the author asserts that democracy is far from established in formerly communist nations, he never goes so far as to claim that communism will always exist. The author states in the beginning of the passage that "a major historical process—the death of communism—is taking place."
    B:      No. The author is certainly concerned that democracy has not yet been firmly established, but the central concern of the passage is to chart the troubled course of change in formerly communist nations, not to glorify democracy.
    C:      No. This choice is true according to the passage, but too broad and vague to express the main idea.
    **D:      Yes. This answer choice reflects the concern that the author expresses in every paragraph of the passage.**

2.  B       This is an Inference question.
    A:      No. This is more or less what the author says did happen (paragraph 4)—it is not what was initially expected to happen.
    **B:      Yes. See paragraph 3. The expected order of events was: 1) change the economy; 2) "explode... totalitarian structure"; and then 3) transform political structures.**
    C:      No. There is no suggestion that elections could be held under Communist rule.
    D:      No. This choice misrepresents the anticipated order; market mechanisms, not democracy, were expected to undermine totalitarianism (paragraph 3).

3.  A       This is an Inference question.
    **A:      Yes. This is implied by the author when he writes that "[w]e have freedom, but we still have not achieved the democratic order" (paragraph 3).**
    B:      No. Note that choices A and B are opposites of each other. If a country can have freedom without having democracy, then democracy does not necessarily accompany freedom. According to the passage, the formerly Communist states now have freedom, but not democracy (paragraph 3).
    C:      No. The author states that "democracy is freedom institutionalized" (paragraph 2), meaning that freedom is an inherent part of democracy.
    D:      No. This choice is too extreme. The passage does not suggest that a democratic state places no limits on freedom whatsoever, or that a country with limited freedom now can never have democracy in the future.

4.  C       This is a Tone/Attitude question.
    A:      No. In fact, the author writes that "we still have not achieved the democratic order" (paragraph 3).
    B:      No. Although he is disillusioned with the nature of the "democracy" that has emerged, there is no indication in the passage that he wants to return to the totalitarian system. He even alludes to the continuing authority of the old leaders as a sign that he and his colleagues are "losing" (paragraph 5).
    **C:      Yes. This best describes the author's closing position, where he details the nature of the "masquerade" of democracy while at the same time acknowledging his positive attitude toward the end of the dictatorships. Note, also, that the author identifies himself with the democratic opposition (paragraph 5).**
    D:      No. While the passage is clearly in favor of the end of communism, the author expresses concern that things are sliding away from democracy and back towards communism (paragraph 5). The author states that "no one can say where we are headed" and that "the political horizon is cloudy."

5.  B       This is an Inference question.
    A:      No. A shift away from authoritarianism is a theme of the passage, but it is not the point of this reference.
    **B:      Yes. The author writes, "In Yugoslavia, we will see whether the federation can survive without communism"; it is this potential for a federation of states to dissolve that he claims we will witness "on a larger scale" in the Soviet Union (paragraph 1).**
    C:      No. There is nothing in the passage about "general distribution systems."
    D:      No. There is nothing in the passage about state-owned farms. Be careful not to use outside knowledge.

6.  B       This is an Inference/Roman numeral question.
    **I:      True. The author writes that all formerly Communist countries have had trouble institutionalizing freedom (paragraph 2), which he later relates to the pain and trouble of "negotiating the empty space of freedom" (paragraph 4).**
    II:     False. While the author admits that they were mistaken in their expectations, he does not go so far as to claim that the mistaken predictions actually caused problems.
    **III:    True. In the third paragraph, the author states that it was assumed that it would be easy to introduce changes into the economy. The author notes, however, that the opposite proved to be true, and that economic transformation came at the end, not the beginning, of the process (paragraph 4).**

7.  C       This is an Inference question.
    A:      No. The author writes that "one thing seems common to all these countries...freedom has won" (paragraph 2).
    B:      No. While the author earlier writes that "we will see whether the federation can survive without communism" (paragraph 1), he does not connect this issue to the loss mentioned in paragraph 5.
    C:      **Yes. This aptly summarizes the initial reasons the author gives for feeling that the people are losing: in both Bulgaria and Romania, former Communist officials are winning the elections (paragraph 5).**
    D:      No. This is contradicted in paragraph 5: "dozens of groups and parties [have been] created."

## Passage 9

This is a Now passage.

**Main Points:**

P1:   Marshall thought main reason for economic study is reduction of poverty
P2:   Contrast with modern economists who assume poverty will always exist
P3:   Poverty has become problem of a minority
P4:   Poverty now relative to community—degrading

**Bottom Line:** Modern poverty is degrading but economists assume it will exist.

1.  C       This is a Main Idea question.
    A:      No. The author barely mentions past strategies, and does not see contemporary economists as even interested in eliminating poverty (paragraph 2). The extreme word "radical" in this choice makes it even more problematic.
    B:      No. This is merely a point made in the last paragraph. The answer for a main idea question should encompass ideas in the whole passage.
    C:      **Yes. This answer covers much more ground than the others, including all the major themes. See in particular the final sentence of paragraph 1 and the first and final sentences of paragraph 2.**
    D:      No. This is merely a point made in the third paragraph. The author mentions the decreasing prevalence of poverty in the service of a larger goal: to explain poverty's 'peculiar modern form.'"

2.  B       This is an Inference question.
    A:      No. "Improve people" is too general and "entirely" is extreme.
    B:      **Yes. Marshall clearly has the interests of the poor at heart and thinks economic studies can help (paragraph 1).**
    C:      No. This is a misinterpretation of the word "interest." Marshall speaks of the interest of economic studies and not of interest accumulated or charged financially.
    D:      No. This choice is too extreme: the author does not suggest that "all humanity" should be primarily interested in economics.

3.  B       This is a Retrieval question.
    A:      No. Although relative vs. absolute forms of poverty are mentioned in the fourth paragraph, the passage does not state that such designations are a result of the change in poverty after the turn of the century, or that poverty itself changed because of the way it is or was measured.
    **B:**      **Yes. In the third paragraph, the author writes that the "general affliction...was ended by increased output.... The result was to reduce poverty from the problem of a majority to that of a minority."**
    C:      No. Although sales tax is mentioned (paragraph 2), it is not discussed in the context of the change in poverty.
    D:      No. "Social welfare programs" are never mentioned and are therefore beyond the scope of the passage.

4.  C       This is an Inference question.
            Note: This Inference question particularly highlights the need for effective annotation and consistency in question approach. Avoid the common tendency to dismiss C, the credited response, because it is from paragraph 4 rather than paragraph 3 (to which the stem refers). The correct answer may be based on information in a different paragraph, if that paragraph also relates to the issue raised in the question stem. Here, the final paragraph starts with "For," which indicates that the author is explaining what he said in the previous paragraph.
    A:      No. The author writes that poverty is the problem of a numerical minority (end of paragraph 3); he is not referring to racial minorities.
    B:      No. The author in fact claims that more people have the minimum necessities now than they did in Marshall's time (paragraph 3).
    **C:**      **Yes. The idea that poverty is defined by community standards of decency, whether or not they have enough for survival, is the focus of the last paragraph and a major point of the passage.**
    D:      No. We cannot infer from the text either that the unemployment is a significant problem or that the economy is expanding. This answer is Out of Scope.

5.  C       This is an Inference question.
    A:      No. Unemployment isn't mentioned in the passage. Remember that poverty is not necessarily related to unemployment.
    B:      No. Race isn't mentioned in the passage. Be careful not to misconstrue the word "minority" in paragraph 3. Notice that this Attractor appears in several questions.
    **C:**      **Yes. In paragraph 2, the author states that war displaced the concern for poverty.**
    D:      No. Concern for the environment is not mentioned in the passage. Be careful not to use outside knowledge or opinion. Out of Scope Attractors are common in Inference questions.

6.   D      This is a Weaken question.
     A:     No. This may be true, but does not deal with the validity of the quote. The fact that others may have other definitions does not by itself suggest that the author's definition is wrong. This choice does not go far enough to weaken the author's argument.
     B:     No. The author refers to "community" (paragraph 4) in the context of general or average living standards, not of specific neighborhoods. Therefore, evidence that poor people tend to live with or near other poor people does not undermine the author's argument that an "adequate" yet comparatively low income constitutes poverty. Avoid interpreting words in particular ways in order to make answer choices fit; stick the the meaning suggested by the context of the passage alone.
     C:     No. If anything, this answer strengthens the author's statement. Furthermore, the quote discusses income, while this answer deals with standard of living.
     **D:     Yes. This does weaken the statement by asserting that poverty is defined only as failing to earn the minimum necessary for survival, rather than by community standards and status. If this were true, a person who had the minimum necessary for survival would not be considered poor no matter how disparate his/her standard of living were from that of his/her community.**

# Passage 10
This is a Later passage.

**Main Points:**

P1:  Illustration of information processing in humans
P2:  Long term memory determines whether info is relevant
P3:  Long term memory acts as its own filter
P4:  Filtering of info necessary for sanity
P5:  Semantic memory repository of knowledge about world
P6:  Only pertinent info reaches awareness

**Bottom Line:** Long term memory helps the human mind sort information and limit distraction so that only what is relevant reaches awareness.

1.   C      This is an Inference question.
     A:     No. The author never mentions objectivity.
     B:     No. The author does not suggest that our memories are distorted—but he does claim that current sensations are filtered, if not actually distorted.
     **C:     Yes. This is the point of the second paragraph: that sensory input is sorted in relation to what we have in memory, and is processed according to what we need at the moment (we "immediately tune in or out what matters"). This is a major argument of the entire passage. Do not eliminate an answer just because the language appears extreme; here the "always" is supported by the "only" in paragraph 2.**
     D:     No. While we know that past experiences influence our perception of reality (paragraph 2), the point of all this sorting is to keep our consciousness uncluttered (see paragraph 4).

2.  C   This is an Inference/LEAST question.

Note: "Semantic memory" is explained in paragraph 5—"the repository of meanings and knowledge about the world"—and that the author provides an example of what would be stored in semantic memory. Also note that you are being asked what would NOT be stored in semantic memory.

A:  No. Dates are a kind of knowledge about the world.

B:  No. A title is a collection of words, which is something like part of the example provided.

C:  **Yes. There is nothing in the passage to suggest that (physical) skills would be stored in semantic memory—although the ability to explain how to drive a car might be.**

D:  No. This choice resembles the example of knowing that a grunt is not a word.

3.  A   This is a Structure/NOT question.

A:  **Yes. This assertion is made in paragraph 2; it is followed by an explanation of its significance but not by an example of how or under which circumstances the judgment might be made.**

B:  No. This assertion is followed by the example of not seeing gas station signs when you are looking for restaurants (paragraph 6).

C:  No. The importance of the "filter" is underlined by the example of schizophrenics, who suffer from a lack of the ability to filter (paragraph 4).

D:  No. This assertion is followed by the example of how we process the sound of a grunt (paragraph 5).

4.  D   This is an Inference question.

A:  No. No evidence is given for this interpretation (no actual brain parts are included in the model, for example).

B:  No. Once again, the flow chart appears to be a model of function only, not of physical structure or organization.

C:  No. While Erdelyi's assertion (paragraph 3) suggests that the model may need a slight modification, there is nothing in the passage to imply that it is a misrepresentation. This choice is too extreme.

D:  **Yes. This interpretation emphasizes the functional nature of the flow chart.**

5.  B   This is a Strengthen question.

Note: The long stem does not provide new information; rather, the new information is in the answer choices, which is one marker of a Strengthen question (even though the stem does not use classic Strengthen question language). The correct answer provides new information that would improve the graphic model by making it more consistent with Erdelyi's argument, as it is described in paragraph 3.

A:  No. While Erdelyi does state that Long-Term Memory can "itself become the filter," he also claims that the filter decides "what to block from short-term storage," implying that Sensory Store and Filter is a separate item.

B:  **Yes. This has Long-Term Memory acting as the filter, and placed before the Sensory Store, best summarizing the end of paragraph 3.**

C:  No. See the explanation for B; note in particular the reversal of before and after.

D:  No. The author writes that Long-Term Memory filters what will get as far as Awareness, so Awareness cannot come first.

## Passage 11

This is a Later passage.

**Main Points:**

P1: Multiculturalism recognizes difference as positive
P2: College students are consumed by identity politics
P3: Majority of multiculturalists, the hard-liners, see difference as absolute
P4: This attitude is a reversal of traditional values of assimilation
P5: Problem with claim that impartiality cannot exist: leaves us without any consensus on knowledge

**Bottom Line:** Multiculturalists may have good intentions in honoring difference, but their philosophy poses several problems to traditional American values.

1. **D**   This is an Inference/NOT question.
   Note: This question asks you what is NOT true of multiculturalists' beliefs. If you annotated effectively you would have seen that in paragraph 3 the author states that multiculturalism's "hard-liners" comprise a majority of the movement; these multiculturalists, the author goes on to explain, claim objectivity or impartiality is not possible.

   A:   No. This is a central tenet of multiculturalist ideology (see paragraph 1).

   B:   No. While the passage stresses the multiculturalist emphasis on difference, the author also emphasizes that the purpose of this emphasis is to fight racism and oppression, which any assumption of racial superiority would represent.

   C:   No. The hard-line multiculturalists champion these ideas, and hard-liners "make up a majority of the movement" (see paragraphs 3 and 4).

   **D:   Yes. According to the author, multiculturalists claim that "impartial knowledge...is not possible," and that "objectivity is a mask for oppression" (paragraph 5). Stereotyping is mentioned in paragraph 2 as something to be overcome, but objectivity is never advanced as a means to that end.**

2. **B**   This is a Retrieval question.

   A:   No. The author never explicitly connects such a belief with liberalism. Be careful not to use outside knowledge.

   **B:   Yes. See paragraph 4: "This [denouncing of the tradition of assimilation] is an extraordinary reversal of the traditional liberal commitment to a 'truth' that transcends parochialisms" (that is, that transcends narrow or selfish views). In other words, traditional liberalism holds that there are some truths that extend beyond any individual's or group's particular interests.**

   C:   No. There is no mention of granting minorities dispensation; "dispensation" (paragraph 4) is here used to refer to a new way of ordering knowledge and authority. This Attractor garbles the language of the passage to change its meaning.

   D:   No. This might be a commonsense understanding of the liberal position, but the author refers to liberalism in quite a different way; the author does not address the priority of the common good with regards to liberalism.

3.   A     This is a New Information question.

              Note: Your first step after reading this question stem should be to go back to the passage and establish what this "kindlier version" is. The passage states that it involves minority groups playing a part in molding larger culture while being molded by it. The credited response will therefore involve a diminished distinction between majority and minority groups.

        A:    **Yes. If the larger and smaller cultures continued to "mold" each other, so that each took on the others' characteristics, it is possible that eventually there would be no new traits to introduce, and everyone would belong to one common culture. The word "may" in this answer choice makes it moderate enough to be supported.**

        B:    No. This implies the dominant culture would remain the same, but the author states minorities mold, as well as are molded by the larger culture.

        C:    No. The multiplicity would not remain because of the reciprocal influences between the original majority and the minorities.

        D:    No. Individual ethnic groups would lose their distinctive cultural identity. This is why hard-line multiculturalists oppose assimilation in any form.

4.   B     This is an Inference question.

              Note: This is a variation on an Inference question, such that the answer choices contain new information. As such, you can approach it similarly to a Weaken question: the correct answer will be the scenario that is most inconsistent with hard-liner beliefs, as they are described in the passage.

        A:    No. According to the author, multiculturalists are interested in preserving gender differences as well as other differences (paragraph 4).

        B:    **Yes. Making everyone speak one language represents the "sameness" the multiculturalist abhors (paragraph 3).**

        C:    No. Although not explicitly mentioned, such a proposal would help to preserve ethnic identity and so would appeal to multiculturalists.

        D:    No. Such a proposal would encourage diversity in language as well as in cultural practices. Therefore, it would likely be accepted by hardline multiculturalists.

5.   D     This is an Inference question.

        A:    No. The reference here is to a "curriculum" (paragraph 2), which suggests learning, not political action. Be careful not to overinterpret the word "politics" in the reference or to apply outside knowledge. This option is Out of Scope.

        B:    No. The context of this passage focuses on ethnic politics, not national politics; that is, the point of identity politics is to reassert one's membership in a particular group (paragraph 3), not one's identity as an "American."

        C:    No. There is no mention of actual therapy in the passage. This choice is a misinterpretation of "therapeutic curriculum" (paragraph 2). This is a Garbled Language Attractor.

        D:    **Yes. The politics of identity leads students to want a therapeutic curriculum that counteracts ignorant stereotypes about minorities—and allows them to discover their ethnic identities (paragraphs 1 and 2).**

6.    B       This is a Tone/Attitude question.
      A:      No. This answer choice is too extreme; remember that the author finds the beginning premise "unexceptional" and says it "sounds like an inflection of traditional American pluralism" (paragraph 1), which the author appears to admire by speaking positively about American traditional values in paragraph 4.
      **B:      Yes. The author is clearly critical of the hard-line approach, but he does acknowledge the good in the "kindlier version" (paragraph 1). He also refers to Phillip Green as a "thoughtful proponent of multiculturalism," which implies a positive assessment of Green's position.**
      C:      No. The author condemns the hard-liners, but he makes no suggestions regarding how multiculturalists could get back on the "right" track. Criticizing reality is not the same thing in and of itself as advocating a change in that reality. This choice goes beyond the scope of the passage.
      D:      No. The author's language is far from detached. See for example paragraph 5. Effective annotation will help you to recognize attitude markers in the passage text.

# Passage 12

This is a Later passage.

**Main Points:**

P1:   Too many laws curb judges' authority
P2:   Best laws are general; better to have none than too many as currently
P3:   Human laws are flawed compared to those of nature

**Bottom Line:** No laws whatsoever would be preferable to France's current surplus of laws.

1.    D       This is a Main Point question.
      A:      No. He does suggest that simple cultures have fewer laws (paragraph 3), but this is not the main point of the passage.
      B:      No. The morality of lawyers is not the main point of the passage.
      C:      No. This idea of basing law on similarity rather than difference is never developed in the passage.
      **D:      Yes. The author writes, for example, that "as formerly we suffered from crimes, now we suffer from laws," and asks: "What have our legislators gained by… [their] hundred thousand laws?" (paragraph 2).**

2.  D    This is an Inference question.
    A:    No. The author opposes inventing more and more laws (see paragraph 2).
    B:    No. In the Indies example (paragraph 3), the author suggests that lawyers will never stop producing lawsuits, but he never attributes to lawyers the wish to make themselves indispensable.
    C:    No. This is a distortion of the first sentence of the passage. In particular, the author does not suggest that all laws are entirely unrelated.
    D:    **Yes. This is the main point of the second paragraph, where the author discusses multiplicity of French laws.**

3.  B    This is an Inference question.
    A:    No. The author does refer to "curb[ing] the authority of judges" (paragraph 1), but he never suggests that lawyers should be involved.
    B:    **Yes. The metaphor of cutting up the judges' meat suggests that some ("the man") wish to eliminate judicial discretion by creating a law for every possible circumstance. The judge then would not have to (or be able to) take a general law and decide how to interpret and apply it to a specific situation, just as he or she would not have to look at a big piece of meat and decide how best to approach eating it.**
    C:    No. The goal as described in the passage is not simplification of the legal process but elimination of judicial discretion and the conflicts it causes (paragraph 1). The method proposed is not breaking judicial procedure into smaller steps (this would be an overly literal reading of "cutting up their meat"), but creating laws specific to all possible circumstances.
    D:    No. The author never refers to less-sophisticated judges; if anything, he implies that they are very sophisticated, as indicated by their ability to interpret laws in so many different ways.

4.  A    This is a Structure question.
    A:    **Yes. See his allusions to the Golden Age, when legal systems were unknown, and to other simpler ways other cultures have of dealing with "quarrels" or disputes (paragraph 3).**
    B:    No. Rural French culture is not mentioned.
    C:    No. Though the author may have some belief in the innate or natural wisdom of humanity, he does not imply that this wisdom "emerges" in natural settings.
    D:    No. The author's religious beliefs are not discussed in the passage.

5.   B   This is an Inference question.
     A:   No. The author never really addresses what laws actually accomplish; he simply complains about how many there are.
     **B:   Yes. This is the main point of the second paragraph, which deals with the ever-expanding number of legal cases while "there is little relation between our actions, which are in perpetual mutation, and fixed and immutable laws."**
     C:   No. The author does not distinguish between law and behavior on these grounds. If anything, he suggests the opposite when he writes that "nature always gives us better laws than we give ourselves" (paragraph 3).
     D:   No. The author does not suggest that human behavior is simple; in fact, it is in "perpetual mutation" (paragraph 2).

6.   A   This is a Tone/Attitude question.
     **A:   Yes. The author shows both concern and frustration with questions such as, "What have our legislators gained by selecting a hundred thousand particular cases and acts and applying to them a hundred thousand laws?" (paragraph 2).**
     B:   No. The author demonstrates the contrary, a solid understanding of the situation.
     C:   No. The author is not poking fun at the system, or ridiculing it.
     D:   No. The author definitely cares about the situation; he's not indifferent.

# Passage 13
This is a Now passage.

**Main Points:**

P1:  Pre-WWII Mexican theater adapted to suit audience and economy
P2:  Los Angeles and San Antonio theatrical centers
P3:  Record of this period incomplete but gives some indication of popular venues

**Bottom Line:** Mexican theater in Southwest before WWII adapted to market, found popularity in Los Angeles and San Antonio.

1.   C   This is an Inference question.
     A:   No. The author never explicitly links mastering multiple styles, in general terms, with success.
     B:   No. It's not entirely clear that any of these actors performed in English; it's possible that their song and dance routines could be appreciated by English-speaking audiences even if they were performed in Spanish. In any case, playing to English-speaking audiences is also not explicitly linked to success.
     **C:   Yes. The author connects both the ability to get work and high salaries with performance in vaudeville (e.g., in reference to Nelly Fernandez's career) (paragraph 1).**
     D:   No. While Leonardo Garcia Astol eventually worked in both radio and television (paragraph 1), the author does not connect such work explicitly with success. Be careful not to let a single example stand for the whole unless the author draws such a conclusion him/herself.

2.   D      This is a Retrieval question.
     A:     No. The Depression led to changes in the nature of the theater that people wanted to see, namely variety acts and vaudeville (paragraph 1). This choice is inconsistent with the passage.
     B:     No. The amount of activity seems to have been fairly stable. The example is given of Nelly Fernandez earning $1,000 a month during the Depression. This is meant to indicate that the theater did okay while the rest of society struggled. The nature of theater did change, however.
     C:     No. It is the actors trained in serious drama who had to switch to variety acts and vaudeville, but there is nothing to indicate that drama became more serious.
     **D:     Yes. The passage discusses the artistic changes that took place, namely the switch to vaudeville and the like (paragraph 1).**


3.   C      This is an Inference question.
     A:     No. The passage states that people from all over "were drawn here for employment," not that the manpower pool came mainly from Los Angeles natives (paragraph 2). Just as importantly, this answer doesn't describe "Los Angeles as a cultural center" (question stem).
     B:     No. Los Angeles is said to be "the most populous Mexican city of the United States," not the largest city overall (paragraph 1).
     **C:     Yes. This is a legitimate extrapolation from the description of the booming theater and film industries in Los Angeles: "Both Los Angeles and San Antonio went through a period of intense expansion and building of new theatrical facilities in the late teens and early twenties" (paragraph 2).**
     D:     No. We have no reason to think this, especially given that the Hispanic theater fed off the booming Hollywood film industry (paragraph 2). Beware of superlatives; they must be supported by the passage to be justified in the answer. This is an Extreme Attractor."


4.   D      This is an Inference question.
     A:     No. This inference, from paragraph 1, relates to before and during, not after, the Depression.
     B:     No. This might be intuitively attractive, since Depression-era preferences were for lighter fare like vaudeville, but no mention is made of this. Theater after the Depression is not described.
     C:     No. No mention is made by the author of a new generation of actors.
     **D:     Yes. The passage gives us no information about the state of the theater after the Depression. The latest date mentioned in the passage is 1935 (paragraph 2). The text of the passage tells us that 1933 was during the Depression (paragraph 1), and no end date for the Depression is provided.**

5.  B   This is an Inference question.
    A:  No. Nothing in the passage suggests a worsening of racial tension or discrimination.
    **B:  Yes. The passage describes two processes which indicate that cultural mixing occurred: First, Hispanic theater is said to have spread into Canada, and a Hispanic production is described as "clearly catering to an English-language audience" (paragraph 1). Second, that same paragraph explicitly mentions that "a number of Mexican performers were able to cross over into the Anglo-American circuits."**
    C:  No. Nothing suggests isolation of Hispanics: just the contrary.
    D:  No. The passage suggests that the flourishing Hollywood film industry helped create a favorable environment for Hispanic drama and helped make Los Angeles a "manpower pool for Hispanic theater" (paragraph 2).

6.  D   This is an Inference question.
        Note: Remember that when you have a specific keyword or reference in the question stem, you should return to the passage to answer the question for yourself before reading the answer options.
    A:  No. It was "probably the only *permanent* theater house [emphasis added] serving the Hispanic community" (paragraph 3). Several other theaters are mentioned as hosting Hispanic companies. Beware of this kind of Attractor, which plays on your memory and/ or less-than-careful return to the passage."
    B:  No. The author states that in 1934 the records became obscure, not that the theater closed (paragraph 3).
    C:  No. On the contrary, the author indicates that other theaters attracted business only when the Hidalgo was booked (paragraph 3).
    **D:  Yes. The author states that in 1934, records became obscure (paragraph 3). Therefore, the passage suggests that we do not know what became of the theatre after that time.**

## Passage 14

This is a Later/Killer passage.

**Main Points:**

P1: Film theorists who focus on art in 2 groups: realists and expressionists
P2: Realists emphasize accurate representation of external reality
P3: Kracauer (realist) hostile to distortions in representation
P4: Kracauer: literary adaptations interior rather than exterior focus: dismissed
P5: Kracauer underestimates audience and realism in some nonrealistic films

**Bottom Line:** Kracauer's realist theory prefers films that accurately document reality; some shortcomings in theory.

1.  B       This is a Primary Purpose question.
    A:      No. The author mentions Arnheim in paragraph 1 as a spokesman for the theory of expressionism, but the passage as a whole is a discussion of Kracauer.
    B:      **Yes. The passage first mentions various theoretical approaches (paragraph 1) as context for its discussion of Kracauer and his ideas (paragraphs 2–4). In the final paragraph, the author criticizes Kracauer's perception of how audiences respond to "nonrealistic" movies.**
    C:      No. There is no discussion of to what extent general artistic theories apply specifically to film—the only theories mentioned or described are particular to cinema.
    D:      No. This choice is too narrow. Beware of primary purpose answer choices that capture the main idea of a single paragraph (here, the final paragraph) rather than the purpose of the entire passage. Even though a passage's Bottom Line is frequently indicated in the first and/or last paragraph, this is not always the case, and is not so here. This is a typical MCAT trap.

2.  C       This is an Inference question.
            Note: Kracauer argued that film should (and for the most part does) record the "visible world around us" with minimum interference by or creative presence of the artist (paragraphs 2 and 3). Be sure to establish a clear idea of Kracauer's preferences before proceeding to the answer choices.
    A:      No. Kracauer would reject the validity of a director "interfering" with reality by using angles in order to communicate some message or comment.
    B:      No. Kracauer believes film should "leave the raw materials of reality more or less intact" (paragraph 2), not pick and choose among them.
    C:      **Yes. Kracauer's Realism posits that film should record external reality in its natural and unmanipulated state (paragraphs 2 and 3).**
    D:      No. Kracauer believes film is like photography in that it leaves "the raw materials of reality more or less intact" (paragraph 2).

3.  D   This is a Weaken question.
    A:  No. Refusal of realist filmmakers to manipulate their subject in order to make an ideological point would be entirely consistent with the author's depiction of Realism (paragraph 3).
    B:  No. "Formative tendency" refers to cinematic technique that distorts or manipulates reality. Expressionistic films do exhibit such tendencies (paragraph 3). Thus this statement is consistent, not inconsistent with the author's description of Expressionism.
    C:  No. There is no reason based in the passage to believe that a truly realistic film director cannot draw on foreign literary sources. Thus this does not contradict the author's depiction of Kracauer or of the Realist school. Note that Kracauer dismisses "most" literary and dramatic adaptations, not "all."
    **D:  Yes. Kracauer, who the author describes as an exemplar of Realist theory (paragraph 2), praises the use of natural lighting that does not distort reality (paragraph 3). Therefore, if most realist filmmakers used artificial lighting in order to eliminate as aspect of reality, this would be inconsistent with the author's depiction of realism.**

4.  A   This is an Inference question.
    **A:  Yes. The author criticizes Kracauer for underestimating "the flexibility of an audience's response to nonrealistic movies" (paragraph 5). This, and the rest of the final paragraph, suggests that Kracauer (falsely) believes that only "documentary" style films will be perceived as "real" by audiences. Thus, Kracauer likely believed that a supposed inability of audiences to respond to depictions of historical or fantastical scenes as if they were real necessitated his "photographic" approach to filmmaking.**
    B:  No. Arnheim is described as a spokesperson for Expressionism, which is described (along with Realism) as centered on the work of art (paragraph 1).
    C:  No. This choice is too extreme. The author writes that *most,* not all, Realist theories took a documentary approach (paragraph 2).
    D:  No. Kracauer admits that expressionistic movies exist (paragraph 2). However, the author describes him as fundamentally hostile to the expressionist aesthetic (paragraphs 2 and 3).

5.  B   This is an Inference question.
        Note: Paragraph 4 tells us that Kracauer accepts only literary adaptations that "lend themselves to a realistic presentation" or the depiction of a "slice of life," and rejects those that focus on the characters' thoughts and emotions.
    A:  No. Kracauer would appreciate neither the depiction of insanity ("interior realities") nor the theme of surrealism, which involves distortion of our everyday world.
    **B:  Yes. This work would be most amenable to an approach that seeks only to record and show reality, with no intricate plots or focus on individuals' mental and emotional states.**
    C:  No. Portraying the reaction of the human mind to war necessarily involves focusing the "interior realities" which Kracauer rejects as inappropriate to film.
    D:  No. Fragmentation of plot lines involves distortion and manipulation (see paragraph 3), not depiction of a "slice of life."

6.  C        This is an Inference question.
             Note: Effective annotation will bring you immediately to the final paragraph of the passage to find the author's criticism. This way you can answer for yourself before weighing the answer options.

    A:       No. The author does not argue that Kracauer's emphasis on Realism is too restrictive. Rather, he claims that supposedly "nonrealistic" films (movies set in distant or fantastical places and times) may in fact be perceived by the audience as representing a reality of their own (paragraph 5).

    B:       No. The author describes these two approaches in paragraph 1, but does not indicate a preference for a focus on the artist over a focus on the art itself.

    C:       **Yes. In the final paragraph the author criticizes Kracauer for not fully understanding that an audience may be able to enter into the world created by a historical or fantastical movie. That is, we may experience it as "real" even though it is not portraying our own current daily experience.**

    D:       No. Kracauer claims that film does have much in common with one other art form—photography (paragraph 2). The author does not claim that more such commonalities exist, nor does he call for more interference or manipulation of reality on the part of the artist.

# Passage 15

This is a Now passage.

**Main Points:**

P1:  Three Factors contribute to teenage pregnancy
P2:  One factor poverty
P3:  Another: sex ed inadequate and often too late
P4:  Also underfunded family planning clinics
P5:  Affluent girls have as much sex but lower pregnancy rate.

**Bottom Line:** Poverty, limited sex ed, and underfunded clinics are factors in teenage pregnancy.

1.  B        This is an Inference/LEAST question.
             Note: The credited response will be the statement that most contradicts the passage.

    A:       No. The author indicates that programs in public schools and family planning clinics should in fact be improved to prevent teen pregnancies (paragraph 1).

    B:       **Yes. This answer directly contradicts paragraph 5, where it states that the two groups are equally sexually active. The author would least agree with this statement.**

    C:       No. Part of the main theme of the passage is that in many cases teens should not get pregnant and give birth. In such cases, the author would agree that childbearing could reasonably be postponed for many years.

    D:       No. The author argues that many teens from poor families turn to sex as recreation with destructive results (paragraph 2). Thus the author would agree that teens should be discouraged from having casual sex.

2.  D   This is an Inference/Roman numeral question.
    I:  False. The author suggests easy access to abortion through friends and family as one reason for the lower pregnancy rate among affluent teens (paragraph 5).
    II: **True. The author indicates that parents of affluent teens support the more extensive sex education programs available in private schools, and that the bureaucrats and politicians who are responsible for inadequate public school programs do not (paragraph 5).**
    III: **True. The author states that affluent teens are just as sexually active as poorer teens (paragraph 5).**

3.  D   This is an Inference question.
    A:  No. The author never suggests that teens are less sexually responsible. The passage says that some mothers of teens are themselves promiscuous (paragraph 1) setting a bad example (paragraph 2). Rather, the argument is that teens are less able than adults to responsibly raise children. Be careful to avoid outside knowledge; even though you may have heard such an argument elsewhere, unless the author implies or states it, you cannot use it here.
    B:  No. The author never indicates that the problem lies in the age of the baby itself.
    C:  No. The author argues that sex education needs to be improved, not that biologically mature teens lack an interest in education of any sort.
    D:  **Yes. This is the main point of the passage. See in particular the first sentence: the rest of the passage develops this theme.**

4.  D   This is an Inference question.
    A:  No. The Guttmacher study (paragraph 3) does not, as described, discuss when sexual activity should begin.
    B:  No. The study only discusses the inadequacy of public school sex education (paragraph 3). It is the author who later in the passage compares private and public (affluent and non-affluent) education (paragraph 5). This is a Words Out of Context Attractor.
    C:  No. Make sure to read all the way through the answer choice; the Guttmacher study dealt with sex education in public schools, not through family planning clinics. This choice is half right, but half wrong.
    D:  **Yes. A variety of inadequacies are mentioned, including low number of hours, the subjects covered or not covered, and excessive delay in teaching certain subjects (paragraph 3).**

5.  A   This is a Main Idea question.
    A:  **Yes. The author argues in the first two paragraphs that teen pregnancy is a serious problem, and then discusses the inadequacies in educational and medical institutions that contribute to the problem. While this answer is not perfect (it would be even better if it mentioned the family explicitly), it covers more than the other options and is therefore the "least wrong" answer.**
    B:  No. This choice is too narrow. Family background is only one of the factors discussed (paragraphs 1 and 2). Others include public school programs and family planning resources.
    C:  No. This choice is too narrow. Inadequate hours devoted to sex education in public schools is discussed only in the third paragraph.
    D:  No. School boards are never mentioned. The author indicates that greater power should be given to parents (not school boards) and less to bureaucrats and politicians (paragraph 5).

6.   D      This is an Inference question.
     A:     No. No mention is made of "welfare rolls," and therefore this choice is Out of Scope.
     B:     No. The author discusses bad examples set by parents (paragraph 1), but not by peers.
     C:     No. The problem is age, not marital status, according to the author. Unmarried mothers
            are never discussed. Like choice A, this is an Out of Scope Attractor, which is common
            on Inference questions.
     D:     **Yes. The author sees teenage pregnancy as a problem because teens are often too young
            to be adequately prepared for child rearing (paragraph 1).**


# Passage 16

This is a Now passage.

**Main Points:**

P1:  Americans' diversity produces disharmony
P2:  States emphasized over unity
P3:  US dependent on other nations for resources
P4:  Economy varies greatly between regions
P5:  US still a great nation because of cooperation of diverse elements

**Bottom Line:** America is a divided and diverse nation, but strong because of the interaction of diverse
components.

1.   D      This is a Retrieval question.
     A:     No. While the US is diverse in population and natural resources, diversity in production
            of goods is not mentioned.
     B:     No. The author claims just the opposite; we are "far from independent of the outside
            world" (paragraph 3). This is an Out of Scope Attractor.
     C:     No. While the US has "certain vital deficiencies" in natural resources (such as rubber,
            silk, and a variety of metals (paragraph 3)), it would be too extreme to state that the
            country is generally *severely* lacking in natural resources.
     D:     **Yes. We consume commodities such as rubber, raw silk, and various metals without
            producing them ourselves (paragraph 3).**


2.   B      This is an Inference question.
     A:     No. There is no such recommendation on the part of the author. States' resistance to
            federal power is described (paragraph 2), but not advocated.
     B:     **Yes. In paragraph 2, the author describes states' resistance to federal authority, both
            past and present.**
     C:     No. The author argues that the interaction and cooperation between the diverse compo-
            nents of the US leads to greatness (paragraph 5). However, separation of state and federal
            government is not presented as an aspect of this productive diversity. Finally, the word
            "guarantee" is too extreme.
     D:     No. The Supreme Court mediates between state and federal government (paragraph 2); it
            does not protect the former against the latter. This is a Garbled Language Attractor.

3.   A      This is an Inference question.
     **A:**    **Yes. According to the passage, diversity in the US population has often led to dishar-mony (paragraph 1), greatness among nations (paragraph 5), and wealth (paragraph 5).**
     B:    No. The author never mentions diversity of cuisine (foods). This answer is Out of Scope.
     C:    No. This is directly contradicted by the passage in paragraph 4.
     D:    No. According to the author, there is no such thing (paragraph 1).

4.   D      This is an Inference question.
     A:    No. No information regarding future consumption rates is given in the author's discus-sion of raw silk and rubber (paragraph 3).
     B:    No. We are told that the interaction between different groups has contributed to great-ness (paragraph 5), not that a particular group has contributed more than others.
     C:    No. The author gives no reason or explanation for the wording of the flag salute (para-graph 1).
     **D:**    **Yes. Trade and communication between the diverse components of the nation are giv-en by the author as the reason for the greatness of the US (paragraph 5). Thus we can reasonably infer that there would be a positive, not a negative effect from an increase in this interaction. Therefore, this question can reasonably be answered based on infor-mation in the passage.**

5.   D      This is a Retrieval/Roman numeral question.
     **I:**    **True. Local diversity of the economy is described in paragraph 4.**
     **II:**    **True. Competition among units is mentioned in paragraph 4.**
     **III:**    **True. In paragraph 4 the author describes regional inabilities to produce certain goods.**

6.   A      This is a Retrieval/Roman numeral question.
     **I:**    **True. In paragraph 5, the author proposes that it is the difference between the US and other nations that makes it difficult to pinpoint the source of the United States' great-ness.**
     II:    False. The author states just the opposite (paragraph 3) in the course of describing the dependence of the US on the resources of other countries.
     III:    False. "Homogenous" means to be composed of similar parts. The US is heterogeneous, or made up of diverse and dissimilar parts.

## Passage 17

This is a Later/Killer passage.

**Main Points:**

P1:      Deductive argument: true premises always mean true conclusion; Inductive: conclusion's truth probable but not certain.

P2:      Induction less certain than deduction

P3:      Induction's conclusion based on past patterns

P4-P7:  Valid logical structures

P8-P9:  Invalid deductions

P10:    Induction example

P11:    Large sample size important in induction

P12:    Statistical connection does not mean a causal one

**Bottom Line:** Various aspects of valid and invalid arguments.

1.   B      This is an Inference question.

      A:     No. The passage does not discuss deductive reasoning in terms of general versus specific.

      B:     **Yes. In the second paragraph, the author contrasts deductive with inductive reasoning. Conclusions drawn by induction are less certain "because they make claims not already made by their premises." From this we can infer that the claims made by deduction are included in their premises, as this is given as the point of distinction between the two.**

      C:     No. The passage indicates just the opposite. It is in deductive reasoning that the truth of the premises is enough to prove the truth of the conclusion (paragraph 1). This is a Reversal Attractor.

      D:     No. The second part of this choice is incorrect. The passage does not indicate that the truth of an inductive conclusion proves the validity of the premises. Always be careful to read all parts of an answer choice carefully—partially correct choices are entirely wrong. This Half right/half wrong Attractor type is common on specific questions.

2.   A      This is an Analogy question.

           Note: The correct answer will be the statement that can be judged to be deductively invalid based on the passage. It will therefore be either the Fallacy of Denying the Antecedent or Fallacy of Asserting the Consequent. Put the choices in terms of A and B as in the passage, then see which one fits.

      A:     **Yes. This statement illustrates the fallacy of denying the antecedent (paragraph 8). The fact that one condition for trustworthiness (not promising to solve all the problems of society) is met is not sufficient proof that all conditions necessary for trustworthiness are fulfilled.**

      B:     No. This argument fits into the valid deductive form of a hypothetical syllogism (paragraph 7).

      C:     No. This claim, in the form of *Modus Ponens* (paragraph 4) is deductively valid. Notice that we cannot use common sense or real-life experience (plants generally need more than just sunshine to grow). The question does not ask what is true or false, but what is or is not logically valid by deduction. By valid deduction, if the premises are all true, the conclusion must also be true.

      D:     No. This argument, in the form of a disjunctive syllogism (paragraph 6), is deductively valid.

3.  D   This is an Inference question.

    A:  No. An argument that attempts to use deduction does not necessarily do so correctly. This answer choice compares an inductive argument with one that merely "attempts to use deductive logic," not one that is deductively valid.

    B:  No. Inductive reasoning is based on probability (paragraph 1), but not such that the likelihood of the truth of the conclusion is *greater* than or equal to the probability of the truth of all of its premises. The opposite would be true—the truth of the conclusion is less probable than the truth of its premises (paragraph 2). This is a Reversal Attractor.

    C:  No. According to the passage, inductive reasoning "often" looks for causal connections (paragraph 11); it does not necessarily always look for them. This choice is too extreme.

    **D:  Yes. See paragraph 10. The author states in the third-to-last paragraph that "We can think of induction, or patterning, as a principle of reasoning that moves from evidence about some members of a class to a conclusion about all members of that class." In the next paragraph the author states that "the quality of a sample is important. We want a sample to be representative of the population it was drawn from."**

4.  D   This is a New Information question.

    A:  No. First, no clear standard for inductive validity is given. This argument is based on a large sample size (all known sufferers of the disease) that is likely to be representative. The argument fulfills some conditions for inductive validity, but there may be others (paragraph 10). Secondly, even inductively valid conclusions (unlike deductively valid conclusions) are only probably, not certainly true (paragraphs 1 and 11).

    B:  No. The lack of 100 percent certainty applies to all inductive arguments, therefore it is not an indication of invalidity (paragraph 1).

    C:  No. This is an inductive, not a deductive argument (see paragraph 10).

    **D:  Yes. Given the fact that the study includes all those known to suffer from the disease, the sample could be representative, and the conclusion could (but not must) be true (paragraphs 1 and 11). Compare the moderate wording of this choice to the extreme wording of choice A.**

5.  C   This is a New Information question.
        Note: Put the question stem information into the A/B form indicated in the passage before weighing the answer options.

    A:  No. See paragraph 8 for the structure of the fallacy of denying the antecedent—this argument does not match.

    B:  No. This argument, unlike one in the form of *Modus Ponens*, is not logically valid. Fulfilling one condition for decency (aiding others) is not enough to assure decency. There may be other necessary conditions that Otto does not fulfill.

    **C:  Yes. See paragraph 8 for the form. If one is decent, one will aid others. Otto aided others, and so the argument fallaciously assumes that he must then be decent. Imagine, if Otto then went down the road and robbed a liquor store, would we still consider him to be decent? There may be more than one condition or action necessary for decency.**

    D:  No. Inductive reasoning, according to the author, argues by patterning. It asserts something to be true of an entire group because it is true of a portion of that group (paragraph 9). This argument is not structured in that way.

6.  B      This is an Inference question.

    A:     No. The fallacy of denying the antecedent is a (flawed) form of deductive reasoning. The author discusses causal arguments only in the context of inductive reasoning (paragraph 11).

    **B:     Yes. See paragraph 8. This answer choice puts into fuller words the logical structure depicted in the passage.**

    C:     No. The fallacy in the question is a form of flawed deductive reasoning. The argument described in this choice reasons inductively by enumeration (paragraph 9).

    D:     No. This fallacy is not described in the passage, and does not fit the form of the fallacy mentioned in the question.

## Passage 18

This is a Later passage.

**Main Points:**

P1:  Economic change for  Kel Ahaggar
P2:  Tourism helped then failed
P3:  Forced to settle in villages—encouraged by Algerian government
P4:  Led to Increased Islamization with negative effects on women
P5:  Also decline of matriline
P6:  Nomadic to settled life has had detrimental effects on women

**Bottom Line:** 1960s saw Kel Ahaggar change from nomadic life to settlement, with negative effects on women.

1.  D      This is an Inference question.

    A:     No. The first part of the choice is accurate. However, the relationship between the Tuareg in Algeria and the Algerian state was characterized by antagonism in the early years of the new regime (paragraph 3). This is a Half right/Half wrong Attractor.

    B:     No. The passage provides no evidence to support this statement. We know that instability existed elsewhere (paragraph 2), but not that it precluded the development of tourism in those areas. This Attractor is both Out of Scope and Too Extreme.

    C:     No. As in choice B, the passage does not provide enough information to support this inference about areas outside of Algeria. This is Out of Scope.

    **D:     Yes. This is directly supported by the passage. The second paragraph mentions uprisings in Mali and Niger, and the author states that "a revolt by Algeria's Tuareg has always been most unlikely" (paragraph 3).**

2.  C    This is a New Information question.
   A:   No. This choice rests on a misinterpretation of the statement that the men stayed close to base camp for longer periods of time. Sedentarization as described in the passage means settlement in villages and agricultural centers (paragraphs 2 and 3).
   B:   No. While the author does make this claim in paragraph 3, the effect of the development of tourism described in the question stem does not directly support this claim—they are two separate issues.
   C:   **Yes. The author explains the decline in the status of women as a result of Islamization (paragraph 4), decline of the matriline (paragraph 5), and sedentarization (paragraph 6). All three of these factors arose from the decline in tourism and state socioeconomic policies which compensated for that decline. The information in the question, if true, suggests that tourism itself could have contributed to the change in the position of women in Tuareg society. Men are spending more time at home "in the domestic domain," a factor identified by the author as a reason for declining status of women (paragraph 6). Furthermore, contact with cultures characterized by different gender relationships could also have an effect.**
   D:   No. The author never suggests that the state contributed to the tourist trade. Rather, state socioeconomic policy compensated the Kel Ahaggar for the decline in tourism (paragraph 3).

3.  B    This is an Inference question.
   A:   No. The first part of the answer choice (arid desert) is not supported by evidence in the passage. The second part (unable to support agriculture) is inconsistent with the author's references to Tuareg gardens (paragraph 1) and to Tuareg settlements in "small cultivation centers" (paragraph 3).
   B:   **Yes. In paragraph 4, the author states that traditional Tuareg society "spaced births in accordance with prevailing ecological conditions" and that the increase in the birth rate had negative health-related and demographic effects.**
   C:   No. The author never describes the topography of the region as a whole.
   D:   No. The author does not explain why tourists traveled to the area. It could have been for cultural elements, for example; there is nothing to suggest it was necessarily related to landscape.

4. C    This is a Strengthen question.

  A:    No. The author presents Islamization as the cause of the increasing birth rate (paragraph 4). This answer choice would weaken, not strengthen the author's explanation by suggesting that the increase could instead be the result of sedentarization.

  B:    No. According to the author, the position of women was stronger when men were away on business (and so had more contact with outsiders) for longer periods of time. When men began to spend more time at home, the status of women eroded (paragraph 6). This answer choice suggests that the opposite would be the case; men would hold more of the power in traditional society, and less power after the advent of sedentarization.

  C:    **Yes. This claim supports the author's argument that the status and power of women declined when political power began to be mediated through or "subsumed within" the state, and traditional land rights were abolished (paragraph 5).**

  D:    No. This claim would not contribute to the author's explanation. First, the passage states that the socialist policies of the new Algerian regime had a negative impact on women's status (paragraphs 1, 3, and 4). Second, women in traditional Tuareg society were not relegated to the sociopolitical margins—just the opposite (paragraph 5).

5. D    This is an Inference question.

  A:    No. In traditional Kel Ahaggar society, access to political rights and office were "transmitted through the matriline" (paragraph 5), but the passage does not indicate that women held a majority of leadership positions. This is an Extreme Attractor.

  B:    No. The author indicates that in this particular case Islamization led to a decline in status of women (paragraph 4), but does not suggest that Islam itself is fundamentally inconsistent with matrilineal systems. Furthermore, in the case of the Kel Ahaggar, it was the transfer of a certain amount of political power to the state and the abolition of traditional land rights, not Islamization, that directly contributed to a weakening of the matrilineal structure (paragraph 5).

  C:    No. The word "only" makes this choice too extreme. Land rights were transferred through the woman's family line, but we do not know that only female heads of households could actually own land.

  D:    **Yes. The author writes that "land rights were transmitted through the matriline" (paragraph 5), that is, through the mother's family.**

6. C    This is a Retrieval question.

  A:    No. The government helped compensate the Tuareg for the loss of tourism (paragraph 3), but the author does not give any evidence to support the statement that tourism itself was supported by the state. This is a Words out of context (Decoy) Attractor.

  B:    No. Banditry is never mentioned in the passage. This is a Not the Issue (Out of Scope) Attractor.

  C:    **Yes. Tuareg uprisings in Mali and Niger are cited as a cause of the decline in tourism (paragraph 2). Note that highlighting dates during your first reading of the passage would help bring you back faster to the relevant part for this question.**

  D:    No. This is a reversal. While the first part of the choice is supported, the second part misrepresents the causal relationship presented in the passage. Tourism was not impeded by the shift away from a nomadic life. Rather, the loss of tourism *contributed to* a shift away from a nomadic or semi-nomadic lifestyle (paragraph 3). Furthermore, it was the Tuareg uprising and the "Algerian crisis" that handicapped tourism (paragraph 2).

# Passage 19

This is a Now passage.

**Main Points:**

P1: Before late 19th/early 20th century, only African art with Greek elements was appreciated—contrast with "Black art"

P2: Black art compelling for spirituality

P3: Now appreciated because of desire to understand forces beyond immediate

P4: Even more impressive because of relatively crude technologies

P5: Appreciation of Black art requires study of African culture

P6: Early enthusiasm meant lack of judgment; this rectified with time

**Bottom Line:** Black art took some time to be appreciated but now enjoys recognition.

1. B     This is an Inference question.

    A:    No. The author never links lack of appreciation (paragraph 1) to lack of quality of the pieces themselves.

    **B:    Yes. In paragraph 1, the author states that until the turn of the century, only pieces that reflected Greek ideals were appreciated. The author labels these pieces "African art" and distinguishes them from "Black art."**

    C:    No. While the author describes Black art as spiritual (paragraph 2), he or she does not connect its spirituality to its underappreciation by earlier scholars. Nor does the author place any responsibility on the art itself for its lack of being appreciated. The fault lies with collectors. This is a Judgment (Too Extreme) Attractor.

    D:    No. The author argues that Black art was not appreciated because it did not reflect Greek ideals (paragraph 1). Thus the differences between African and Black art were significant and striking to collectors.

2. D     This is an Inference question.

    A:    No. This choice takes words from the passage out of context. While Black art portrays harmony and figures not seen in nature (paragraph 2), the author does not suggest that Black art appeals to a human tendency to see harmony and nature as mutually exclusive or to choose one over the other.

    B:    No. The author states that Black art portrays a harmony between stillness and power (paragraph 2), but does not go so far as to suggest that it appeals to a human desire to escape from some conflict between the two.

    C:    No. Black art is spiritual (paragraph 2), but the passage does not suggest that people feel that spirituality is not respected, nor that Black art addresses some such lack of respect.

    **D:    Yes. In paragraph 3 the author claims that Black art appeals to a human desire to understand hidden governing forces.**

3.   A       This is a Retrieval question.

     Note: If you annotated effectively, you would know from paragraph 5's main point that study of African culture is needed to appreciate Black art; you therefore would have your answer ready before reading the choices.

     A:      **Yes. The author states that an appreciation of African culture is necessary to an appreciation of Black art (paragraph 5). Thus one who studies African culture would have at least some of the required tools.**

     B:      No. This choice reverses a relationship posited by the passage. One fascinated by artistic motives of Black sculptors would wish to study African culture (paragraph 5), not the other way around.

     C:      No. Study of African culture helps a person to appreciate Black art (paragraph 5). The passage does not suggest that such study would have the opposite effect on one's understanding of "African art."

     D:      No. The passage argues just the opposite; study of African culture increases ones appreciation of Black art (paragraph 5).

4.   A       This is a New Information-Weaken question.

     A:      **Yes. The correct answer will be a claim made in the passage that is inconsistent with the discovery described in the question. This statement would contradict the author's argument that the crudeness of the available technology required "extraordinary technical care and caution" (paragraph 4).**

     B:      No. This claim (paragraph 2) does not rest on the assertion that only crude tools and technology were available.

     C:      No. This claim (paragraph 2) does not depend on the unavailability of advanced technology.

     D:      No. The claim that Black art is important to world art (paragraph 1) has no direct relationship to the author's claim later in the passage that Black artists were constrained and challenged by the low level of available technology.

5.   C       This is a New Information question.

     A:      No. The correct answer will be an analogy with the discovery of Black art that can be supported by the passage. Once Black art received recognition or attention, it was also admired, according to the author's description in the first paragraph. There is no indication in the passage of a necessary lag time between attention and admiration.

     B:      No. Classic conceptions of art are described solely as one set of standards that were adhered to at one particular time (paragraph 1).

     C:      **Yes. The author admits that when Black art first gained recognition, there was little distinction between degrees of quality, and that this is true of newly discovered art in general (paragraph 6).**

     D:      No. The author's discussion of the relevance of technique (paragraph 4) is specific to Black art, not generalizable to newly discovered art in general. Furthermore, the author does not suggest that the public was more interested in the technique than in the meaning of Black art.

6.   B     This is a Retrieval/EXCEPT question.

   A:    No. Emotional power is mentioned in paragraph 2.

   **B:    Yes. This contradicts the author's claim that lack of advanced tools and technology required a high level of technical competency on the part of the artist (paragraph 4). Be careful to distinguish between technology and technical competency. This answer constitutes a Reversal (Decoy) of information in the passage that makes it an appropriate answer for this EXCEPT question.**

   C:    No. The straightforward nature is discussed in paragraph 2.

   D:    No. The author mentions achievement of a higher truth in paragraph 2.

# Passage 20

This is a Now passage.

## Main Points:

P1:   Ways art teachers can aid creative experience

P2:   Child needs psychological space but within limits

P3:   This space varies among children

P4:   Sometimes teachers overly restrict space

P5:   Time and choice two crucial factors

P6:   Art time varies in formal settings but needs to be flexible

**Bottom Line:** An art teacher of children can best encourage creativity by giving children time for art and choice in activity.

1.   A     This is a Structure question.
         Note: Recall that the author mentions time as a critical factor in the passage's fifth paragraph. Since this is a Structure question, though, the answer is not necessarily limited to that paragraph but rather considers the relationship of this claim to the passage as a whole.

   **A:    Yes. Allocation of time is given as one necessary factor in the "facilitation of the aesthetic/creative experience" (paragraph 5).**

   B:    No. The author argues that apportioning regular time periods to artistic work is crucial (paragraph 5). The author does not equate regularity with flexibility, nor does he or she contrast regularity with strict routines.

   C:    No. The passage argues that sufficient time should be allocated, not that limited time facilitates creativity. This choice is an Opposite Attractor.

   D:    No. This choice is too extreme. The passage discusses time as a factor in facilitating the aesthetic/creative experience (paragraph 5), but does not go so far as to claim that it or the classroom experience more generally produces highly creative and aesthetic children.

2.   D        This is an Inference question.

     A:        No. The author discusses how to maximize the creative experiences of children, not how to produce artists of high quality. This is a Not the Issue (Out of Scope) Attractor.

     B:        No. This contradicts the author's recommendation that schools schedule regular periods for artistic work (paragraph 6).

     C:        No. The passage advocates giving children a fair degree of freedom to assert their own creative impulses (paragraphs 1 and 2), not forcing creativity on children. This is a Negation (Decoy) of passage information.

     **D:        Yes. Throughout the passage, the author advocates devoting a variety of resources to the facilitation of children's artistic creativity.**

3.   C        This is an Inference question.

     A:        No. Psychological room, according to the author, is safe only if boundaries are set (paragraph 2). The "always" makes this an Absolute (Extreme) Attractor, in the context of passage information.

     B:        No. Leaping into the air is safe only when there is ground to land on (paragraph 2). The "always" makes this an Absolute (Extreme) Attractor, in the context of passage information.

     **C:        Yes. The analogy indicates that leaping into the air is safe if one has the security of ground on which to land; in the same way, psychological room or freedom is safe if the child is given the security of limits and boundaries (paragraph 2).**

     D:        No. Leaping is only safe with a landing ground, and psychological room is only safe within boundaries (paragraph 2). The "always" makes this an Absolute (Extreme) Attractor, in the context of passage information.

4.   B        This is a Structure question.

     A:        No. What constitutes "enough room" varies from child to child (paragraph 3), and so cannot be specified.

     **B:        Yes. This choice is a much less extreme version of choice A. The techniques listed are general guidelines to help teachers encourage creativity.**

     C:        No. Psychological freedom is one factor but not the only factor discussed. (Always be suspicious of extreme words like "solely.")

     D:        No. The author explicitly advocates giving sufficient time and choice later in the passage (paragraph 5). The techniques listed in the beginning are entirely consistent with this recommendation; time and choice are recommended, not discredited. This is an Opposite (Decoy) Attractor.

5.  A   This is a Main Idea question.
    **A:**   **Yes. The passage as a whole discusses a variety of techniques (variety, tolerance, freedom within limits, time, and choice) to facilitate aesthetic/creative growth of children.**
    B:   No. This choice is too narrow, and the definition of a connection between time and choice is not an issue in the passage.
    C:   No. The passage as a whole is a discussion of various ways to facilitate creativity. Whether or not the author would agree with the statement would depend on how narrowly one defined "approach." Most importantly, the passage is structured as a positively oriented discussion of various recommendations, not a negatively oriented attempt to disprove a claim that a single "approach" is sufficient.
    D:   No. This choice is too narrow. In addition, flexibility helps facilitate creativity—it does not compensate or substitute for lack of creativity.

6.  B   This is an Inference question.
        Note: Appropriate annotation techniques would have led you to highlight "two most critical factors" in paragraph 5, which would make that phrase easy to find as you attacked the question; then answer choice B would stand out.
    A:   No. "Learning-with-feeling" is the goal to be achieved through use of time and choice (paragraph 6); time and choice are themselves the "two most critical factors."
    **B:**   **Yes. Time and choice are described as the "two most critical factors in facilitating the aesthetic/creative experience" (paragraph 5).**
    C:   No. This choice is too vague. Neither element is specifically discussed or suggested by the author as a crucial factor.
    D:   No. Tolerance is one element discussed (paragraphs 1 and 4), but it is not presented as the most important factor. Innovation on the part of the teacher is never addressed in the passage.

## Passage 21

This is a Later passage.

**Main Points:**

P1: Two functions of photography at end of 19th century—news and art reporting
P2: Photography led to a distinction between making art and reporting on it
P3: People started using photographs as a way of seeing the world, and this influenced art
P4: Outcome has been positive because merely technically impressive work is no longer valued as highly artistic

**Bottom Line:** Photography's increased acceptance led to a distinction between technical skill and creativity in art; a good outcome.

1. D      This is a Primary Purpose question.

   A:      No. While the author does state that photography was mocked at first (paragraph 1), the author never suggests that photography was eventually accepted by the public as an art form. Rather, the passage discusses how photography led people to realize that some works they had previously considered to be art were really just pictures of works of art, not artistic creations in their own right (see paragraph 2). This is a Half right/half wrong (Decoy) Attractor.

   B:      No. This choice, while supported by the passage (paragraph 2), is too narrow to be the primary purpose of the passage. Most importantly, it leaves out the author's discussion of how photography affected how people viewed and perceived nature (paragraph 3). This "Too Narrow" Attractor is a good reminder to always consider all four answer options before making your choice.

   C:      No. The second part of this choice is not supported by the passage. While the etcher Jacquemart's work was devalued ("the ground was cut from under [his] feet" [paragraph 2]) due to revelations brought about by photography, the author does not indicate that this was unfair or "unfortunate." In fact, the author suggests that he agrees with those who "realized" that Jacquemart was "merely a reporter of works of art and not a maker of them" (paragraph 2). The passage also does not suggest that reevaluation and devaluation of any other artists was unjust, nor does the author use a negative tone in the second paragraph. Finally, this choice does not include the main idea of the third paragraph, which is an important theme in the passage. This is a Half right/half wrong (Decoy) Attractor.

   D:      **Yes. The first and second paragraphs discuss how photography changed how the public views and evaluates both "pictorial expression" and "pictorial communication of statements of fact." The third paragraph explains how photography "conditioned" people to "think photographically, and thus to see for themselves things that previously it had taken the photograph to reveal". That is, photography changed how people saw nature, or reality, itself. In this paragraph the author also states that "Just as nature had once imitated art, now it began to imitate the picture made by the camera". That is, our perception of nature was affected by the depiction of nature, or reality, in photographs. (Note that the author uses "nature" in a general way, to refer to "the appearance of everything".) Finally, the author sees the effects of photography as "a permanent gain", which supports the positive tone of this answer choice. Remember that your Bottom Line should include the author's tone, and that Primary Purpose answers must match that tone.**

2.  A       This is a New Information question.

    A:      **Yes. A main theme of the passage is that once it was realized that a photograph could better depict "the quality and character of something" (paragraph 2), people came to distinguish between skilled representations of objects on one hand, and works of art on the other. Therefore, we can infer that the author of the passage might agree with a statement that discusses the necessary conditions for creating art, in this case artistic photographs, and so suggests that not all photographs qualify as art. Notice the moderate wording of this answer choice; we can infer that the author would agree that the statement in the question stem "may be true," even if we don't know for sure that the author would entirely or definitively agree. Finally, there is no other answer choice that is better supported by the passage.**

    B:      No. While the passage does say that eventually photography was common, it also states that this happened slowly (paragraph 1). Therefore, the passage does not suggest that the technical aspects can be quickly mastered. Furthermore, Stieglitz's statement is about taking photographs that qualify as art, not simply the capacity to take a photograph (i.e., to master the technical aspects). Thus there is no reason, based on the passage, to believe that the author would be skeptical on this basis.

    C:      No. The author never discusses photography as an art form, nor does he describe any photographs as "artistic" (while he also does not rule out the possibility that they could be art). The passage in large part describes how the fact that photographs could so accurately depict works of art made the public realize that depictions of works of art (including those made by photographers) do *not* qualify as art. Therefore, we cannot conclude that Stieglitz's statement is, or would be accepted by the author as, a natural continuation of the author's own analysis.

    D:      No. The author does in fact discuss "qualities of artistry" to the extent that some things do not qualify as art (second and third paragraphs).

3.   B      This is an Inference question.

Note: If you did a question preview, you likely had an easier time locating "nature" (paragraph 3) for this question.

A:   No. The author never discusses art's fundamental goal, only that certain pictorial representations do not qualify as art.

B:   **Yes. See paragraph 3. The author states that as people became accustomed to the view of nature shown by photographs, they "began to think photographically, and thus to see for themselves things that it had previously taken the photograph to reveal to their astonished and protesting eyes." The author also states, "Just as nature had once imitated art, now it [nature, meaning our perception of nature] began to imitate the picture made by the camera". These lines indicate that viewing photographs changed how people viewed the world around them. Finally, the author then states that "willy nilly many of the painters began to follow suit," meaning that this new view of the world then affected how painters depicted or represented nature. Note that the author does not use "nature" in a way that is limited to certain parts of the world (trees, wild animals, etc.). Rather, he uses it as a synonym for the world around us, or "the appearance of everything".**

C:   No. It was photographs, not theoretical discussions, which changed how we perceive and represent nature (see the explanation for choice B). This choice is only "partially correct"; everything but "theoretical discussions" is fine, but those words are enough to make the choice as a whole incorrect.

D:   No. This choice is too extreme. While the author does indicate that the work of some (e.g., Jacquemart) who represented works of art (that is, represented objects that represent nature) came to be less valued than it was previously (paragraph 2), this is not enough to show that artistic creation is *always* more highly valued. Furthermore, this choice does not deal with the issue of the question, which is the relationship between the depiction of nature and the perception of nature itself.

4.   C      This is an Inference question.

A:   No. Be careful not to use outside knowledge or to interpret the cited words out of the context of the passage. The passage never discusses how photographers might purposefully or consciously manipulate images.

B:   No. This choice is too extreme. The author states that "many of the painters began to follow suit" (paragraph 3); that is, painters began to depict reality in a way that imitated photographs. This suggests that some paintings do distort the picture in the same way as a photograph would.

C:   **Yes. The author states that photographic distortion "only meant that the camera had not been taught, as human beings had been, to disregard perspective in most of its seeing" (paragraph 3). This indicates than when we see things directly, without the mediation of a photographic image, we interpret the relative physical relationship between objects (perspective) in a way that a photograph does not.**

D:   No. Be careful not to use outside knowledge or to take the words of the passage out of context. The passage describes "distortion" as something inherent to the nature of a photograph (paragraph 3), not as a side effect of primitive or inadequate technology.

5.   A   This is an Inference/Roman numeral question.

   I:   **True. See paragraph 2. The author suggests that a new distinction came to be drawn between artists and non-artists. Jacquemart was now shown to be "merely a reporter of works of art" and was no longer seen as an artist. By using changing public opinion about Jacquemart to illustrate how a new distinction came to be drawn between "pictorial expression [art] and pictorial communication of statements of fact [not art]," the author indicates that Jacquemart was once seen as a good artist. Note that the distinction between good and poor artists was, before photography, drawn on the basis of skill, and that Jacquemart is described as highly skilled.**

   II:   False. See the final sentence of paragraph 2. The word "only" makes this choice incorrect. While it is true that photographs were more accurate, this is not the only reason his work was devalued. Rather, the fact that photographs were so accurate led to a new distinction being drawn between art and representations of art. It was this new distinction or perception that was the main cause of the change in perception of Jacquemart's work.

   III:   False. See paragraph 2. Note the words "not only and "but also". This transition tells us that Jacquemart was not a "humble workaday factual illustrator." While it is possible, only given that wording, that he was some other kind of illustrator than a "humble workaday" one, the description given of his work gives no indication that he made illustrations, or that his reputation was one of an illustrator. Instead, the passage suggests that he was once seen as an artist; artists and illustrators are not equated in the passage.

## Passage 22

This is a Later passage.

**Main Points:**

P1:  Spanish Inquisition agents wished to quash threats against tradition
P2:  Support for Church and monarchy across social scale
P3:  Small minority wanted change
P4:  To minority, news of Revolution exciting; to others, terrifying
P5:  Eventually Spain/France and England/Portugal alliances formed
P6:  Napoleon invaded Portugal and behaved like king; Portugal wanted democracy

**Bottom Line:** The French Revolution caused political upheaval in Portugal: conflict between status quo and change.

1.  C      This is a Structure question

    A:      No. This would be a too literal reading of the phrase cited in the question stem. The passage does not indicate that Napoleon actually took the throne, only that he "behaved" like a king while ruling Portugal. Furthermore, there is no indication that Napoleon, while behaving like a king, claimed that his rule was sanctioned by God or the Church ("divine rights of a monarch"). This is a Words out of context (Decoy) Attractor.

    B:      No. While the passage indicates earlier (paragraph 3) that the Portuguese monarchy restricted these rights, the author never argues that all or most traditional orders do so. Also, the issue in this part of the passage is the specific behavior of Napoleon. The passage does not suggest that Napoleon is a traditional ruler, nor does it generalize from his behavior to that of other rulers.

    **C:      Yes. This part of the passage contrasts the hopes of the Portuguese liberals with the reality of Napoleonic rule. By saying that the liberals flocked to Napoleon with the hope of representative government, and yet that Napoleon "humored" them, "secretly laughed at them" and then behaved like a king (and monarchies are not representative regimes, as we know from paragraph 3), it suggests that the liberals' hopes were dashed.**

    D:      No. There is no indication that Junot intended to institute a representative government, or that Napoleon's and Junot's goals differed. There is also no indication that Napoleon at any point acted against Junot's wishes, or vice versa. The passage describes them both as laughing at and humoring the liberals, suggesting that neither Napoleon as ruler, nor Junot as military commander, intended to grant the liberals' wishes.

2.  B   This is an Inference/Roman numeral question.
    I:   False. See paragraph 5. Portugal's dependence on Britain is described as military and political, not economic (the author's statement that economic factors led to alliances does not necessarily mean there was a relationship of economic dependence between the two countries). Portugal needed to make terms with the British government to ensure safe passage for its imports of gold from its colonies. Portugal also depended on England to protect it from France and Spain. No mention is made in the passage of industrial imports, nor of imports of any kind from England.
    II:  False. According to the passage, there was *no* middle class in Portugal (paragraph 5). Secondly, according to the passage, the lower classes were not demanding political representation; most supported the traditional monarchical order (paragraph 1).
    III: **True. The author argues that Portugal's lack of "progressive agriculture and technological industry" left it dependent on imports of precious metals from its colonies (paragraph 5). When England took control of the seas, Portugal made terms and cooperated with the British in order to ensure safe passage for these imports (paragraph 5). Portugal's dependence on England made it a target for Napoleon, who invaded Portugal in order to undermine England (paragraph 6).**

3.  C   This is an Inference question.
    A:   No. The Inquisition existed before the coming of the Revolution (paragraphs 1 and 4). This is also an Out of Scope Attractor since the author does not indicate the origin of the Inquisitors.
    B:   No. The passage states that John was regent in 1799 and king between 1816 and 1826 (paragraph 2), but no role by the Inquisition or Inquisitors in placing him on the throne is mentioned or suggested. Like A, this choice is an Out of Scope Attractor.
    C:   **Yes. In the first paragraph the author describes how the Inquisition sought to eliminate or "repel" the new ideas brought to Portugal by the Marquès. The Marquès is portrayed as a rebel against the traditional order, while the Inquisition protected that order (paragraph 1).**
    D:   No. This choice is too absolute. The Marquès and his new ideas must have had a fair amount of influence in the 1760s, if Portugal was "struggling to return to the traditional order" in the 1780s. Furthermore, a "small minority" of dissenters against tradition existed in Portugal at the time of the French Revolution. These dissenters rejected the past in favor of new philosophical and political ideas (paragraph 3).

4.  D   This is a Structure question
    A:   No. This assertion is explained in paragraph 5.
    B:   No. The author gives examples of those at the bottom who supported the traditional order, and explains the reasons for their support (paragraph 1).
    C:   No. Examples of members of this minority are given (paragraph 3), and the passage explains why they wanted a representative government (they were "irked by the despotism of the past," and wanted freedom of trade, assembly, press, and thought).
    D:   **Yes. This statement is made in paragraph 2, but it is never explained how the barons acted as models of manners, and no examples of their behavior in this context are given. The author does mention that the barons were among those that saw the Church as a "support of private morals," but this is not an explanation or example of the barons' own (public) manners.**

5.  B    This is a New Information question.

    A:   No. There is no information in the passage to suggest that the author makes this assumption. The Portuguese monarchy was vulnerable because of its economic system (paragraph 5), not, as far as we know from the passage, because of the lack of political representation. The author makes no argument that traditional or unrepresentative systems are inherently weak or vulnerable. Remember that just because the question stem indicates that every answer choice is an assumption made by the author, this is not necessarily actually the case.

    B:   **Yes. See paragraph 5. The author states that economic factors led to the political and military dependence of Portugal on England and contributed to the invasion of Portugal by France and Spain. The author also indicates that Spain's economic dependence on imports from its colonies led to its (failed) attempt to fight Britain and thus to its eventual alliance with and dependency on France.**

    C:   No. While this is an assumption made by the author (paragraph 5), it is not directly relevant to or supported by the new information given in the question. There is no indication in the passage or the question stem that France lacked a strong middle class, or that it lacked industrialization and was dependent on colonial resources.

    D:   No. The passage never suggests that the Portuguese monarchy levied high taxes or that it built up its naval forces. This is an Out of Scope Attractor.


6.  B    This is an Inference question.

         Here is an overview of the shifting alliances described in the passage. At first Spain, Portugal, and England all waged war on France in 1793 (paragraph 4). Then, Spain negotiated a separate peace with France (paragraph 4), and the two eventually joined forces (paragraph 5). France refused to negotiate a separate peace with Portugal (paragraph 4), who eventually joined forces with England in order to protect itself against Spain and France (paragraph 5).

    A:   No. While the Portuguese royal family fled to Brazil (paragraph 6), no military alliance is suggested.

    B:   **Yes. Spain joined with France in invading Portugal (paragraph 5). In 1793, Portugal "followed Spain in a holy war against France" (paragraph 4).**

    C:   No. No alliance between Spain and Brazil is mentioned.

    D:   No. The passage suggests that Charles III and Louis XV had some similar ideas (paragraph 1), but no alliance, military or otherwise, is mentioned.


7.  D    This is an Inference question.

    A:   No. While the author suggests that economic dependency may in some cases lead or contribute to political dependency (as in the case of Portugal), he says nothing about the reverse, i.e., that political dependency may lead to economic dependency. This is a Reversal (Decoy) Attractor.

    B:   No. It was Portugal's reliance on imports of gold and other metals from its colonies (paragraph 5) that impeded the development of both its agricultural and industrial sectors.

    C:   No. There was a minority in Portugal who hoped for greater representation and liberty (paragraph 3), but they are not described as "well-organized" (the fact that "liberal leaders" existed is not enough to support this inference). Secondly, while they did "flock" to Napoleon after the fact (paragraph 6), the passage does not indicate that this "timid minority" (paragraph 3) actually played a role in, or paved the way for, Napoleon's invasion.

    D:   **Yes. If the "small minority" described in paragraph 3 "dreamed of . . . free trade," then free trade must not have existed under the Portuguese monarchy.**

# MCAT
# Critical Analysis and Reasoning Skills

## Practice Test 1

## Passage I (Questions 1-5)

That placebos can cure everything from dandruff to leprosy is well known. They have a long history of use by witch doctors, faith healers, and even modern physicians, all of whom refuse to admit their efficacy. Modern distribution techniques can bring this most potent of medicines to the aid of everyone, not just those lucky enough to receive placebos in a medical testing program.

Every drug tested would prove effective if special steps had not been taken to neutralize the placebo effect. This is why drug tests give half the patients the new medication and half a harmless substitute. These tests prove the value of placebos because approximately five percent of the patients taking them are cured even though the placebos are made from substances that have been carefully selected to be useless.

Most people feel that the lucky patients in a drug test get the experimental drug because the real drug provides them a chance to be cured. Analysis shows that patients getting the placebo are the lucky ones because they are going to be cured without risking any adverse effects the new drug may have. The drug may well be found worthless and to have severe side effects. No harmful side effects result from placebos.

Placebos regularly cure more than five percent of the patients and would cure considerably more if the doubts associated with the tests were eliminated. Cures are principally due to the patient's faith, yet the patient must have doubts knowing that he may or may not be given the new drug, which itself may or may not prove to be an effective drug. Since he knows the probability of being given the true drug is about fifty percent, the placebo cure rate would be more than doubled by removing these doubts if cures were linearly related to faith.

The actual curing power of placebos probably stems from the faith of the patient in the treatment. This suggests that cure rates in the forty percent range could be expected even when patients know their problems are incurable if given placebos under the guise of a proven cure.

It may take a while to reach the forty percent level of cure because any newly established program shall not have cultivated the word-of-mouth advertising needed to insure its success. One person saying, "I was told that my problem was beyond medical help, but they cured me," can direct countless people to the treatment with the required degree of faith. Also note that when only terminal illnesses are treated, those not cured tell no one of the failure.

Unfortunately, placebo treatment centers cannot operate as nonprofit businesses. The nonprofit idea was ruled out upon learning that the first rule of public medicine is never to give free medicine. Public health services know that medicine not paid for by patients is often not taken or not effective because the recipient feels the medicine is worth just what it cost him. Even though the patients would not know they were taking sugar pills, the placebos cost so little that the patients would have no faith in such a cheap treatment. Therefore, though it is against higher principles, treatment centers must charge exorbitant fees for placebo treatments. This sacrifice of principles is a small price to pay for the greater good of the patients.

Adapted from "Placebo Cures for the Incurable," *Journal of Irreproducible Results,* © 1985 T. G. Kyle.

1. This passage was most likely written by:

   A. an expert explaining science to the layperson.
   B. a scientist suggesting further research.
   C. a businessperson describing a product and how to market it.
   D. a scientist recommending an exciting new treatment.

2. According to the passage, the curative properties of placebos are primarily ascribed to:

   A. proper experimental procedure.
   B. psychological phenomena.
   C. secondary effects of harmless substances.
   D. unknown effects of drugs being tested.

3. Which of the following is the best argument against charging excessive fees for placebos?

   A. The high cost of placebo treatments may limit the number of patients who use such treatments, impeding "word-of-mouth" advertising.
   B. The correlation between a consumer's faith in a drug and its cost has never been clearly proven.
   C. A high-priced placebo is the only way to ensure its success.
   D. Higher priced over-the-counter drugs do not sell any better than their cheaper counterparts.

4. According to the passage, all of the following contribute to the curing power of placebos EXCEPT:

   A. word-of-mouth regarding the efficacy of a given treatment.
   B. the elimination of doubt in the mind of the patient.
   C. exorbitant fees for the treatment.
   D. the lack of harmful side effects associated with placebos.

5. According to the passage, which of the following is NOT one of the benefits of placebos?

   A. Unlike some drugs, they have no side effects.
   B. Unlike most drugs, they are effective against an extremely wide range of illnesses.
   C. For patients, placebos could be an inexpensive way to cure illnesses.
   D. They could result in a cure rate of more than forty percent, if patients believed the placebos were an actual cure.

## Passage II (Questions 6-12)

A being of volitional consciousness has no automatic course of behavior. He needs a code of values to guide his actions. "Value" is that which one acts to gain and keep, "virtue" is the action by which one gains and keeps it. "Value" presupposes an answer to the question: of value to whom and for what? "Value" presupposes a standard, a purpose and the necessity of action in the face of an alternative. Where there are no alternatives, no values are possible.

Happiness is the successful state of life, pain is an agent of death. Happiness is that state of consciousness which proceeds from the achievement of one's values. A morality that dares to tell you to find happiness in the renunciation of your happiness—to value the failure of your values—is an insolent negation of morality. A doctrine that gives you, as an ideal, the role of a sacrificial animal seeking slaughter on the altars of others, is giving you *death* as your standard. By the grace of reality and the nature of life, man—every man—is an end in himself, he exists for his own sake, and the achievement of his own happiness is his highest moral purpose.

It is for the purpose of self-preservation that man needs a code of morality. The only man who desires to be moral is the man who desires to live.

This much is true: the most *selfish* of all things is the independent mind that recognizes no authority higher than its own and no value higher than its judgment of truth. You are asked to sacrifice your intellectual integrity, your logic, your reason, your standard of truth—in favor of becoming a prostitute whose standard is the greatest good for the greatest number.

If you search your code for guidance, for an answer to the question: "What is the good?"—the only answer you will find is "*The good of others*." The good is whatever others wish, whatever you feel they feel they wish, or whatever you feel they ought to feel. "The good of others" is a magic formula that transforms anything into gold, a formula to be recited as a guarantee of moral glory and as a fumigator for any action, even the slaughter of a continent. Your standard of virtue is not an object, not an act, nor a principle, but an *intention*. You need no proof, no reasons, no success, you need not achieve *in fact* the good of others—all you need to know is that your motive was the good of others, *not* your own. Your only definition of the good is a negation: the good is the "non-good for me."

Your code—which boasts that it upholds eternal, absolute, objective moral values and scorns the conditional, the relative, and the subjective—your code hands out, as its version of the absolute, the following rule of moral conduct: If you wish it, it's evil; if others wish it, it's good; if the motive of your action is your welfare, don't do it; if the motive is the welfare of others, then anything goes.

Under a morality of sacrifice, the first value you sacrifice is morality; the next is self-esteem. When need is the standard, every man is both victim and parasite. As a victim, he must labor to fill the needs of others, leaving himself in the position of a parasite whose needs must be filled by others. He cannot approach his fellow men except in one of two disgraceful roles: he is both a beggar and a sucker.

Adapted from A. Rand, "'Value Yourself' from *Atlas Shrugged*," in *Philosophy and Contemporary Issues (4th. ed.)*, John R. Burr and Milton Goldinger, eds., © 1984 MacMillan.

6.  The author suggests which of the following about value and virtue?

    A.  Something is valuable when it is a necessity of life; that is, a person has no alternative but to pursue it.
    B.  A virtuous action is one that maximizes happiness and minimizes pain for the community as a whole.
    C.  The existence of value and virtue depends on the existence of alternative choices.
    D.  The most virtuous act is to sacrifice one's own needs for the good of others.

7. Which of the following statements best expresses the main idea of the passage?

    **A.** The fact that an act was performed with good intent does not in itself justify that act; whether or not a good result was achieved must also be considered.

    **B.** The maximization of happiness defines and constitutes the highest moral purpose of a human being.

    **C.** No absolute, objective, or eternal moral standards exist; good and evil are defined by, and will be different for, each individual man and woman.

    **D.** The rule that dictates that we must act with the goal of maximizing the good of others is wrong and injurious; those who behave selfishly to ensure their own well-being act according to the highest ethical standards.

8. Which of the following maxims is most consistent with the author's beliefs, as they are presented in the passage?

    **A.** "From each according to his ability, to each according to his need."

    **B.** "Do unto others as you would have them do unto you."

    **C.** "Pull yourself up by your own bootstraps."

    **D.** "It's the thought that counts."

9. As it is used in the passage, the phrase "man—every man—is an end in himself" (paragraph 2) most likely means that:

    **A.** morality is relative—no individual has the right to judge the moral codes of other individuals or societies.

    **B.** good intentions do not justify or excuse destructive or ineffectual actions.

    **C.** the end justifies the means—actions that increase the general level of happiness for the whole may require the individual sacrifice of a few individuals.

    **D.** human beings should not be valued in terms of the extent to which they help fulfill the needs of others.

10. Suppose that a political leader wished to incorporate the author's ethical standards into national policy. Of the following programs or policies, which would best embody those ideas?

    **A.** The elimination of governmental welfare benefits

    **B.** A system of socialized medicine in which the state provides care free of charge

    **C.** Reinstatement of national conscription (the draft) in times of war or national emergency

    **D.** An increase in the minimum wage in order to raise all those who are gainfully employed above the poverty line

11. According to the author's views, an individual's self-esteem is best assured when one acts:

    **A.** to fulfill one's own needs just as much as the needs of others.

    **B.** according to a code of values and virtues.

    **C.** only on the basis of one's own reason and beliefs.

    **D.** with only the best of intentions.

12. In paragraph 2 the author claims that, "A morality that dares to tell you to find happiness in the renunciation of your happiness—to value the failure of your values—is an insolent negation of morality." This statement, in the context of the passage as a whole, is intended to:

    **A.** illustrate the internal contradiction inherent within the concepts of value and morality.

    **B.** criticize moral standards that validate an ethic of selfishness.

    **C.** reject "morality" and "value" as empty and meaningless terms.

    **D.** indicate how morality and value must be defined in terms of the preservation of one's own life and the maximization of one's own happiness.

## Passage III (Questions 13-19)

The romantics were prompted to seek exotic subjects and to travel to far-off places. They failed to realize that, though the transcendental must involve the strange and unfamiliar, not everything strange or unfamiliar is transcendental.

The unfriendliness of society to his activity is difficult for the artist to accept. Yet this very hostility can act as a lever for true liberation. Freed from a false sense of security and community, the artist can abandon his plastic bank-book, just as he has abandoned other forms of security. Both the sense of community and of security depend on the familiar. Free of them, transcendental experiences become possible.

I think of my pictures as dramas; the shapes in the pictures are the performers. They have been created from the need for a group of actors who are able to move dramatically without embarrassment and execute gestures without shame.

Neither the action nor the actors can be anticipated, or described in advance. They begin as an unknown adventure in an unknown space. It is at the moment of completion that in a flash of recognition, they are seen to have the quantity and function which was intended. Ideas and plans that existed in the mind at the start were simply the doorway through which one left the world in which they occur.

The most important tool the artist fashions through constant practice is faith in his ability to produce miracles when they are needed. Pictures must be miraculous: the instant one is completed, the intimacy between creation and the creator is ended. He is an outsider. The picture must be for him, as for anyone experiencing it later, a revelation, an unexpected and unprecedented resolution of an eternally familiar need.

The presentation of this drama in the familiar world was never possible, unless everyday acts belonged to a ritual accepted as referring to a transcendent realm. Even the archaic artist, who had an uncanny virtuosity, found it necessary to create a group of intermediaries, monsters, hybrids, gods, and demigods. The difference is that, since the archaic artist was living in a more practical society than ours, the urgency for transcendent experience was understood, and given an official status. As a consequence, the human figure and other elements from the familiar world could be combined with, or participate as a whole in the enactment of the excesses which characterize this improbable hierarchy. With us the disguise must be complete. The familiar identity of things has to be pulverized in order to destroy the finite associations with which our society increasingly enshrouds every aspect of our environment.

Without monsters and gods, art cannot enact our drama: art's most profound moments express this frustration. When they were abandoned as untenable superstitions, art sank into melancholy. It became fond of the dark, and enveloped its objects in the nostalgic intimations of a half-lit world. For me the great achievement of the centuries in which the artist accepted the probable and the familiar as his subjects were the pictures of the single human figure—alone in a moment of utter immobility.

Adapted from M. Rothko, "The Romantics Were Prompted" in *Possibilities I*, © 1948.

13. According to the passage, "the unfriendliness of society to his [the artist's] activity" (paragraph 2) is:

    A. an unexpected, but ultimately positive development from the transcendental movement.
    B. unfortunate in that it distances the artist from the very thing that gives him his creative inspiration.
    C. good insofar as it discourages the artist from relying on false societal securities.
    D. neither good nor bad, but simply a fact of the artist's existence.

14. Which of the following best describes the author's intended meaning in paragraph 5?

    A. A completed work of art is by definition a wholly unpredictable development from the artist's original conception.
    B. Artistic aspiration, though admirable, is not necessarily practical.
    C. A finished work of art in no way reflects the needs or desires of the artist.
    D. A completed work of art is not of this world.

15. Which of the following best describes the "miraculous" quality of pictures mentioned in paragraph 5?

    A. The picture's ability to give shape to gods and monsters.
    B. The picture's ability to represent reality in other forms.
    C. The picture's ability to exist instantly upon completion as an autonomous entity.
    D. The picture's ability to convey the unique desire of the artist.

16. Which of the following best describes the author's use of drama as an analogy for art?

    A. Both are representations of reality from one individual's perspective.
    B. The individual components of a painting interact like actors on a stage, free of external influences.
    C. Both require the careful contemplation of our world.
    D. The painting is isolated from reality by a frame, and drama by a stage.

17. According to the passage, what led to art's present state of melancholy?

    A. disillusion with art's ability to express human emotion
    B. the increasing skepticism about the existence of gods and monsters
    C. a gradual devaluation of art's role in society
    D. the limited relationships ascribed by society to all parts of our environment

18. Which of the following, if true, would NOT *weaken* the author's points made in the sixth paragraph?

    I. Finite associations were more often made by archaic than modern peoples with regard to their environmental surroundings.
    II. No society has ever been more practical than ours.
    III. Modern artistic disguises of hybrids, gods, and demigods are often labored and unsuccessful.

    A. I only
    B. III only
    C. I and II only
    D. II and III only

19. All of the following may be inferred from the passage EXCEPT:

    A. The most important artistic tool is the artist's faith in his or her own ability to do the miraculous.
    B. Art's most profound moments utilize the presence of monsters and gods.
    C. One of the greatest artistic achievements involved portraits of single human figures.
    D. Transcendent experiences are dependent on isolation and feelings of insecurity.

### Passage IV (Questions 20-25)

If ecologists are to study urban ecosystems, they must decide two questions first: what an urban ecosystem is, and what measures appropriately describe its interactions with other ecosystems?

Among the traditional ways to look at an ecosystem is by examining how it balances primary production (photosynthesis, or solar-energy conversion by plants) with respiration, by which energy is converted to unusable form. For most ecosystems the overall calculation is fairly well balanced between inputs and outputs. An urban ecosystem, a concentration of people and human activity, is an energy-intensive ecosystem, and viewed in traditional ecological terms it is more unbalanced than most other ecosystems. Its unique energy signature, then, is one way of distinguishing an urban ecosystem.

Howard T. Odum noted that a typical city daily transforms into heat about 70 times more usable energy per square meter than a close nonhuman equivalent to a city—an oyster reef. A natural ecosystem is likely to be self-powered by photosynthesis or chemosynthesis. By contrast a city is a *heterotrophic* ecosystem, one that depends primarily on external sources of energy. Heterotrophic ecosystems are rare on earth, including some marshes, the deep ocean and streams, but even among such systems cities are extreme. The different characteristics of urban ecosystems may call for some nontraditional ways of assessing how dependent they are on other ecosystems.

William Rees employs in his analysis an instructive measure of urban energy dependence called an "ecological footprint." The footprint of a city is the total area of productive land required to support its activities in a sustainable way. In other words, that land must produce an amount of resources equivalent to the sum of all resources consumed by the city—and assimilate an amount of waste equivalent to that produced by the city. Cities' footprints can be impressive—tens or hundreds of times larger than their actual area—because in addition to the plant, microbial, and animal metabolisms that characterize all ecosystems, cities have an "industrial metabolism"—a metaphorical hunger whose satisfaction requires mining of nonrenewable resources as well as exploitation of renewable ones.

In many cases the patterns of human activity, unlike those of most animals, do not follow natural rhythms but seem to alter them. In other cases human activity, of course, has tended to follow natural cycles: We are active by day and sleep by night; throughout human time our festivals have tracked harvests or grown out of the need to fill winter nights. It is unclear whether people living in modern urban ecosystems are as likely to develop social rhythms responding to natural cycles as are rural human societies that depend vitally on a local resource—hunter-gatherer societies or subsistence-agriculture villages, for example.

Is there a possibility of simply stretching current ecological theory to encompass urban ecosystems? Human beings, we might argue, are like other organisms. It could be that the differences in the ways in which people and other organisms evolve, interact with, and influence their surroundings are merely quantitative, not qualitative.

Or one can take the position that current ecological theory is insufficient to capture the key patterns and processes in these human-dominated or urban ecosystems. The emergence and influence of culture, the constraints and opportunities afforded by our institutions, and our ability to create strategies in response to anticipated (rather than realized) selection pressures mean that standard ecological and evolutionary theories and principles apply only imperfectly to human populations. This view would obligate would-be urban ecologists to seek out a great deal of interaction with, or "borrowing from," the social sciences to advance ecology in general to a point where it can explain patterns and processes in human-dominated systems.

Adapted from J. P. Collins, et. al., "A New Urban Ecology," in *American Scientist,* Vol. 88 #5, © Sept 2000.

20.  The passage suggests which of the following to be true of traditional approaches to the study of ecosystems?

   **A.**  Such approaches indicate that cities cannot sustain themselves, given their high population density and level of human activity.
   **B.**  They utilize the concept of an "ecological footprint" of a city in order to analyze an urban center's rates of primary production and respiration.
   **C.**  They all calculate the balance between photo-synthesis and production of waste in order to describe the way in which ecosystems function.
   **D.**  One approach demonstrates that urban centers show a greater disequilibrium between inputs and outputs than a majority of natural ecosystems.

21. As it is used in the passage, the term "industrial metabolism" (paragraph 4) most likely means:

    A. the chemical and physical processes through which plants and animals utilize resources.
    B. cities' need for resources beyond those that they can themselves produce.
    C. the rhythm of life created by the social and cultural institutions that structure modern industrial societies.
    D. an analogy that can be drawn between urban and natural ecosystems.

22. Which of the following statements, if shown to be true, would most strengthen the position, as it is described in the final paragraph of the passage, that an innovative approach to the study of urban ecosystems is required?

    A. Heterotrophic qualities are much more commonly found in urban centers than in natural environments.
    B. Humans commonly dam and channel rivers in order to eliminate the risk of flooding, and plant and animal species in the affected areas must then adapt to these changes in their environment.
    C. Efforts to lessen the progression of global warming by banning the use of CFCs (chlorofluorocarbons) have had little or no impact.
    D. More natural ecosystems than previously thought have been found to depend on external sources of energy.

23. In paragraph 3 the author cites a colleague's comparison of a typical city and an oyster reef. What is the purpose of this comparison?

    A. To illustrate the fact that heterotrophic systems, though rare in nature, do exist in ecosystems other than urban centers
    B. To provide an example of a natural ecosystem sustained through photosynthesis or chemo-synthesis
    C. To demonstrate how concentrations of people and human activity may have different energy signatures than do dense nonhuman populations
    D. To support the claim that the differences between how humans and other organisms influence their environments are quantitative, not qualitative

24. Suppose it were demonstrated that urban industrial laborers working the night shift and subsistence farmers in small villages consumed on average the same number of calories, ate meals at roughly the same times, and spent the same amount of time with their families. What relevance would this finding have for the author's consideration of whether or not urban ecosystems have unique characteristics?

    A. It would prove that those who live in urban settings follow natural cycles to the same extent as do those in rural societies.
    B. It would undermine Rees's claim that industrial regions consume more than they produce.
    C. It would be useful in an evaluation of whether or not urban systems are structured by nature in the same way that some non-urban communities are.
    D. It would show the importance of taking culture into account when studying urban ecosystems.

25. According to the author's description of Rees's model, what does the impressive nature of many cities' footprints show us about the distinctive nature of urban ecological systems?

    A. Because of the volume of waste produced, heterotrophic systems have a destructive effect on the surrounding natural ecologies.
    B. Urban ecologies are essentially different from natural ecologies, which always balance inputs with outputs over the long run.
    C. Natural ecosystems are internally powered either by photosynthesis or by chemosynthesis, while cities are driven solely by industrial exploitation of externally derived resources.
    D. Cities are on average more dependent on other ecosystems than are most natural ecologies.

## Passage V (Questions 26-30)

I have written this book to sweep away all misunderstandings about the crafty art of punnery and to convince you that the pun is well worth celebrating…. After all, the pun is mightier than the sword, and these days you are much more likely to run into a pun than into a sword. [A pun is a witticism involving the playful use of a word in different senses, or of words which differ in meaning but sound alike.]

Scoffing at puns seems to be a conditioned reflex, and through the centuries a steady barrage of libel and slander has been aimed at the practice of punning. Nearly three hundred years ago John Dennis sneered, "A pun is the lowest form of wit," a charge that has been butted and rebutted by a mighty line of pundits and punheads.

Henry Erskine, for example, has protested that if a pun is the lowest form of wit, "It is, therefore, the foundation of all wit." Oscar Levant has added a tag line: "A pun is the lowest form of humor—when you don't think of it first." John Crosbie and Bob Davies have responded to Dennis with hot, cross puns: "… If someone complains that punning is the lowest form of humor you can tell them that poetry is verse."

Samuel Johnson, the eighteenth century self-appointed custodian of the English language, once thundered, "To trifle with the vocabulary which is the vehicle of social intercourse is to tamper with the currency of human intelligence. He who would violate the sanctities of his mother tongue would invade the recesses of the national till without remorse… "

Joseph Addison pronounced that the seeds of punning are in the minds of all men, and tho' they may be subdued by reason, reflection, and good sense, they will be very apt to shoot up in the greatest genius, that which is not broken and cultivated by the rules of art.

Far from being invertebrate, the inveterate punster is a brave entertainer. He or she loves to create a three-ring circus of words: words clowning, words teetering on tightropes, words swinging from tent tops, words thrusting their head into the mouths of lions. Punnery can be highly entertaining, but it is always a risky business. The humor can fall on its face, it can lose its balance and plunge into the sawdust, or it can be decapitated by the snapping shut of jaws.

While circus performers often receive laughter or applause for their efforts, punsters often draw an obligatory groan for theirs. But the fact that most people groan at, rather than laugh at, puns doesn't mean that the punnery isn't funnery. If the pun is a good one, the groan usually signifies a kind of suppressed admiration for the verbal acrobatics on display, and perhaps a hidden envy.

Edgar Allan Poe…neatly…summed up the situation when he wrote, "Of puns it has been said that those most dislike them who are least able to utter them…."

Step right up and into a circus of words. All the humor will be in tents, guaranteed to whet (and wet) your appetite for more…. You'll find that, indeed, a bun is the doughiest form of wheat.

Adapted from R. Lederer, *Get Thee to a Punnery: An Anthology of Intentional Assaults Upon the English Language*, © 2006 Gibbs Smith.

26. Based on information in the passage, you can infer that Edgar Allen Poe believed that:

    A. people who dislike puns envy those who can make them.
    B. people who make puns have sophisticated senses of humor.
    C. humor is not limited to puns, but is expressed in other ways as well.
    D. people who make puns are the funniest people in our society.

27. Samuel Johnson's statement cited in paragraph 4 of the passage indicates that Johnson would most likely agree with which of the following?

    A. People should be wary of making puns that are too playful.
    B. People who make puns are unintelligent.
    C. Punning is a frivolous and transgressive use of language.
    D. If we did not have puns we would not be intelligent.

28. Which of the following facts would most *challenge* the claim that the punster is a brave entertainer?

    A. Sexually oriented humor causes people to laugh.
    B. Punsters are rarely, if ever, in danger of being ridiculed or embarrassed when they perform.
    C. Audiences often do not laugh at puns.
    D. Some puns cause hysterical laughter.

29. It has been said elsewhere that a pun is the highest form of wit. Which of the following claims made or cited in the passage would most support this claim?

    A. "A pun is a witticism involving the playful use of a word..."
    B. "If the pun is a good one, the groan usually signifies a kind of suppressed admiration for the verbal acrobatics on display..."
    C. "The seeds of punning are...apt to shoot up in the greatest genius...."
    D. "Far from being invertebrate, the inveterate punster is a brave entertainer."

30. The author asserts that, most fundamentally, punning is:

    A. slanderous.
    B. destructive.
    C. entertaining.
    D. courageous.

## Passage VI (Questions 31-37)

I think we have to begin thinking about stories at a much more fundamental level, so I want to talk about one quality of fiction which I think is its least common denominator—the fact that it is concrete—and about a few of the qualities that follow from this.... The beginning of human knowledge is through the senses, and the fiction writer begins where human perception begins. He appeals through the senses, and you cannot appeal to the senses with abstractions. It is a good deal easier for most people to state an abstract idea than to describe and thus re-create some object that they actually see. But the world of the fiction writer is full of matter, and this is what the beginning fiction writers are very loath to create. They are concerned primarily with unfleshed ideas and emotions.... They are conscious of problems, not of people, of questions and issues, not of the texture of existence, of case histories and of everything that has a sociological smack, instead of with all those concrete details of life that make actual the mystery of our position on Earth.

One of the most common and saddest spectacles is that of a person of really fine sensibility and acute psychological perception trying to write fiction by using these qualities alone. This type of writer will put down one intensely emotional or keenly perceptive sentence after another, and the result will be complete dullness. The fact is that the materials of the fiction writer are the humblest. Fiction is about everything human and we are made out of dust, and if you scorn getting yourself dusty, then you shouldn't try to write fiction.

Now the word *symbol* scares a good many people off, just as the word *art* does. They seem to feel that a symbol is some mysterious thing put in arbitrarily by the writer to frighten the common reader—sort of a literary Masonic grip that is only for the initiated. They seem to think that it is a way of saying something that you aren't actually saying, and so if they can be got to read a reputedly symbolic work at all, they approach it as if it were a problem in algebra. Find $x$. And when they do find or think they find this abstraction $x$, then they go off with an elaborate sense of satisfaction and the notion that they have "understood" the story. Many students confuse the *process* of understanding a thing with understanding it.

I think that for the fiction writer himself, symbols are something he uses as a matter of course. You might say that these are details that, while having their essential place in the literal level of the story, operate in depth as well as on the surface, increasing the story in every direction.

The type of mind that can understand good fiction is not necessarily the educated mind, but it is at all times the kind of mind that is willing to have its sense of mystery deepened by contact with reality, and its sense of reality deepened by contact with mystery. Fiction should be both canny and uncanny. In a good deal of popular criticism, there is the notion operating that all fiction has to be about the Average Man, and has to depict average ordinary everyday life, that every fiction writer must produce what used to be called " a slice of life." But if life, in that sense, satisfied us, there would be no sense in producing literature at all...

Adapted from F. O'Connor, *Mystery and Manners: Occasional Prose*, ©1961 Farrar, Straus & Giroux.

**31.** The author of the passage would be most likely to consider a literary effort successful if it:

A. developed the theme of good and evil through a series of philosophical conversations.
B. used concrete details that involved the senses of the reader.
C. explained the process of understanding so that readers could comprehend it.
D. presented a "slice of life" with which the average person could identify.

**32.** Given the information in the passage, which of the following reactions is common when some readers come across symbols in a story?

I. The readers believe that assigning the correct meaning to the symbol allows them to understand the story.
II. The readers feel that they may be excluded from fully understanding the story.
III. The readers only appreciate symbols with sociological meanings.

A. I only
B. I and II only
C. I and III only
D. I, II, and III

**33.** The author of the passage would probably support the statement that:

A. intelligence and perception are not the only requirements for writing literature.
B. to read literature with understanding, a person must be educated in the classics.
C. the theme of a story is more important than its incidental details.
D. psychology and sociology are not appropriate subjects for fiction.

**34.** In the context of the passage, the word "mystery" (paragraph 5) refers to the:

A. enigmatic aspects of human existence.
B. difficulty of understanding literature.
C. suspense intentionally created by the writer.
D. subjective problems caused by attempting to assign meanings to symbols.

**35.** Which of the following statements, if true, would most *weaken* the author's contention that "the world of the fiction writer is full of matter" (paragraph 1)?

A. Most people are more comfortable expressing ideas than feelings.
B. Books about theoretical principles are not usually popular with the general audience.
C. Some writers are able to write abstractly in a way that engages the senses of the average reader.
D. Emotional writing tends to have more significance for the writer than for the reader.

**36.** According to the author, the reason literature is written at all is that:

A. it supplies something lacking in everyday life.
B. some of the people who try to write have talent.
C. it is the foundation of human knowledge.
D. it gives people another way to engage their senses.

**37.** The author of the passage recommends that writers take advantage of the concrete nature of fiction because:

A. she does not enjoy reading fiction that is about ideas rather than people.
B. she believes that beginning writers do not have the skills to write abstract fiction.
C. readers understand ideas more easily than mystery.
D. fiction is more appealing to readers when it engages their senses.

## Passage VII (Questions 38-42)

1929 was a watershed year in many ways for American society and politics. The Great Depression changed the thinking of farmers, industrial workers, younger intellectuals, and ultimately even lawmakers. This change created the foundation for the New Deal to come in the next decade. The profound shifts in political allegiance were the undoing of the dominance of the Republican Party, which had prevailed since and because of the War Between the States. These shifts also provided the opportunity for the Democrats to return to power for the first time in more than a quarter century.

In 1921, a depression, relatively minor in comparison to that which was to hit the whole economy at the end of the decade, devastated the farmers. The price of produce plummeted but their costs, chiefly mortgage payments to banks, remained high. Other rural dwellers, such as blacks in the South and the whites of Appalachia, continued to live in hopeless poverty. The 1921 depression, however, had little effect on national politics. Industrial production and employment remained high and even increased steadily. Between 1925 and 1929 the number of manufacturing establishments rose from 183,900 to 206,700; the nation produced 5,358,000 automobiles in 1929—1,000,000 more than three years earlier. Although wages increased slowly, prices remained stable. In the elections of 1924 and 1928, as well as in the intervening congressional elections, the Republicans easily defeated the Democrats again.

The crash of 1929 and the deep depression that followed brought the industrial workers out in force. Unemployment rose precipitously. Workers no longer accepted the free-wheeling capitalism that had driven the economy since the Civil War. The middle-class began to consider organized labor a legitimate facet of a predominantly capitalist society. In 1933 fewer than 3,000,000 workers were organized into unions; by the early 1940s that figure had more than quadrupled. The giant automobile, steel, rubber, and electrical manufacturing employers, for example, were forced to bargain collectively. At about the same time, young, active intellectuals began to suggest that the old

order was incapable of solving the new problems. They called for governmental regulation and oversight of the largely unfettered employers and securities markets. Some, William O. Douglas to name just one, left their academic posts to become the regulators of the capitalists. The dissatisfaction of farmers and laborers led the Democrats to landslide victories in the elections of the 1930s.

Throughout the 1930s the Democratic President and Congress enacted a plethora of statutes to benefit their new constituents. These included, but were hardly limited to, the National Labor Relations Act, the Agricultural Adjustment Acts, the Agricultural Marketing Agreement Act of 1937, the Bituminous Coal Act, the Securities Exchange Acts of 1933 and 1934, as well as wage, hour, child labor, and social security laws. Although the Supreme Court held some of the New Deal legislation unconstitutional, much of it survived and formed the basis for the strongly regulated capitalism that contrasts so starkly with the economic policies that existed prior to 1929.

**38.** The primary purpose of the passage is to:

    **A.** describe the events of the Great Depression in chronological order.

    **B.** explain the causes and effects of the defection of particular groups from unregulated capitalism to regulated capitalism.

    **C.** argue that unlike the Great Depression, the depression of 1921 had only minor effects on national policy.

    **D.** explain the history of the labor movement in the United States.

**39.** With the information provided, one can most reasonably conclude that the shift from Republican to Democratic political dominance occurred because of:

    **A.** the crash of 1929.

    **B.** Marxist ideas.

    **C.** the effects of the labor movement.

    **D.** the 1921 depression.

**40.** One can most reasonably infer from the passage that a chief expense for farmers in the early 1920s was:

    **A.** purchase of farming equipment.

    **B.** cost of seed and grain.

    **C.** repayment of debt.

    **D.** acquisition of manufactured goods.

**41.** According to the passage, which of the following played the strongest role in encouraging workers to unionize?

    **A.** Wage increases

    **B.** Young intellectuals' calls for change

    **C.** High levels of rural poverty

    **D.** Rising unemployment

**42.** Which of the following scenarios would be most similar to the causal relationship between the events described in the passage?

    **A.** The need for female factory workers during World War II led to a change in societal attitudes about the proper role of women in the labor forces, which led to an increase in the political power of women and to legislation against discrimination in the workplace.

    **B.** Belief in basic ideals of liberty and justice led to the Fourteenth Amendment granting voting rights to African Americans, which created a backlash in the south, leading to Jim Crow laws which sought to limit the political power of the newly enfranchised.

    **C.** Increasing industrialization in the North led to a migration of labor from the South to the North, which led to a further weakening of the agriculturally based southern economy.

    **D.** An economic crisis in the US caused in part by competition from foreign agricultural producers led to increased subsidies and price supports for US farmers, which led to a decrease in the cost of domestic agricultural goods and increased competitiveness with foreign producers.

## Passage VIII (Questions 43-48)

Researchers in cognitive psychology and the area of computer science known as artificial intelligence (AI) have come to strikingly similar conclusions about the knowledge-bound character of all cognitive skills. AI research demonstrates that the ability of humans to exercise a skill depends on their possession of specific schemata that are sufficiently numerous and detailed to handle the many varieties of the tasks they are called on to perform. It is more accurate to speak of "reading *skills*" than of "reading skill." Graphs showing community college students' high degree of skill in reading an essay on friendship but their lack of skill in reading about Grant and Lee accord with the recent discovery of AI and cognitive psychology that a skill is not a unified system of intellectual muscles that can be developed by calisthenics into a vigorous all-purpose ability.

Dr. Herbert A. Simon, a leading figure in AI research, once wryly remarked that saying an expert performance is caused by a "skill" is like Molière's doctor saying that the sleep-inducing properties of opium are caused by its "dormative power." Simon, a Nobel laureate, has been working since the 1950s on the detailed structure of cognitive skills. The discoveries that he and his coworkers have made should induce a deep skepticism toward the belief that our schools can teach reading, writing, and critical thinking as all-purpose general skills applicable to novel problems. Simon and his colleagues have cast doubt on the idea that there are *any* general or transferable cognitive skills. All cognitive skills depend on procedural and substantive schemata that are highly specific to the task at hand.

AI research shows that experts perform better than novices not because they have more powerful and better oiled intellectual machinery but because they have more relevant and quickly available information. What distinguishes good readers from poor ones is simply the possession of a lot of diverse, task-specific information.

Probably the most dramatic illustrations of the knowledge-bound character of human skills came from some remarkable experiments conducted by Adriaan de Groot, a Dutch psychologist, who described his findings in a book entitled *Het Denken van den Schaker* (literally, "the thinking of chess players"). De Groot discovered that chess masters are astonishingly skilled at remembering and reproducing chess positions after a very brief exposure to them. The subjects in his experiments were players of various abilities, as indicated by their official chess rankings. In one experiment, de Groot displayed for five to ten seconds a chess position from an actual game in which twenty-five pieces were left on the board. The subjects were asked to reproduce the position from memory. Grandmasters performed this feat with 100 percent accuracy, masters with 90 percent accuracy. Weaker players were lucky if they could correctly place five or six pieces.

Then de Groot varied the conditions of his experiment in one respect. Instead of placing the twenty-five pieces in positions from an actual game, he placed them on the board randomly. The results were unexpected. All his subjects—grandmasters, masters, class A players, and class B players—performed the same as novices did, placing only five or six pieces correctly.

When the configuration of a task is significantly changed, past skills are not transferred to the new problem. In normal circumstances, of course, elements from past problems appear in present ones, and experts perform well with duplicated elements. But beyond analogous circumstances, skill is not transferred.

Adapted from E. D. Hirsch, Jr., *Cultural Literacy*, © 1987 Houghton Mifflin Co.

**43.** The main point of this passage is that:

**A.** it is not general skill but specific knowledge that enables people to excel in a particular field.

**B.** research in the fields of artificial intelligence and cognitive science has produced remarkably similar results concerning the nature of human intelligence.

**C.** in any given field, "experts" are not necessarily more intelligent than "novices."

**D.** intelligence is essentially a measure of general knowledge.

**44.** Within the passage, the reference to the opinions of Dr. Herbert A. Simon serves to:

**A.** support the central thesis, because Simon is a recognized authority in a field that deals with cognitive skills.

**B.** introduce a contrary opinion that complicates the relationship between artificial intelligence and human intelligence.

**C.** confirm the relationship between artificial intelligence and human intelligence.

**D.** make an irrelevant point, because Simon is an expert in artificial intelligence, not cognitive science.

**45.** Simon most likely uses the story of Molière's doctor in order to do which of the following?

**A.** To demonstrate a weakness of the medical profession

**B.** To show that cognitive skills and diagnostic skills are closely related

**C.** To make the claim that a "skill" and an "expert performance" are essentially identical

**D.** To imply that the reverse is actually true—that giving expert performances causes skills to be acquired

**46.** Adriaan de Groot's experiments with chess players imply each of the following EXCEPT that:

**A.** a player's ability and ranking are to some degree dependent on his or her memory.

**B.** chess masters possess a greater store of general knowledge than do chess novices.

**C.** novice chess players might play checkers as well as master chess players.

**D.** the ability to remember something is dependent upon previous familiarity with schemata that fit whatever is to be remembered.

**47.** Suppose that de Groot's chess players were given one minute, rather than five seconds, to study the randomly placed pieces, and that, with the extra time, the master players were able to remember more pieces while the novice players were not. Assuming that de Groot's theories are correct, this new information implies that:

**A.** master chess players learn more quickly than do novice chess players.

**B.** master players are faster thinkers than are novices.

**C.** this new situation is more analogous to ordinary chess playing than was previously suspected.

**D.** it is primarily practice that separates novices from master chess players.

**48.** The claim that "it is more accurate to speak of 'reading *skills*' than of 'reading skill' " (paragraph 1) most directly suggests that:

**A.** reading ability is more accurately characterized as the sum of the abilities of a population than as an individual achievement.

**B.** the ability to read is attained by developing skills in familiar subjects before skills in unfamiliar subjects are sought.

**C.** the capacity to understand one text is not necessarily representative of the reader's capacity to comprehend all texts.

**D.** the ability to read is defined by the specific capacity to comprehend a wide variety of texts.

## Passage IX (Questions 49-53)

Since the 1970s, industrialized nations have been experiencing a "health food" movement in which unscrupulous vendors of doubtful products with unproven claims play on our beliefs, fears, and hopes. The truth is that there is no such thing as health food. The term is both false and misleading—misleading because it suggests that other foods are unhealthy. Furthermore, apart from human milk for babies, no single food supplies all the nutrients we need.

Many of the traditional foods that we have eaten since biblical times—such as olives, honey, and dates—are very poor sources of nutrients even when they are "natural," that is, not even dried by the sun. Yet they are often promoted as "health foods" because they are of ancient origin and are unprocessed. In fact, fresh dates are sixty five percent sugar. Honey is a mixture of two sugars, glucose and fructose, and apart from its pleasant flavor, has only small traces of any other nutrients. Fresh olives contain less than one percent protein and most of the rest, apart from water, is fat.

Attempts have been made from time to time to define "health food," but since the concept itself is artificial, none of these definitions will ever be accepted by medical science and neither will the health food industry itself. For example, one attempt defined health foods as "whole foods," presumably meaning whole wheat as compared with white flour or milled cereals. This would mean that unpeeled potatoes, apples, and oranges could be called "health foods," but that their peeled counterparts could not.

The fact that "health food" cannot be defined does not stop health food shops from making extravagant claims. They sell a variety of foods, food supplements and extracts, pills and potions. Some are useful, some are useless but harmless, and some are dangerous. When foods of various kinds are promoted as so-called health foods, far-ranging claims are made for them. It is these claims that are criticized by scientists. Few if any of the claims have ever been investigated, which makes it impossible for their promoters to substantiate them.

At one time not too long ago, vast numbers of Americans rushed out to buy an extract of apricot stones—wrongly called vitamin B17—because it had been claimed to cure cancer. Many of these misguided patients chose not to undergo surgical treatment which might have saved their lives. The health food movement, therefore, poses a true danger to the public health. When the manufacture and sale of "vitamin B17" were banned in some states, the demand was so great that the useless extract was smuggled in from Mexico. In 1948, the strength of public opinion compelled the British Minister of Health to organize a clinical trial of a cancer cure that the medical profession knew did not even merit testing.

Surely people are right to believe that food is related to health. Nutrition is a legitimate medical science originating, perhaps, with Alcmaeon's equilibrium principle. It is understandable that an individual should be prepared to try anything in the hope of relieving chronic pain or curing terminal disease. What is most deplorable is the way in which the purveyors of health food exploit the hopes of the sufferers and profit from their distress.

**49.** The author of the passage believes that the term "health food":

A. was originally named by concerned vendors of useful products.
B. suggests all foods are healthy.
C. is defined as foods that meet all the dietary needs of most people.
D. is inaccurate and deceptive.

**50.** According to the author, human milk differs from other foods in that human milk:

A. should be called "health food," and other foods should not.
B. is deficient in some vitamins but most other foods are not.
C. is the only food that can supply all necessary nutrients for some people.
D. cannot be sun-dried although other foods can be.

**51.** The author states that "food is related to health" (paragraph 6) in order to:

A. qualify the author's earlier criticism of the "health food" movement.
B. give one reason why sick people might believe the claims of "health food" purveyors.
C. suggest effective ways in which people with terminal diseases might alleviate their suffering.
D. indicate that parts of the medical establishment have played a role in perpetuating the fraud of "health food."

**52.** Which of the following, if true, would most *weaken* the author's claim that "health food" is an artificial concept?

A. Many people believe that the consumption of large amounts of vitamin C can help prevent colds.
B. Several methodologically valid studies have shown that a diet rich in antioxidants can help prevent the development of certain cancers.
C. High levels of sugar consumption can contribute to the development of diabetes.
D. Consumption of extract of apricot stones is not in and of itself harmful.

**53.** Suppose it were demonstrated that certain foods eaten in ancient times contain high levels of many important nutrients. What impact would this have on the author's claim that it is impossible to define "health food"?

A. It would weaken it by suggesting that olives, honey, and dates may be more healthful than indicated by the author.
B. It would have no impact on it, as the author does not argue that no traditional foods have nutritional value.
C  It would have no effect on it, as the author's claim that traditional foods are not necessarily healthy has no direct relationship to the author's claim that health food cannot be defined.
D. It would strengthen it, by supporting the author's claim that nutrition is a legitimate and ancient science.

---

## END OF TEST 1

# ANSWER KEY — TEST 1

| Passage I | Passage II | Passage III | Passage IV | Passage V | Passage VI | Passage VII | Passage VIII | Passage IX |
|-----------|-----------|-------------|------------|-----------|------------|-------------|--------------|------------|
| 1.  C | 6.  C | 13.  C | 20.  D | 26.  A | 31.  B | 38.  B | 43.  A | 49.  D |
| 2.  B | 7.  D | 14.  A | 21.  B | 27.  C | 32.  B | 39.  A | 44.  A | 50.  C |
| 3.  A | 8.  C | 15.  C | 22.  B | 28.  B | 33.  A | 40.  C | 45.  C | 51.  B |
| 4.  D | 9.  D | 16.  B | 23.  C | 29.  C | 34.  A | 41.  D | 46.  B | 52.  B |
| 5.  C | 10.  A | 17.  B | 24.  C | 30.  D | 35.  C | 42.  A | 47.  C | 53.  B |
|  | 11.  C | 18.  B | 25.  D |  | 36.  A |  | 48.  C |  |
|  | 12.  D | 19.  B |  |  | 37.  D |  |  |  |

# Test Assessment Log

Use this Log to evaluate your performance on this CARS Practice Test. Diagnose what led you to select (or seriously consider) wrong answers, or to spend more time than necessary to identify the correct answer.

Approximate the time you spent on the Now passages and on the Later passages. Consider if you are spending the time needed on easier passages to get most of those questions right, or, if you are spending more time than necessary and not getting to as many questions as you could while still maintaining good accuracy. If you find that you are spending most of your 90 minutes on harder passages with a low level of accuracy, consider how best to reapportion your time on your next practice test. Finally, evaluate your ranking; are you choosing the right passages and doing them at roughly the right time within the section?

## Now Passages

| Now Passage # | Q # and Type (for questions you got wrong) | Attractors (for wrong answers you picked or seriously considered) | What did you do wrong? |
|---|---|---|---|
| | | | |
| | | | |
| | | | |
| | | | |
| | | | |
| | | | |

Approximate time spent on Now passages _____

Total Now passages attempted _____

Total # of Q's on Now passages attempted _____

Total # of Now Q's correct _____

% correct of Now Q's attempted _____

## Later Passages

| Later Passage # | Q # and Type (for questions you got wrong) | Attractors (for wrong answers you picked or seriously considered) | What did you do wrong? |
|---|---|---|---|
| | | | |
| | | | |
| | | | |
| | | | |
| | | | |
| | | | |

Approximate time spent on Later passages _____

Total Later passages attempted _____

Total # of Q's on Later passages attempted _____

Total # of Later Q's correct _____

% correct of Later Q's attempted _____

# Final Analysis

Total # of passages attempted (including partially completed) _____

Total # of questions attempted _____

Total # of correct answers _____

Total % correct of attempted questions _____

## Revised Strategy

| | |
|---|---|
| **Pacing** | |
| **Passage choice/ranking** | |
| **Working the Passage** | |
| **Attacking the Questions** | |

# MCAT
# Critical Analysis and Reasoning Skills

# Practice Test 1
# Solutions

# TEST 1 SOLUTIONS

## Passage I

This is a Now passage.

**Bottom Line:** Placebos effective and safe—could cure even more with increased faith of patients.

1.  C     This is a Tone/Attitude question.
    A:    No. The author does not explain any in-depth scientific issues that a layperson would have difficulty understanding.
    B:    No. Further research is not suggested anywhere in the passage. Furthermore, given the lack of any real scientific explanation in the passage, you cannot infer that the author is a scientist.
    **C:    Yes. The author describes the effectiveness of placebos in non-scientific language and discusses the possibility of widely increasing their use through word-of-mouth advertising, as well as the need to charge a high price. Given that the other three choices state or suggest that the author is a scientist, this is the "least wrong" answer.**
    D:    No. There is no real science discussed in the passage. Therefore, you cannot conclude that the author is a scientist. Furthermore, treatment through placebos is not new; the author states in paragraph 1 that the effectiveness of placebos is historically "well known."

2.  B     This is a Retrieval question.
    A:    No. The procedure causes some subjects to doubt the efficacy of what they are given (paragraph 4).
    **B:    Yes. "Faith," mentioned in paragraph 4, is responsible for the curative properties.**
    C:    No. These harmless substances have no secondary effects, other than their psychological impact (paragraph 3).
    D:    No. This does not indicate why placebos are effective.

3.  A     This is a Weaken question.
    **A:    Yes. If so few people purchase the placebo due to its exorbitant fee and word-of-mouth is stifled, then this vital form of advertising (paragraph 6) would preclude the program's success.**
    B:    No. The lack of clear proof for a correlation does not constitute evidence against it. This choice gives no reason to doubt the opinion of the public health services referred to in paragraph 7.
    C:    No. This strengthens the argument that high fees are necessary for successful treatment.
    D:    No. The argument claims that high fees lead to success of the treatment, not to higher sales. Evidence that high fees do not correlate to high sales is out of the scope of the argument.

4.  D     This is a Retrieval/EXCEPT question.
    A:    No. This is mentioned in paragraph 6.
    B:    No. This is mentioned in paragraph 4.
    C:    No. This is mentioned in paragraph 7.
    **D:    Yes. Although a lack of harmful side effects is mentioned in the passage (paragraph 3), it is not described as contributing to the effectiveness of placebos.**

5.   C      This is a Retrieval/NOT question.
     A:     No. The passage states, "No harmful side effects result from placebos" (paragraph 3).
     B:     No. Placebos are effective against a wider range of illnesses than any other drug. "That placebos can cure everything from dandruff to leprosy is well known" (paragraph 1).
     **C:     Yes. Exactly the opposite is true. Although placebos could be inexpensive, the author claims that "treatment centers must charge exorbitant fees for placebo treatments" (paragraph 7).**
     D:     No. Support for this statement is found in paragraphs 5 and 6.

# Passage II
This is a Killer passage.

**Bottom Line:** Morality should be based on self-interest, not good of others.

6.   C      This is an Inference question.
     A:     No. In the first paragraph, the author argues that value is nonexistent when no alternatives are available.
     B:     No. Actions are virtuous when they achieve values (paragraph 1). Value is defined by the author as one's own happiness, not the happiness or good of the community or others within the community (paragraph 2). This choice contradicts the author's ethic of selfishness as it is expressed throughout the passage.
     **C:     Yes. In the opening paragraph, the author claims that "'value' presupposes...the necessity of action in the face of an alternative." Virtue is defined as the actions one takes in order to achieve values. If you have no choice but to pursue a given course of action, your actions are not virtuous.**
     D:     No. This statement directly contradicts the author's repudiation of a morality based on self-sacrifice (paragraphs 2 and 7).

7.   D      This is a Main Idea question.
     A:     No. This claim is supported in paragraph 5, but it is too narrow to be the main point of the entire passage.
     B:     No. Happiness for whom? This choice is too vague to capture the author's advocacy of an ethic of selfishness, and fails to include the passage's critique of self-sacrifice.
     C:     No. While the author rejects the "eternal, absolute, objective" moral standards of those who define value as the good of others (paragraph 6), she does not (either specifically or in the passage as a whole) argue against the existence of *any* eternal or objective standards.
     **D:     Yes. The author presents her arguments for selfishness in the first half of the passage, and then moves on to a related critique of moralities based on self-sacrifice for the good of others.**

8.  C   This is an Inference question.
    A:  No. The author rejects moralities based on need (paragraph 7).
    B:  No. This choice is inconsistent with the theme of the passage, which is that morality is entirely defined by the achievement of one's own happiness (paragraph 2). The author does not advocate treating others badly, but neither does she accept the idea that morality is to be defined by reference to anyone but oneself (paragraph 4).
    C:  **Yes. The passage portrays dependency on others in a strongly negative light (paragraph 7). The author clearly would support the theme of self-reliance embodied in this motto.**
    D:  No. This is inconsistent with the author's critique in paragraph 5 of those who use intention as a "standard of virtue."

9.  D   This is an Inference question.
    A:  No. The author's own express purpose is to evaluate and reject moral codes (those based on self-sacrifice) held by others.
    B:  No. The author does reject intention as a standard of virtue (paragraph 5), but this is not the meaning of the cited phrase in the context of the second paragraph. This answer choice is the right answer to the wrong question.
    C:  No. This choice contradicts the main idea of the passage, which holds that individuals should not sacrifice themselves for the good of the whole. Beware of choices that take words ("end") out of context.
    D:  **Yes. In this part of the essay (the second paragraph) the author argues that every individual exists only for himself, and should act only in order to secure his own happiness ("the highest moral purpose") rather than the happiness of others.**

10. A   This is a New Information question.
    A:  **Yes. The author claims that those who sacrifice for others become in turn dependent, "in the position of a parasite whose needs must be filled by others" (paragraph 7). By depicting the "disgraceful role" of such a "beggar," the author gives evidence that she would support the elimination of any system or policy whose mission was to fulfill the needs of those that do not or cannot support themselves.**
    B:  No. The author places high value on self-reliance and self-sufficiency (paragraph 7). Socialized medicine would contravene, not embody, those principles as she defines them.
    C:  No. Conscription into the military entails forcing the individual to (potentially) sacrifice his own life to protect the nation. This contradicts the central thrust of the passage.
    D:  No. This choice is similar to choice B. The author would reject a policy that provided a guaranteed benefit or standard of living, turning citizens into (in the mind of the author) "beggars" and "parasites."

11. C   This is a Retrieval question.
    A:  No. This choice is only partially correct (and therefore wholly incorrect). The author calls on us to prioritize our own desires and needs, not to balance them against the needs of others.
    B:  No. This choice is too vague. Self-esteem is maximized when we act in accordance with the specific code of value set out in the passage, as the author suggests in the final paragraph (paragraph 7).
    C:  **Yes. Self-sacrifice destroys self-esteem (paragraph 7); maintaining independence of mind would have the opposite effect (paragraph 4).**
    D:  No. The author criticizes those who use their intentions as justification for their actions (paragraph 5).

12.   D     This is a Structure question.

       A:    No. The author uses similar ironic wording throughout the passage (see for example paragraph 7). By referring to morality that negates morality, the author is suggesting how wrong and destructive she believes a morality of self-sacrifice to be, rather than indicating an internal contradiction within the concepts themselves. She herself puts forward a moral code based on a reasonably clear and consistent definition of value.

       B:    No. The author advocates such standards (paragraph 4).

       C:    No. The author rejects a certain moral code, not the ideas of value and morality themselves.

       **D:    Yes. By claiming that a morality that requires self-sacrifice is a negation of morality, etc., the author underscores the absolute and fundamental nature of her critique. She also highlights the contrast between this supposedly debased code of false values and her own "highest moral purpose" based in selfishness.**

# Passage III

This is a Later passage.

**Bottom Line:** Transcendence in art requires abandoning what is familiar, secure, and predictable.

13.   C     This is a Retrieval question.

       A:    No. The author claims that society's unfriendliness helps make transcendental experiences possible (paragraph 2), not that it develops from transcendental movement.

       B:    No. This contradicts the passage, which claims that society's unfriendliness is a positive factor that contributes to transcendental experiences (paragraph 2).

       **C:    Yes. This is the main idea of the second paragraph.**

       D:    No. In the second paragraph, the author clearly believes alienation from society to be a positive influence on artistic inspiration.

14.   A     This is an Inference question.

       **A:    Yes. Paragraph 4 describes how the author's original conception is only a starting point. The finished product can be neither predicted nor anticipated. In paragraph 5, the author says that each painting is an "unexpected and unprecedented resolution."**

       B:    No. The passage states that archaic societies were more practical (paragraph 6), but never claims that artistic inspiration is impractical.

       C:    No. While the end product may be unpredictable, it does represent "resolution of an eternally familiar need" (paragraph 5). Thus it reflects the needs and desires of all people, including the artist.

       D:    No. This is a misreading of paragraph 4. The author is stating that the finished work ends up in a different "world" or place than that in which it began, not that it leaves "this world" or this reality as a whole. (Be careful not to take words out of context.)

15.  C   This is an Inference question.

A:   No. According to the author, the "miraculous" nature of art is its ability to provide an unexpected revelation to all who experience it (paragraph 5). Gods and monsters are discussed later in paragraphs 6 and 7, in a different context.

B:   No. The representation of reality in other forms is discussed later in the passage (paragraph 6). The "miraculous" nature of art relates to a different issue—the unpredictability of the final product.

**C:   Yes. The author describes art as "miraculous" because at the moment of completion, it becomes an entity independent of the intentions and original conceptions of the artist (paragraph 5).**

D:   No. The picture conveys "eternally familiar" needs and desires, not the specific desires the artist may have intended to express (paragraph 5).

16.  B   This is a Structure question.

A:   No. According to the author, art does not express the artist's individual perspective (paragraph 5).

**B:   Yes. The author uses the analogy to describe the independence of the finished work from the intentions of the artist (paragraph 3). The components of the painting move and interact by their own volition, as do actors on a stage.**

C:   No. Contemplation of the world is never discussed in this context.

D:   No. The analogy between stage and frame is neither made nor implied by the author.

17.  B   This is a Retrieval question.

A:   No. The author does not suggest that modern art is less able to express emotion.

**B:   Yes. In paragraph 7, the author describes the loss of belief in gods and monsters as a source of frustration and melancholy.**

C:   No. The value of art's role in society is never discussed.

D:   No. This choice takes the reference to "finite associations" in paragraph 6 out of context. It is not these finite relationships themselves that lead to melancholy, but the unavailability of gods and monsters to express and portray transcendence.

18.  B   This is a Weaken/EXCEPT question.

I:   False. The correct choice(s) will NOT undermine the author's contrast between archaic and modern art and society. This statement *would* attack the author's claim that finite associations are increasingly made in modern society (paragraph 6).

II:   False. The author claims in paragraph 6 that the archaic artist lived in a more practical society than ours. Thus this statement would weaken the author's claims.

**III:   True. This statement would have no effect on the author's claims. The depiction of monsters and gods is no longer an essential means of artistic expression (paragraph 7). If such depictions are often poorly done, it would have no relevance to the author's points about the difference between archaic and modern art.**

19.     B       This is an Inference/EXCEPT question.

        A:       No. This statement can be inferred from paragraph 5. The correct answer will be the statement that is least supported by the passage.

        **B:       Yes. According to the author, modern art's most profound moments express the frustration arising from our lack of belief in gods and monsters (paragraph 7). Archaic art utilized gods and monsters (paragraph 6), but the author does not use their presence or absence as a standard of profundity.**

        C:       No. This is directly stated by the author in paragraph 7.

        D:       No. This is directly supported by the author's discussion of transcendence and separation from society in paragraph 2.

# Passage IV

This is a Later passage.

**Bottom Line:** Urban ecosystems rely on external resources and factors; perhaps need new way of understanding them.

20.     D       This is an Inference question.

        A:       No. In traditional ecological terms, urban ecosystems are less well balanced than other ecosystems (paragraph 2). However, the third paragraph tells us that they can survive by drawing on external sources of energy. Nontraditional methods may be needed to understand how dependent these systems are on other ecosystems (paragraph 3), but the traditional methodologies described in the passage do not indicate that urban systems cannot sustain themselves in this way.

        B:       No. The author presents the "ecological footprint" as a nontraditional approach (paragraph 3).

        C:       No. The passage describes this calculation as one "among the traditional ways to look at an ecosystem" (paragraph 2), indicating that not *all* traditional approaches use this type of calculation.

        **D:       Yes. In "traditional ecological terms," urban ecosystems are less well balanced than most other ecosystems (paragraph 2).**

21.     B       This is an Inference question.

        A:       No. This is a dictionary definition of "metabolism" that does not capture the meaning of the term as it is used in this part of the passage.

        **B:       Yes. This does capture the meaning of the term as it is used in the context of the author's discussion of the "metaphorical hunger" of cities, which necessitates the consumption of resources from and disposal of wastes in other ecosystems (paragraph 4).**

        C:       No. "Industrial metabolism" refers to the dependence of cities on other ecosystems for resources and waste disposal (paragraph 4), not to the social or cultural effects of urban institutions. This theme, discussed elsewhere in the passage, is not connected by the author to the issue of industrial metabolism.

        D:       No. The existence of an industrial metabolism indicates how urban and natural ecosystems are different, not how they are similar or analogous.

22.　B　This is a Strengthen question.

A:　No. The fact that urban areas are more heterotrophic than natural systems falls within the scope of traditional approaches, as they are described by the author (paragraph 3).

**B:　Yes. The author claims that "our ability to create strategies in response to anticipated… selection pressures" (for example, to prevent flooding in the future) may indicate the need to draw on the social sciences in order to fully understand urban ecosystems (paragraph 7). The same paragraph also indicates that current ecological models do not now borrow from these other disciplines.**

C:　No. A failure of a current policy to solve a specific ecological problem does not in itself show that current ecological theories are inadequate.

D:　No. Traditional theorists do not deny the existence of heterotrophic natural systems (paragraph 3). There is no reason given in the passage or the question to believe that the discovery of even more such systems would contravene the theoretical underpinnings of traditional models.

23.　C　This is a Structure question.

A:　No. The passage does not describe the oyster reef as a heterotrophic system.

B:　No. Natural systems are *likely* to be powered by photosynthesis or chemosynthesis (paragraph 3). Using only information provided in the passage, we can infer from this wording that other self-powering methods exist, and we are never told how an oyster reef sustains itself.

**C:　Yes. Odum states that a typical city transforms 70 times more energy into heat than does an oyster reef. He uses this "close nonhuman equivalent" (paragraph 3) in order to illustrate that ecosystems with concentrated human populations are more energy intensive and less well balanced than comparable nonhuman communities.**

D:　No. This choice takes the quantitative comparison between the energy signature of a reef and of human cities out of context. The question of whether or not the fundamental differences between urban and natural systems are quantitative or qualitative is raised but not fully answered by the author later in the passage (paragraph 6).

24.　C　This is a New Information question.

A:　No. The author raises but does not answer the question of whether or not urban societies are less likely to follow natural cycles than are rural communities (paragraph 5). One new example showing both urban and rural communities following the same cycle (the question does not indicate whether or not it corresponds to natural cycles) is not enough to "prove" that urban communities are no different in this respect.

B:　No. This example has no direct relevance to Rees's discussion of consumption or production rates (paragraph 4).

**C:　Yes. The author raises the question of whether or not "social rhythms" in urban and rural communities are equally likely to correspond to natural cycles (paragraph 5). This example demonstrating a similarity in this respect would provide useful data, but not conclusive proof. Note the moderate wording of this choice compared to answer choice A.**

D:　No. We do not know, based on information provided, whether or not this example indicates a qualitative difference between human-dominated and natural ecosystems (see paragraph 6).

25. **D**   This is a Retrieval question.
    A: No. Heterotrophic systems draw on external sources of energy (paragraph 3) including, in the human case, nonrenewable resources (paragraph 4). This does not necessarily mean, however, that they *destroy* other ecologies, particularly in the case of natural heterotrophic systems. This choice is too extreme.
    B: No. Natural heterotrophic ecological systems exist and do not, by definition, balance inputs with outputs (paragraph 3).
    C: No. This is usually, but not always true of natural ecosystems (paragraph 3). Furthermore, cities depend primarily but not entirely on external resources. This choice is too extreme.
    **D: Yes. The passage supports this in paragraphs 2 and 3. Notice the moderate wording of this choice compared to choices A and C.**


# Passage V

This is a Now passage.

**Bottom Line:** Punning is brave and worthy of respect.

26. **A**   This is an Inference question.
    **A: Yes. In paragraph 8, the passage states that Poe "neatly summed up the situation" in that quote. The situation referred to is in the previous paragraph, in which a groan in reaction to a good pun may indicate "a hidden envy."**
    B: No. Neither Poe nor the author depicts puns as a sophisticated form of humor.
    C: No. Poe's statement relates only to puns, not to other forms of humor.
    D: No. This choice is too extreme. Poe does not imply that punning is funnier than other forms of humor.

27. **C**   This is an Inference question.
    A: No. Johnson is condemning punning itself, not singling out particularly playful puns for criticism.
    B: No. This choice is too extreme. While punning may, according to Johnson, involve the misuse of the tools with which intelligence is expressed (i.e., words), we cannot infer from this that he believes that punners are themselves unintelligent.
    **C: Yes. Johnson describes punning as "trifling" with words, and compares it to grand larceny (invading the national till, in paragraph 4). Thus he sees it as both frivolous and illicit.**
    D: No. This choice contradicts Johnson's meaning. He views punning as undermining, not as embodying, intelligent expression.

28.  B       This is a Weaken question.
     A:      No. People's reaction to sexual humor has no relevance to the punster's courage (or lack thereof).
     B:      **Yes. This fact would indicate that punning is not particularly risky, and so undermine the author's claim in paragraph 6 that punning requires bravery.**
     C:      No. This would strengthen, not weaken, the author's argument that punsters risk failure and public humiliation (paragraph 6).
     D:      No. This choice is too weak to challenge the passage. The author does not argue that all puns fail to be entertaining (he or she writes "Punning can be highly entertaining" in paragraph 6). Thus the success of some puns has no effect on the passage's claims.

29.  C       This is a New Information-Strengthen question.
     A:      No. The correct answer will indicate that puns sit on top of a hierarchy of humor. This choice is part of the author's definition of a pun (paragraph 1), but does not compare puns to other forms of wit.
     B:      No. This statement suggests that puns may be skillful, but not that they are more skillful than other forms of humor.
     C:      **Yes. This quote (paragraph 5) indicates that punning arises from the greatest form of genius, and so would lend the most support to the claim that punning is a superior form of humor.**
     D:      No. This statement describes what punsters do (paragraph 6), but not their great skill at doing it compared to other humorists.

30.  D       This is a Retrieval question.
     A:      No. Slander is telling a destructive lie about another person. The author has a positive, not a negative attitude towards punning.
     B:      No. The author thinks puns can be skillful and entertaining, not destructive.
     C:      No. The author says that good punning *can be* entertaining, but not that *all* puns entertain (paragraph 6).
     D:      **Yes. The inveterate punster is brave, and punning is "always a risky business" (paragraph 6). Thus punning *most fundamentally* involves courage.**

## Passage VI
This is a Later passage.

**Bottom Line:** Good fiction combines real experience and mystery.

31.  B       This is an Inference question.
     A:      No. This choice is inconsistent with the passage. The author believes that good fiction deals with the senses and concrete details, not philosophical abstractions (paragraph 1).
     B:      **Yes. The author writes that human knowledge, and so fiction, begins with the senses, and that the way to appeal to the senses is through the use of concrete detail (paragraph 1).**
     C:      No. Successful fiction portrays the details and mysteries of life. The author never discusses literature that explains the process of understanding.
     D:      No. The author argues that fiction should go beyond simply presenting a "slice of life" (paragraph 5).

32.  B      This is an Inference/Roman numeral question.
     I:     **True. In paragraph 3, the passage indicates that many readers believe that defining or assigning meaning to a symbol equates with understanding the story.**
     II:    **True. Many readers are put off by symbols because they see them as something that only an elite group, of which they are not a member, can comprehend (paragraph 3).**
     III:   False. The passage never refers to symbols with sociological meaning. Sociology is mentioned in the first paragraph as a concern of beginning writers, but is never connected to the use or appreciation of symbols.

33.  A      This is an Inference question.
     A:     **Yes. The author argues that a successful author must address the details and mystery of life as well (paragraph 2).**
     B:     No. The author directly states that readers who do not have educated minds may understand good fiction (paragraph 5).
     C:     No. In paragraph 5, the author criticizes those who believe that identifying the theme is the key to understanding. The author believes that it is the details that make for good fiction (paragraph 1).
     D:     No. This choice is too extreme. Psychological insight and sociological themes do not alone create good fiction (beginning of paragraph 2), but the passage never claims that psychology and sociology should be excluded altogether from literature.

34.  A      This is an Inference question.
     A:     **Yes. "Mystery" is contrasted with reality and the "canny" or knowable aspects of life. Thus mystery in this context indicates the enigmatic or hidden elements of existence.**
     B:     No. "Mystery" in the context of the passage refers to a quality of life that is communicated by good literature, not to difficulties in understanding literature itself.
     C:     No. Be careful not to take words out of context of the passage. Nowhere does the author refer to the genre of mystery or suspense novels, or to the use of suspense as a technique.
     D:     No. The author uses the word "mystery" to describe qualities of good writing, not problems encountered by writers or readers.

35.  C      This is a Weaken question.
     A:     No. The author states that people are more comfortable expressing abstract ideas than offering concrete descriptions (paragraph 1). The passage never makes any comparison between people's comfort level expressing ideas in general versus expressing feelings. Thus the answer choice is not relevant to the passage and does not weaken the author's claim.
     B:     No. The author makes the claim about the world of the fiction writer in order to argue that good fiction concerns itself with the details or "dust" of life. The unpopularity of theoretical texts has no direct relevance to that issue.
     C:     **Yes. In the first paragraph, the author writes, "[The fiction writer] appeals through the senses, and you cannot appeal to the senses with abstractions." Thus good writers concern themselves with "matter" or concrete details. If writers were able to engage the senses through abstraction, it would weaken the author's contention.**
     D:     No. The comparative significance of emotional writing for writer and reader has no direct relevance to the author's contention about the use of concrete detail.

36.  A      This is a Retrieval question.

     **A:**    **Yes. The final sentences of the passage suggest that if everyday life were all we needed, literature would not exist. Therefore, literature must include or provide something beyond a depiction of everyday life.**

     B:      No. While this makes common sense, it is never an issue in the passage.

     C:      No. The foundation of human knowledge is in the senses, and so good literature appeals through those senses (paragraph 1). However, literature itself is not described as the foundation of human knowledge.

     D:      No. Engagement of the senses is a quality of, not a motivation for, the writing of good literature. Also, literature as an additional way to engage the senses is never discussed.


37.  D      This is an Inference question.

     A:      No. The author does say that fiction which is only based on emotion and perception is dull (beginning of paragraph 2). However, this is not the same distinction as that between ideas and people, and the author does not use his or her own enjoyment as a standard.

     B:      No. All writers should avoid abstraction, not just beginning writers (middle of paragraph 2). Level of skill is not the issue.

     C:      No. The author does not draw a distinction between ideas and mystery, nor does the author imply that people have difficulty in understanding mystery.

     **D:**    **Yes. This is directly supported by the middle of paragraph 1, and by the discussion of "dullness" in the beginning of paragraph 2.**


# Passage VII

This is a Now passage.

**Bottom Line:** The Great Depression caused political transformation which led to regulated capitalism.

38.  B      This is a Primary Purpose question.

     A:      No. The Great Depression is one of a series of events described in the passage. Also, the passage does not follow chronological order (see the first sentences of paragraphs 1 and 2).

     **B:**    **Yes. The first paragraph sets out the main theme of shifts in political allegiance. Each following paragraph discusses how various groups came to reject unregulated capitalism and the effects those defections had on political power and policy.**

     C:      No. This choice is too narrow; this is just one of the points made by the author (middle of paragraph 2).

     D:      No. How unionization progressed is discussed in the third paragraph only; the passage as a whole is not a history of unionization.

39.  A     This is an Inference question.
     **A:**    **Yes. 1929 was a "watershed year," in which the crash started a profound political shift from Republican to Democratic power (beginning of paragraph 1).**
     B:    No. Marxist ideas are never mentioned.
     C:    No. Both the political shift and the labor movement were effects of the crash and subsequent economic depression. The depression changed the thinking of workers, which then resulted in both increased unionization and political realignment.
     D:    No. The 1921 depression "had little effect on national politics" (paragraph 2).

40.  C     This is an Inference question.
     A:    No. The correct answer must be based on the passage, not common sense or outside knowledge. Farming equipment is never mentioned.
     B:    No. The cost of seed and grain is never discussed.
     **C:**    **Yes. In 1921, prices for farm products fell but the farmers' "costs, chiefly mortgage payments to banks, remained high" (beginning of paragraph 1).**
     D:    No. Acquisition of manufactured goods is never discussed.

41.  D     This is a Retrieval question.
     A:    No. Wages were increasing slightly between 1921 and 1929, but no related increase in unionization is described in the passage. No figures on wage levels during the post-1929 unionization drive are given.
     B:    No. Young intellectuals are described as calling for "governmental regulation and oversight" (paragraph 3). No direct connection is drawn by the author between their activities and unionization.
     C:    No. Rural poverty (paragraph 2) is not given by the author as a causal factor.
     **D:**    **Yes. The sharp increase in unemployment following the crash encouraged the rejection of unregulated capitalism and facilitated the organization of labor into unions (beginning of paragraph 3).**

42.  A     This is an Analogy question.
     **A:**    **Yes. The passage describes how economic changes (the crash of 1929 and the ensuing depression) contributed to a change in attitudes and beliefs about the legitimacy of organized labor and of the old political order (paragraph 3). This led to the increase in political weight and power of farmers and laborers (end of paragraph 3) and to the passage of new kinds of legislation (beginning of paragraph 4). Similarly, in this answer choice, an economic change leads to a change in attitudes, which contributes to political and legislative changes.**
     B:    No. In the passage, economic change causes a change in attitudes or beliefs. In this choice, beliefs and attitudes come first. Furthermore, although the passage states that not all of the New Deal legislation survived (paragraph 4), most of it did; to characterize the Supreme Court's actions as a "backlash" would be too extreme.
     C:    No. The passage describes changes in beliefs and attitudes as playing a fundamental role (beginning and middle of paragraph 3). No such factor exists in this answer choice.
     D:    No. As in choice C, this answer lacks any discussion of changes in attitudes. Furthermore, there is no international factor at play in the passage.

## Passage VIII

This is a Later passage.

**Bottom Line:** No such thing as generalized transferable skills.

43.  A    This is a Main Point question.
  A:  **Yes. The point of the chess experiments, and of the passage in general, is that "all-purpose" skills (paragraph 2) don't exist, regardless of the field.**
  B:  No. While this restates the beginning of the first paragraph, it is too narrow to be the passage's main point.
  C:  No. The passage is about types of skills, not about intelligence.
  D:  No. The passage focuses on skills, not intelligence. No definition of intelligence is ever given, for example.

44.  A    This is a Structure question.
  A:  **Yes. Simon's research on cognitive skills, mentioned in the second paragraph, reinforces the author's claim that general "skill" does not exist. (The reference to Simon's Nobel Prize posits Simon as an authority.)**
  B:  No. Simon's opinion is not contrary to the author's.
  C:  No. While some relationship between AI and human knowledge is assumed, the author never discusses human intelligence, nor does the passage suggest that knowledge and intelligence are the same thing. In fact, by stating that experts perform better "not because they have more powerful and better oiled intellectual machinery but because they have more relevant and quickly available information" (paragraph 3), the author suggests that intelligence and knowledge are not in fact the same.
  D:  No. Simon studies cognitive skills, and he clearly addresses the issue of general vs. specific skills (paragraph 2).

45.  C    This is a Structure question.
  A:  No. This is too literal a reading of the anecdote.
  B:  No. There is no mention of diagnostic skills. Again, beware of reading analogies too literally.
  C:  **Yes. "Dormative power" is merely the power to send someone to sleep; thus, the story, by analogy, demonstrates that "skill" and "expert performance," like "sleep-inducing properties" and "dormative power," are essentially the same thing.**
  D:  No. This is a misreading of the analogy. It would imply that the skills are only fully acquired after (at the end of) the performance. This is inconsistent with the author's claim that skills and expert performances are essentially the same thing.

46.  B    This is an Inference/EXCEPT question.
      Note: The credited response will NOT be supported by the author's discussion of de Groot.
  A:  No. Memory is at least one factor in this skill, as is implied in paragraph 4.
  B:  **Yes. The passage suggests that master chess players possess more diverse, task-specific knowledge about chess (paragraph 3), but not that they have a greater store of general knowledge.**
  C:  No. We can infer that checkers requires a different set of specific schemata than does chess, which chess masters would not necessarily have mastered.
  D:  No. This is the main thesis of the passage. Without previously recognizable patterns, master chess players could not remember better than novices.

47.    C        This is a New Information question.
       A:       No. The passage does not address learning speed.
       B:       No. There is nothing in the passage about faster thinking, only about the number and variety of mental schemata available to more experienced players.
       C:       **Yes. See paragraph 6. If de Groot's claims are true, then the superior performance of the chess masters in this situation indicates that they were able to transfer some of their previous skills to this less-than-truly-random situation.**
       D:       No. Presumably, for the purposes of these experiments, novices had as much opportunity to practice as did masters.

48.    C        This is an Inference question.
       A:       No. The focus of the passage is on the skills possessed by a single individual, not on the accumulated skills of an entire population.
       B:       No. Nothing in the passage suggests that skills are or should be attained by reading familiar material first: the contrast between familiar and unfamiliar reading material is Out of Scope.
       C:       **Yes. The author argues that "reading," like other cognitive skills, is not a single ability that applies to all tasks or contexts, but that it is specific to individual tasks (see the first paragraph).**
       D:       No. The example of a college student who can read and comprehend one kind of text but not another (paragraph 1) contradicts this claim.

# Passage IX

This is a Now passage.

**Bottom Line:** No such thing as health food, but some use concept to exploit people.

49.    D        This is an Inference question.
       A:       No. The passage does not tell us who conceived of the term "health food." The author does assert that the term is artificial and false; he or she would not agree that such products are "useful" (paragraph 1).
       B:       No. The term, according to the author, falsely suggests that "health foods" are healthier than non-"health foods" (paragraph 1).
       C:       No. The passage asserts that the term cannot be defined (paragraphs 1 and 3). The statement in this answer choice (meeting all the dietary needs of most people) is suggested as one of the false or misleading definitions that people use (paragraph 1).
       D:       **Yes. The term is labeled "false and misleading" in the middle of paragraph 1.**

50.    C        This is a Retrieval question.
       A:       No. The author completely rejects the term "health food" as misleading and impossible to define.
       B:       No. Human milk is not described as being more deficient in vitamins than any other food. In fact, it is described as the most nutritionally complete food (end of paragraph 1).
       C:       **Yes. The passage claims that human milk (for babies) is the only food that by itself supplies all necessary nutrients (paragraph 1).**
       D:       No. Sun-drying of milk is never discussed. The correct answer must be based on information given in the passage, not on common sense or outside knowledge.

51.  B      This is a Structure question.

   A:      No. The author never accepts that the health food movement may in fact have some connection to good nutrition.

   **B:      Yes. The author makes this statement in the context of explaining why sick people are especially vulnerable to the false claims made by purveyors of "health food" (paragraph 6).**

   C:      No. While the author states that food is related to health, he does not go so far as to claim that nutrition can be used to cure disease.

   D:      No. The author never criticizes the medical establishment; if anything he presents it in a positive light, in opposition to the health food movement (paragraphs 3 and 5).

52.  B      This is a Weaken question.

   A:      No. A belief that something is true, even a widespread belief, does not constitute valid evidence that it is in fact true.

   **B:      Yes. The author claims that few of the health food movement's claims have been tested, and that none can be substantiated (paragraph 4). If valid tests have been done showing that a particular type of food does in fact promote health, it would undermine this part of the author's argument. It would also suggest that there may in fact be, in the future, some way of defining "health foods."**

   C:      No. The author accepts that food and nutrition is generally related to health (paragraph 6).

   D:      No. This is not inconsistent with the author's argument. The passage never claims that the extract was harmful in and of itself, only that it did not have beneficial effects (paragraph 5), and that it caused people to forgo potentially beneficial treatments.

53.  B      This is a New Information question.

   A:      No. The question stem does not indicate that olives, honey, and dates are among the nutritious ancient foods.

   **B:      Yes. The author argues that traditional foods are not necessarily more nutritious (paragraph 2), but not that all traditional foods are non-nutritious. Therefore, the new information in the question stem would have no impact on the author's argument.**

   C:      No. This choice is partially correct, and therefore wrong. While the first half is supported by the passage, the second half is not. The author discusses traditional foods as one way of arguing that "health food" cannot be defined (paragraphs 1 and 3).

   D:      No. The fact that nutritious foods were eaten in the past has no direct relevance to nutrition as a science. Furthermore, the author's statement that nutrition is a legitimate science (paragraph 6) is not part of his argument against the possibility of defining "health food."

# MCAT
# Critical Analysis and Reasoning Skills

## Practice Test 2

## Passage I (Questions 1-6)

Sociologists have long debated over what can be said to be the distinguishing features of a minority. In 1945, Louis Wirth wrote a definitive text in which he defines a minority as a group of people who, because of their physical or cultural characteristics, are singled out from the others in the society in which they live for differential and unequal treatment, and who therefore regard themselves as objects of collective discrimination. According to Wirth, the existence of a minority in a society implies the existence of a corresponding dominant group with higher social status and greater privileges. Minority carries with it the exclusion from full participation in the life of the society.

This definition contains several key ideas. First, a minority must possess distinctive physical or cultural characteristics that can be used to distinguish its members from the majority. Such characteristics are used both as a reminder to the majority that the minority is different and as a means for determining whether a given person is a member of a minority. This is more evident in the case of physical characteristics than it is for cultural ones. Culturally, a minority member can "pass" as a member of the majority by a change in name, the loss of an accent, or the adoption of the majority's culture.

Second, whatever its numerical size, the minority is dominated by the majority. This dominance is reflected especially in a society's stratification structure. In almost any society there are desired goods, services, and privileges. Because these "good things" are usually in limited supply, there is competition for them. The majority dominates largely because it has accumulated enough power to obtain an unequal share of the desired goods, services, and privileges. The dominant group can deny minority group members access to desirable resources by limiting opportunities to compete on an equal basis. Minorities, for example, can be denied good jobs by limiting them to inferior schooling or by not hiring even those who are qualified.

Most disturbingly, members of a minority are denied equal treatment. The distinctive cultural or physical traits of a minority are usually judged by the majority to be inferior to their own. This presumed inferiority is then used as justification for the unequal treatment given the minority. In other words, the alleged inferiority of a minority becomes part of the majority's ideology, or set of ideas, that is used to justify and defend the interests and actions of a group. If, for example, its ideology contains the belief that members of the minority are a shiftless and lazy lot, then it is justified in discriminating against them in the workplace.

The definition of minority has been elaborated by sociologists since Wirth's time. Charles Wagley and Marvin Harris (1964) have added characteristics to Wirth's definition. For example, minorities have a sense of collective identity. In addition to the special traits such as language and national origin which members of a minority share, minority members also often feel a sense of isolation, suffering, and common identity. To the extent such feelings develop, self-consciousness creates social bonds which may act to keep the group together, enhance already-existing or emerging cohesion, and perhaps help the group as it seeks to change its situation. All minorities experience such in-group feelings to some extent, even in the face of great conflicts within the group. In part, a minority identity is a group identity—and this can bring something positive to an otherwise difficult and unfair socioeconomic position.

Adapted from J. M. Shepard, *Sociology (Second Ed.),* © 1984 Jon M. Shepard.

1. The passage suggests which of the following about the majority in a society?

    I.  If there is an oppressed minority in a society, then the majority enjoys advantages that the minority does not.
   II.  Social equality will require sacrifices on the part of the majority.
  III.  Members of both minorities and the majority have recently changed the way they view their place in society.

    A.  I only
    B.  II only
    C.  I and III only
    D.  I, II, and III

2. Which of the following best expresses the main idea of the passage?

    A.  Changing definitions of "minority" have affected the ways in which minorities are treated by the majority.
    B.  There are many ways in which a minority occupies an inferior social role in its particular society.
    C.  The unhappiness experienced by members of a minority actually gives the minority strength as a group.
    D.  The discriminatory behavior of a majority toward a minority is a moral wrong.

3. The term "ideology," as it is used in the passage (paragraph 4) is best defined as which of the following?

    A.  Beliefs which carry the weight of religious conviction
    B.  A set of laws which institutionalize the attitudes of the majority
    C.  A formula according to which people determine what is morally superior
    D.  The collective beliefs by which a group defines and regulates its behavior

4. Based on the passage, which of the following CANNOT be inferred to be part of Louis Wirth's characterization of minorities?

    A.  They understand themselves to be the recipients of unequal treatment.
    B.  They see themselves as being a cohesive group that stands apart from the majority.
    C.  Their ability to act within their society is less than that of the majority.
    D.  They may actually outnumber the majority.

5. The author's attitude toward the treatment usually received by members of minority groups can best be characterized as exhibiting:

    A.  measured disapproval.
    B.  cautious optimism.
    C.  scholarly detachment.
    D.  cynical resignation.

6. Which of the following can most properly be inferred about minority members' attempts to pass as members of the majority?

    A.  They are more likely to be successful if the minority characteristics are cultural rather than physical.
    B.  They will inevitably be met with complete indifference on the part of the majority.
    C.  They can bring something positive to the difficult situations experienced by most members of minorities.
    D.  They are actually counterproductive in the sense that they produce an effect opposite to the one desired.

## Passage II (Questions 7-12)

Oddity and fluidity of perspective are widespread features of the culture of modernism and postmodernism. They have, in fact, often been seen as necessary features of authentic or creative modes of experience and expression. The Dadaist Marcel Duchamp, for instance, expressed contempt for standard orientations and declared his devotion to his new category of the "*infra-mince*," which included such unfairly neglected phenomena as the difference in space taken up by shirts before and after they have been laundered. The surrealist Louis Aragon defined poetic imagery as an instrument of radical reversals and caustic irony that would annihilate the world of convention.

Many instances of schizophrenic eccentricity and cognitive slippage closely resemble these modernist examples, with their reversals and their concentration on what is usually ignored by the person engaged in normal activity. One patient I knew said she found it curious that we always walk on the treads rather than the risers of a staircase. Another contemplated how one could tell the back from the front of a blouse—surely a candidate for inclusion in Duchamp's category of the *infra-mince*.

Sullivan, generally an advocate of the primitivity hypothesis, assumed that these peculiar cognitive slants were consequences of regression, of "the inclusion in attention of primitive, diffuse processes" deriving from a "failure to restrict the contents of consciousness to the higher referential processes that can be consensually validated"; but, in reality, the anomalies at issue are more suggestive of a condition of alienation, a homelessness of mind quite foreign to anything characteristic of childhood.

"I ceaselessly ruminate upon what interests me; by dint of regarding it in *different positions of mind* I end up by seeing something new in it, and I make it change its aspect." The words are those of the novelist Stendhal; more generally, they describe Schiller's "sentimental" or "reflective" poet, the kind—increasingly common in modern times—who is "self-divided because self-conscious, and so composes in an awareness of multiple alternatives, and characteristically represents not the object in itself, but the object in the subject." Such techniques are bound up with the modern realization of the importance of point of view or mode of awareness, a realization that might be traced back to Kant's description, at the end of the eighteenth century, of the constituting role of consciousness, and also to his emphasis on the unsurpassable limits of the actual.

What does it *say* about modernism that it should display such remarkable affinities with this most severe of mental illnesses, which some have called the cancer of the mind? What does this parallelism suggest about how we should judge the relevant aspects of the modern sensibility? Can we view the alienation and self-consciousness of the modern mind as the inevitable signs of increasing degrees of complexity, subtlety, or insight, or must we see them as something far less benign—signs of deep pathology, perhaps, of a disease or spiritual decadence corroding the style and sensibility of age?

We might ask as well how these parallels should affect our evaluation of schizophrenia. I have been disputing the condescending and derogatory implications of traditional views of this illness, with their tendency to equate the unintelligible with the unintelligent—but how far in this opposite direction should we go? Do the affinities with modern thought and expression suggest that there is something especially sophisticated, insightful, or self-aware about this condition—or that, perhaps in some tragic sense, such persons are more in touch with the true human condition than is the normal or average individual?

Adapted from L. Sass, *Madness and Modernism: Insanity in the Light of Modern Art, Literature, and Thought,* © 1992 Basic Books.

7. Which of the following best summarizes the main idea of the passage?

   A. Sullivan is incorrect in his hypothesis that the oddity and fluidity of perspective characteristic of schizophrenic thought are attributable to a primitive or regressed state of consciousness.
   B. One can often see essential characteristics of a society or a culture reflected in the unique thought patterns of those afflicted with particular mental illnesses.
   C. The peculiarities of perspective that characterize both schizophrenic and modernist thought may indicate some relationship between the disease and the nature of the human condition.
   D. Schizophrenia is attributable not to biological but to environmental causes.

8. According to the first paragraph, Marcel Duchamp's category of the *"infra-mince"* (paragraph 1) includes:

   A. radical reversals and childlike or regressive imagery.
   B. ironic references and allusions illustrating the standard beliefs that characterize modern society.
   C. subcategories of physical phenomena.
   D. conditions or possibilities not normally considered or imagined in the course of daily life.

9. The author implies that which of the following is most likely to be true of the modern condition?

   A. Schizophrenia is becoming more and more prevalent, perhaps in part because of increasing levels of disorder and insecurity endured by most people today.
   B. The human experience today is characterized at least in part by a degree of complexity and alienation.
   C. The alienation and self-consciousness we see in modernist artistic expression are clear indications of greater levels of insight and sensibility.
   D. Environmental stresses such as homelessness or physical illness can cause or contribute to mental disorders such as schizophrenia.

10. As it is used in the passage, the phrase "the object in the subject" (paragraph 4) most likely means:

    A. the purpose underlying Schiller's depiction of the poet as reflective and sentimental.
    B. subcategories within the larger categories newly created by modernist thinkers.
    C. things as perceived through the individual consciousness, not as they inherently or essentially are.
    D. the tendency of modernist literature to focus on the topics of self-knowledge and self-awareness.

11. Which of the following claims, if shown to be true, would most *weaken* the author's objection to Sullivan's hypothesis?

    A. Schizophrenics display a genuine infantilism with arrest at a definite stage in the development of the emotional life and character formation.
    B. Schizophrenia is often found in "primitive" cultures and non- or pre-industrialized societies.
    C. The schizoid personality experiences a kind of vertigo, a continual collapsing of one frame of reference into the next.
    D. Some kind of biological vulnerability might well be necessary for developing some forms of schizophrenia.

12. As the terms are used by the author in paragraph 6, "unintelligible" is to "unintelligent" as:

    A. foreign is to unconventional.
    B. unnatural is to unknown.
    C. singular is to multiperspectival.
    D. illegible is to illogical.

## Passage III (Questions 13-19)

Because of its unique implications, the privileged communication between a patient and her psychotherapist warrants investigation. Unlike the ancient common law principle protecting intercourse between lawyer and client, the psychotherapist-client privilege is comparatively new, created by state laws on the theory that a failure to protect the confidentiality of psychotherapeutic interactions might discourage the psychologically troubled from seeking treatment.

Yet in recent years there has been considerable erosion of the psychotherapeutic privilege. Nearly all states require therapists to take certain actions to make reports and/or take preventive measures if, in their opinion, a patient represents a violent physical threat to himself or others.

In 1974, an important judicial decision was reached by the California Supreme Court. The court ruled that if a psychotherapist had reason to believe that a patient intended to commit an act of violence against another individual, that other individual could hold the psychotherapist civilly liable for failure to give warning, if in fact physical harm did occur. In that case a patient confided to his psychotherapist an intent to commit a crime against a female acquaintance. The therapist determined that it would violate his professional ethics if he gave warning to the woman in danger. The crime was in fact committed and the psychologist was sued. The court concluded that "the public policy favoring protection of the confidential character of the psychotherapist-client communication must yield to the extent to which disclosure is essential to avert danger to others. The protective privilege ends where the public peril begins."

Although the California decision first caused dismay among the psychotherapeutic community, a consensus has since emerged that psychotherapists should take meaningful preventive action when convinced that a patient poses an imminent threat to another human being. According to prevailing sentiment among psychotherapists, the preventive action need not always involve notice to the police or the potential victim. It might, for example, mean involuntary hospitalization for the patient.

Since the California case, a dozen or more states have enacted laws detailing the obligation of psychotherapists who have reason to believe that their patients pose a public threat. For example, Colorado law provides that a therapist must take preventive action in the case of "serious threat of imminent violence." A therapist is absolved of all liability if he or she in fact notifies the police or the intended victim.

Psychotherapists themselves believe strongly in the privileges and confidentialities that surround the therapeutic relationship, and they are not entirely comfortable with laws that limit it. Nonetheless, they recognize the need to protect individuals and the public from potentially dangerous patients and have gone so far as to have proposed their own law on the subject. A model statute devised by the American Psychiatric Association requires action in the face of an "explicit threat to kill or seriously injure." It is difficult to know whether new laws in this area will help in any way to prevent violent crime by patients in psychotherapy. It is possible that patients, knowing of the new laws, will hesitate to confide to their psychotherapists their plans to commit dangerous or violent acts.

13. The passage suggests that among psychotherapists there is likely to be:

    A. an ongoing acceptance of policies requiring definitive action where patients present a threat of violent crime.
    B. a "renewed" movement to protect the confidentiality of the therapeutic relationship.
    C. a reevaluation of civil liability.
    D. greater hostility toward the legal system.

14. The author indicates that the California case, and the issues it raised, produced among lawmakers:

    A. dismay and disappointment.
    B. a determination to prevent violent crime committed by psychotherapy patients.
    C. an awareness that patients in psychotherapy pose a potential threat.
    D. a greater awareness that the traditional psychotherapist-patient privilege should not be absolute.

15. Considering the information set forth by the author, a reader might reasonably infer that in the future, where serious issues of safety and welfare are at stake:

    A. more laws placing limits on a psychotherapist's right to remain silent may be enacted.
    B. fewer patients' confessions to therapists will be used in court.
    C. therapists will provide more testimony in civil proceedings.
    D. patients will be forced into hospitals even though they have no mental illness.

16. With reference to the new laws described in the passage, the author suggests that psychotherapists have reacted with:

    I. moderate discomfort.
    II. fundamental opposition.
    III. sympathy in principle.

    A. I only
    B. II only
    C. I and III only
    D. I, II, and III

17. The passage indicates that the new laws to which it refers may have a limited effect on violent crime for the reason that:

    I. patients may be reluctant to reveal their feelings to their therapists.
    II. patients will not know about the laws.
    III. many psychotherapists will refuse to obey the laws.

    A. I only
    B. I and II only
    C. II and III only
    D. I, II, and III

18. Under the Colorado law mentioned in the passage, a therapist who fails to notify the police or intended victim of a threat:

    A. will be held liable for the actions of his patient.
    B. may be held liable if his patient commits the threatened violent action.
    C. will be considered an accessory to the criminal action.
    D. could be considered just as guilty as his patient.

19. The information in the passage implies that the psychotherapist-client privilege:

    A. is currently stronger than before 1974.
    B. was first recognized in the 1960's.
    C. is a relatively new phenomenon.
    D. no longer holds any real meaning.

    _____

## Passage IV (Questions 20-25)

When Nietzsche's Zarathustra descended from his mountains to preach to the world, he met a saintly hermit in the forest. Zarathustra asked how the hermit passed the time. He replied, "I make up songs and sing them; and when I make up songs, I laugh, I weep and I growl; thus do I praise God." When alone, Zarathustra thought: "Can it be possible! This old saint in the forest has not yet heard that God is dead!"

*Zarathustra* was first published in 1883. The number of people for whom God is dead has greatly increased since then. And so, after two terrible world wars, there are some who are still trying to come to terms with Zarathustra's message. They are searching for comfort in a universe deprived of its center. For these people the world has become disjointed and purposeless, that is, absurd. Theater of the Absurd is one of the expressions of this search.

For those for whom the world has lost its central explanation, it is no longer possible to accept art as it was. In all art forms there is a basis of standards and concepts, laws of conduct, and ultimate values. For many, the continuation of those standards as a basis for art is no longer valid. Theatre of the Absurd expresses a tragic sense of loss of these ultimate certainties.

A strange paradox has come to exist, though. In the confrontation of a world which has lost its central anchor, Theater of the Absurd has become somewhat of a genuine religious quest. Its purpose seems to be to sing, to laugh and to weep. This is done, if not in praise of God, then at least in search of the Ineffable, to make us aware of ultimate realities. Theater of the Absurd attempts to shock its audience out of an existence that has become trite, mechanical, complacent, and deprived of a deep sense of dignity. Theater of the Absurd forms part of the unceasing endeavor of the true artist to breach this dead wall of complacency and automatism. It wants to re-establish an awareness of the "human situation" by confronting an audience with ultimate realities.

Theater of the Absurd fulfills a dual purpose and presents its audience with a two-fold absurdity. In one way it castigates, satirically, the absurdity of lives lived unaware of ultimate realities. This is the experience that Ionesco expresses in plays like "The Bald Soprano" or "The Chairs." It represents the pillorying of an inauthentic, petty society. This aspect of the Absurdists' movement may be the most easily accessible to the general public. However, it is not its most essential. In its more positive aspect, Theater of the Absurd faces up to a deeper layer of absurdity. The human condition itself, in a world of declined religious belief, is absurd.

Theater of the Absurd, therefore, represents a return to the original function of theater. Like ancient Greek tragedy, it is intent on making its audience aware of the precarious and mysterious position of human beings in the universe. Lacking the central religious foundation, Absurdist theater merely presents an individual's intuition of the ultimate realities.

Theater of the Absurd confronts the audience with characters whose motives and actions are largely incomprehensible. It is impossible to identify with them. Inevitably, characters with whom the audience fails to identify are regarded as comic. If the audience identified with the character that loses his pants, they would feel embarrassment and shame. If, however, identification is blocked, then the audience usually laughs. The subject matter for most plays that are considered Absurdist is somber, violent, and bitter. That is why the Theater of the Absurd transcends the categories of comedy and tragedy. It combines laughter with horror.

Adapted from M. Esslin, *The Theatre of the Absurd*, © 1973 The Overlook Press.

20. The material in this passage is focused on the whole on:

    A. the religious beliefs of playwrights who created Theater of the Absurd.
    B. the characteristics of Theater of the Absurd and its place in the modern world.
    C. the structure of a Greek tragedy.
    D. the progressive absurdity of the human condition.

21. Based on information in the passage, one can most readily conclude that Theater of the Absurd was produced by:

    A. the loss of religious faith and the search for a substitute.
    B. Nietzsche's *Zarathustra*.
    C. a disbelief in ultimate realities.
    D. the search for illusion.

22. Which of the following, based on the passage, is *least* likely to be a technique employed by Theater of the Absurd?

    A. Shocking the audience with violent subject matter
    B. Using satire to raise an audience's awareness
    C. Making people laugh at themselves
    D. Breaking out of traditional theatrical categories

23. One can most reasonably infer from the text that the plays of Absurdist writers essentially:

    A. display intense anger about the human condition.
    B. express the contradiction and irony of human life.
    C. exhibit sadness about the tragedy of existence.
    D. criticize those who believe in God.

24. The fact that Theater of the Absurd represents a return to the original function of theater would most directly cast doubt on an assumption that:

    A. the ancient Greeks were concerned about the meaning of life.
    B. the absurdist can be considered modern.
    C. God is dead.
    D. Theater of the Absurd did not attempt to make audiences aware of their place in the cosmos.

25. The passage implies that the continuation of standards:

    A. is for all people, no longer valid.
    B. is an artificial constraint on the artist.
    C. may, for some people, still be valid.
    D. may, for some people, be the only means of accepting art.

## Passage V (Questions 26-31)

The Cortes, the parliament of Spain, stands halfway up the hill leading from the Prado to the Puerta del Sol. Today, the gilded corridors and salons of the Cortes are used only occasionally, when a few honorific dignitaries give formal assent to decrees issued by the Head of State. On 16 June 1936, however, this building was the centre of all Spain.... "Over five years had then passed since King Alfonso XIII had abandoned the Spanish throne. These had been five years of parliamentary activity. Before the King left, there had been eight years, from 1923 till 1931, when, under the amiable military dictator General Primo de Rivera, the Cortes had been as deserted as it is today. Now, in June 1936, parliamentary life in Spain seemed likely to be destroyed...." An anxious group of middle-class liberals were gathered at the front of the semicircular debating chamber. They admired the pleasing, democratic ways of Britain, France, and America. Yet the men of this government had a fanaticism of their own hardly typical of the practical-minded countries which they desired to reproduce in Spain.

Observe, for example, the Prime Minister, Santiago Casares Quiroga. A rich man from northwest Spain, he had spent much of his life calling for home rule for his own poor province. He was a passionate liberal when the rise of organized labor caused liberalism to seem almost as anachronistic as the liberals' foe of feudalism. Yet since there had not been in Spain a successful middle-class revolution on the model of that in France in 1789, one can hardly blame Casares and his friends for their attitude.

The nature of the crisis in Spain was described on 16 June 1936 by Gil Robles, the sleek leader of the Spanish Catholic Party, the CEDA. His party was conservative, and catholic, and it included those who wanted to restore a monarch, as well as those who desired a Christian democratic republic. Some in the CEDA were almost fascists; and some admired the corporate state. Robles was as hated by monarchists and fascists as he was by socialists. Yet he had created the first middle-class Spanish mass party. Now he recalled that the government had, since the elections in February, exceptional powers. Nevertheless, during those four months, 160 churches, he said, had been burned to the ground, there had been 269 mainly political murders, and 1,287 assaults of varying seriousness. "Let us not deceive ourselves!" concluded Robles. "A country can live under a monarchy or a republic, under communism or fascism! But it cannot live in anarchy. Now, alas, Spain is in anarchy. We are today present at the funeral service of democracy!"

The conditions of the country and the regime were as grave as Robles suggested. Neither Casares Quiroga nor Gil Robles, representing groups which had been prominent in the history of the Second Republic, could any longer control events. Both, indeed, were sustained in the Cortes by the votes of deputies whose aims were different from their own. The elections of the preceding February had been contested by two alliances: the Popular Front, and the National Front. Besides the liberals like Casares, the former had consisted of the large socialist party, the small communist party, and other working-class groups. The National Front consisted not only of the CEDA, but also of monarchists, agrarians, representing the large landowners of the south and center, and some other right-wing parties. It was the political front for all the forces of old Spain.

Adapted from H. Thomas, *The Spanish Civil War*, © 2001 Modern Library.

26. The author would most likely describe the present function of the Cortes as:

    A. critical to the Spanish government.
    B. principally ceremonial.
    C. politically anachronistic.
    D. strictly administrative.

27. According to the passage, the period 1931 to 1936 differed from the period 1923 to 1931 in that:

    A. the later period was marked by dictatorship, and the earlier by parliamentary activity.
    B. the later period was marked by parliamentary activity, and the earlier by dictatorship.
    C. the later period was politically stable, while the earlier was not.
    D. the later period was politically unstable, whereas the earlier was not.

28. It can be inferred from the passage that Casares Quiroga's political ideology differs from that of Robles in that:

    A. Casares had previously held political office.
    B. Casares's party contained fascists.
    C. Casares had a majority of public support.
    D. Casares represented the interests of new social and economic forces.

29. It can be inferred that by 1936:

    A. Casares had a firm grasp on the majority of public support.
    B. both Casares and Robles had finally gained complete control of their political factions.
    C. Casares and Robles were the only two political leaders in Spain with notable public support.
    D. both Casares and Robles were disturbed about the direction of Spanish politics.

30. The author's attitude towards the events he describes can best be described as one of:

    A. nostalgic regret.
    B. moderate optimism.
    C. journalistic neutrality.
    D. strong disappointment.

31. Which of the following can be inferred from the passage?

    A. CEDA was still a relatively new political group in 1936.
    B. CEDA had its origins in the politics of other European governments.
    C. Casares supported some degree of decentralization of the power of the Spanish government.
    D. Both Casares and Robles represented groups that had been present in Spanish politics for some time.

_____

## Passage VI (Questions 32-37)

Man has always had problems with his environment because he did not understand it or his responsibilities to it. Owing to this ignorance and lack of concern, his environment has "rebelled" many times, and as a result, man himself has suffered. Belatedly, man has been forced to recognize his responsibility to his environment and the tremendous penalties that his pollution of his world will exact from him if he does not change his ways.

Pollution is not well-defined in scientific terms. Something described as polluted is commonly thought of as being unclean or defiled. For water to be polluted, then, must a substance merely be present that was not present in the original "pure" water? Or must this new substance be present in a concentration that causes the water to be unfit for its intended purpose? Not knowing the original composition of our environment, we are forced to accept the definition of pollution as being that state in which water, air, or soil is unfit for the intended purpose.

Even the phrase *intended purpose* eludes consistent, accepted definition, as exemplified by the struggle to define a unified "purpose" for New York State's Hudson River: the upper reaches of this major river have a much different "intended purpose" than does the river where it flows into the Atlantic Ocean. A look at the development of standards of water quality throws light on this problem.

In 1965 the Federal Clean Water Act became law. This law required the states to establish standards for all interstate and coastal waters. Nine years later, New York State had succeeded in establishing its standards in a document entitled "Classification and Standards Governing the Quality and Purity of Waters of New York State."

There are six classes of fresh surface water. These include three classes of drinking water and one class each for primary contact recreation (swimming), fishing, and secondary contact recreation (boating). All waters must be suitable for fish survival. Each class is designated for a "best usage," and meeting the criteria for best usage permits all uses included within that "best usage" category.

The best usage in the highest class is "enjoyment of water in its natural condition and, where compatible, as a source of water for drinking." This water, class N, is to be clean enough for human consumption with no treatment other than disinfection (required for all public water supplies) and otherwise is to be left in its natural state. The classes that follow are AA, A, B, C, and D, the lowest quality water permitted. AA and A water can be used for drinking with sufficient treatment. B water has a best usage of swimming; class C, of fishing; class D, of boating.

In this way the surface waters in the state have been classified, although not without great struggle at all levels of government among special interest groups and lobbyists. The upper reaches of the Hudson River have a higher best usage than does the river as it flows past New York City.

Along with the definition of best usage there are limits set on the concentration of various pollutants (chemical and bacterial) plus the level of dissolved oxygen. These data dictate what may or may not be discharged into that water. Since the Federal Clean Water Act also states that the standards and classifications of waters must be directed toward improvement of water quality, the classification of a water cannot give legal permission to degrade quality below that in existence at classification. The result of all this work has been a general improvement of fresh water quality in spite of the presence of areas which some would still term "open sewers."

Adapted from D. Ludington, *Man and His Environment,*
© 1980 David Ludington.

32. The passage suggests that which of the following can be claimed about water quality in New York State today?

   A. Water pollution in New York has steadily increased in spite of the Federal Clean Water Act.
   B. Water quality will probably continue to deteriorate in spite of whatever environmental legislation the state legislature manages to pass.
   C. The overall quality of water in New York has improved since 1965.
   D. The water policy described in "The Classification and Standards Governing the Quality and Purity of Waters in New York State" has at least succeeded in eliminating "open sewer" areas.

33. As described in the passage, the best usage classification:

   A. means that water can be used only for the purposes indicated for that particular classification.
   B. indicates that water can be used for the purpose associated with the "best usage" classification and the uses of all categories below it.
   C. is an absolute standard to be met by each of the various lakes, rivers, and other waterways in a state.
   D. is the ideal usage of water for a particular area.

34. It can be inferred from the passage that the "problem" referred to in paragraph 3 is that:

   A. pollution is an environmental issue not easily resolved or eliminated.
   B. the "intended purpose" of a body of water varies according to the area in which it is located.
   C. it is often more difficult to determine the "intended use" of a river when it is located near an ocean.
   D. different groups with political influence in any area will lobby for different intended purposes.

35. The passage suggests which of the following about environmental issues today?

   A. The problem of water pollution is the most serious environmental issue today.
   B. People's problems with their environment will continue because it is unlikely that people will ever recognize the responsibilities they bear toward their environment.
   C. Recent industrial development has dramatically changed the relationship between people and their environment.
   D. The present problems regarding people and their environment stem from an ongoing conflict between people and nature that has always existed.

36. If a regulator classifies a body of water as "B," but the amount of pollution in the water would be in accordance with a classification of "AA," then which of the following is most likely true?

   A. A change in the regulations must have occurred.
   B. The classification is not consistent with the objectives of the Clean Water Act.
   C. Some portions of the body of water are of lower quality than other portions.
   D. Lobbyists have influenced the regulator's decision.

37. The passage suggests that the author would have which of the following attitudes toward further attempts to classify bodies of water for particular usages?

   A. He would wholeheartedly support any measure aimed at further classification.
   B. He would be cautiously optimistic about further attempts to classify bodies of water.
   C. He would be indifferent to further classifications, as the current system is more than adequate.
   D. He would oppose further measures, because definitions for terms such as "intended purpose" and "best usage" are flawed by their inaccuracy.

## Passage VII (Questions 38-42)

Writing a story or a novel is one way of discovering *sequence* in experience, of stumbling upon cause and effect in the happenings of a writer's own life. This has been the case with me. Connections slowly emerge. Experiences too indefinite of outline in themselves to be recognized for themselves connect and are identified as a larger shape. And suddenly a light is thrown back, as when your train makes a curve, showing that there has been a mountain of meaning rising behind you on the way you've come, is rising there still, proven now through retrospect.

What discoveries I've made in the course of writing stories all begin with the particular, never the general. They are mostly hindsight: arrows that I now find I myself have left behind me, which have shown me some right, or wrong, way I have come. What one story may have pointed out to me is of no avail in the writing of another. But "avail" is not what I want; freedom ahead is what each story promises—beginning anew. And all the while, as further hindsight has told me, certain patterns in my work repeat themselves without my realizing. There would be no way to know this, for during the writing of any single story, there is no other existing.

I have been writing a number of stories more or less after the other, before it belatedly dawned on me that some of the characters in one story were, and had been all the time, the same characters who had appeared already in another story. Only I'd written about them originally under different names, at different periods in their lives, in situations not yet interlocking but ready for it. From story to story, connections between the characters' lives, through their motives or actions, sometimes their dreams, already existed: there to be found.

The characters who go to make up my stories and novels are not portraits. Characters I invent along with the story that carries them. Attached to them are what I've borrowed, perhaps unconsciously, bit by bit, of persons I have seen or noticed or remembered in the flesh—a cast of countenance here, a manner of walking there, that jump to the visualizing mind when a story is underway. (Elizabeth Bowen said, "Physical detail cannot be invented." It can only be chosen.) I don't write by invasion into the life of a real person: my own sense of privacy is too strong for that and I also know instinctively that living people to whom you are close—those known to you in ways too deep, too overflowing, ever to be plumbed outside love—do not yield to, could never fit into, the demands of a story. On the other hand, what I do make my stories out of is the whole fund of my feelings, my responses to the real experiences of my own life, to the relationships that formed and changed it, that I have given most of myself to, and so learned my way toward a dramatic counterpart. Characters take on life sometimes by luck, but I suspect it is when you can write most entirely out of yourself, that a character becomes in his own right another human being on the page.

Adapted from E. Welty, *One Writer's Beginnings*, © 1985 Warner Books.

**38.** The author asserts that the meaning in her stories:

A. is greater for her readers than for her.
B. guides her progress.
C. emerges as an afterthought.
D. overshadows her character development.

**39.** Based on information in the passage, which of the following best describes the author's progression from one story to the next?

A. She pursues a general concept throughout her stories.
B. There is no real progression; her stories have nothing in common with each other.
C. She faces a clean slate at the start of each story.
D. The progression of her stories follows the progression of lessons learned in the author's life.

**40.** According to the author, each of the following helps to create a true work of fiction EXCEPT:

A. memory.
B. experience.
C. imagination.
D. autobiography.

**41.** According to the author, which of the following discoveries occur(s) in the course of writing?

I. Repeated patterns in the writer's work
II. Characters appear from previous works
III. An understanding of cause and effect in the events of a writer's life

A. I only
B. I and II only
C. II and III only
D. I, II, and III

**42.** According to the passage, all of the following may contribute to the development of a character EXCEPT:

A. one's personal experiences.
B. luck.
C. connections to other authors' stories.
D. the plot of a story.

## Passage VIII (Questions 43-47)

During the first Congress of the United States, two measures to amend Article I of the Constitution were considered which, if ratified, would have limited the number of successive terms held by senators and representatives. Those measures were defeated and the issue was not considered again for over 150 years. However, since 1943 when the proposal was first resurrected in Congress, interest in the idea has grown to the point that from January 1981 through February 1992 no less than 69 proposals to limit the tenure of our national legislators were introduced into Congress.

Today the idea of limiting the number of successive terms a member of Congress may hold is hotter than ever. Fanned by the support of the 1988 and 1992 Republican Conventions, and fueled by the efforts of several special interest groups, the idea has achieved high levels of support nationally. A nationwide poll of likely voters conducted two weeks before the 1992 elections showed that 79 percent favored congressional term limitations. In an impressive burst of voter resolve, 16 states have passed amendments to their constitutions that attempt to limit the number of successive terms that their own U.S. representatives and senators may serve in office. Will those limitations survive? We believe that they will not. Either the courts or Congress will negate them.

First, the original intent weighs heavily against congressional term limits. In his polemic *supporting* term limits, George Will acknowledges, and even applauds, the participants at the Constitutional Convention of 1787 for rejecting term limits. Second, Barnicle points out that a precedent has been set, because previous major changes to qualifications for holding federal elected office and the manner of choosing elected officials have come by constitutional amendment.

Opponents of state-imposed congressional limits bolster their case with an argument from Article 1, Sections 2 and 3 of the Constitution, which explicitly states the qualifications for holding a seat in the House and Senate, and from the related Supreme Court case of *Powell v. McCormack*. In that case the Supreme Court determined that Congress could not add requirements to holding a seat in Congress above those expressly stated in the Constitution. Opponents of the limits say that this argument extends directly to states as well.

It should be noted, however, that nine of the 16 term-limit states have fashioned their laws in a manner that some believe may successfully circumvent the "additional requirement" argument. Rather than prohibiting legislators who have used up their eligibility from continuing to hold office, they merely prohibit their names from appearing on the election ballot. Thus incumbents are allowed to run write-in campaigns. This, proponents claim, is constitutional because it does not impose a new qualification for holding office, nor does it bar the incumbent from obtaining office. It simply alters the manner of election, a power which is granted states by the 10th Amendment. The constitutionality of this approach is likely to be the toughest question with which the courts will have to deal.

At any rate, even if state-imposed congressional term limitations of one form or another pass the test of court scrutiny, Congress can and likely will dispose of them with a negating law. Therefore, the only way for proponents to assure the survival of term limits is via an amendment to the Constitution.

Adapted from P.J. Fett and D.E. Ponder, "Congressional Term Limits, State legislative Term Limits, and Congressional Turnover: A Theory of Change" in *Political Science and Politics*, Vol 26 #02, © June 1993.

 © TPR Education IP Holdings, LLC

**43.** According to the passage, the idea of limiting the number of terms served by United States congresspersons originated in:

    **A.**  conventions of major political parties.
    **B.**  state constitutional conventions.
    **C.**  citizen-driven referenda.
    **D.**  proposals of the initial US Congress.

**44.** What is the overall structure of the passage?

    **A.**  Describe a current state of affairs; provide data to bolster that depiction; predict changes likely to occur in the future; present opposition to those changes
    **B.**  Describe a past state of affairs; predict a change for the future; present evidence opposing that prediction; present a qualification to the original prediction
    **C.**  Describe a current state of affairs; provide evidence supporting that description; make a prediction; support that prediction; present attempts to avoid the predicted result; reassert the prediction
    **D.**  Describe a past state of affairs; contrast past and present; make a prediction; show opposition to that prediction; introduce a revised prediction; elaborate on the previous contrast between past and present

**45.** The author cites the Supreme Court's decision in *Powell v. McCormack* in order to:

    **A.**  rely on an established authority on the wisdom of term limits.
    **B.**  demonstrate that the Supreme Court is not infallible.
    **C.**  explain the argument that state term limit laws are unconstitutional.
    **D.**  show historical evidence supporting the idea of term limits.

**46.** The author mentions all of the following as evidence of widening support for term limits EXCEPT:

    **A.**  the 1988 and 1992 Republican Conventions.
    **B.**  Congressional support.
    **C.**  high voter support.
    **D.**  state legislation.

**47.** The author's primary purpose in the passage is most likely to:

    **A.**  argue that attempts to impose term limits, although popular on both a state and national level, will fail.
    **B.**  describe efforts by proponents of term limits to circumvent Constitutional provisions.
    **C.**  suggest that term limits, however popular, if enacted only on a state level will not survive.
    **D.**  argue that term limits are unconstitutional, and should therefore not be supported.

### Passage IX (Questions 48-53)

Most of the opium consumed in America before the turn of the century was in the form of patent medicines. The growth of patent medicines derived in large part from the limitations of the medical profession. The number of physicians in those days was not adequate to deal with the rapidly expanding and geographically mobile American population. Also, compared with the standards of Europe, the quality of American medicine was woefully deficient. Since prescription drugs were expensive and the quality of medical care offered by physicians left much to be desired, people naturally turned to the much cheaper patent medicines.

The patent-medicine industry in the United States was not regulated in the nineteenth century. Labeling was not required, so the public had no way of knowing whether one or another preparation contained opium or any other ingredient. Even many patent medicines that were advertised as "cures" for the opium habit frequently contained large amounts of opiates. This was certainly a valid way of dealing with withdrawal symptoms, but it was not exactly what customers expected when they purchased a "cure."

Since the manufacturer had free license to put almost any ingredient into his preparations, he would usually include opiates, often mixed with generous amounts of alcohol. These two ingredients ensured that there would be a genuine pharmacologic effect. At a minimum, the tranquilizing property of opiates would provide symptomatic relief for a rather broad range of medical complaints. Patients would feel that they were getting something for their money and would come back for more when the supply ran out.

The United States' patent-medicine industry grew almost exponentially in the second half of the nineteenth century, and with it the consumption of opium proliferated. The per capita importation of crude opium increased four- to fivefold from the 1840 figure of less than 12 grains per capita to more than 52 grains in 1890. A grain of opium would represent a fairly substantial dose. Thus, it is not surprising that the United States was home to a quarter of a million opiate addicts in 1900.

The personal characteristics of the typical opiate addict of that day were greatly different from those of today's heroin addict, however. At the turn of the century the typical opiate addict was a middle-aged woman living an essentially normal life, married and raising a family. She purchased opium legally in the form of patent medicine and used it orally. Since she was fairly tolerant to the effects of the drug, her day-to-day activities could proceed much like her neighbors', with no evidence of physical or emotional disturbance. Because the effects of opium last longer when taken by mouth than when injected intravenously, she did not have sudden rushes of euphoria. By the same token, she rarely would experience withdrawal symptoms.

Most of these addicts to oral opiates had no adverse long-term medical effects. Opiate addiction in and of itself is not physically dangerous. Heroin addicts generally die of violent crime, viral hepatitis or AIDS from sharing needles, or from allergic reactions to materials mixed with the injected heroin, or simply from an overdose, which depresses the breathing process. Ingesting opiate extracts by mouth is safer than injecting morphine; but if dosage is reasonably well controlled, even opiates by injection are not inherently dangerous. There are many reported cases of opiate addiction among physicians, who have injected themselves regularly with pure, sterile morphine and continued to practice medicine productively, surviving in robust health to the age of 80 or 90.

Adapted from S.H. Snyder, *Brainstorming: The Science and Politics of Opiate Research*, © 1989 Harvard University Press.

**48.** Based on information in the passage, a nineteenth-century salesman for opium-containing patent medicine might advertise which of the following properties of his product?

   I. Relief from most medical ailments
   II. Sudden rushes of euphoria
   III. Curing opium habits

   **A.** I only
   **B.** II only
   **C.** I and II only
   **D.** I and III only

**49.** According to the passage, a modern opiate addict is LEAST likely to be which of the following?

   **A.** A European physician
   **B.** An American physician
   **C.** An intravenous drug abuser
   **D.** An average housewife

**50.** The author of the passage would most likely agree with which of the following statements?

   **A.** While opiate addiction was widespread in the nineteenth century, it did not pose the problems for society that heroin addiction does today.
   **B.** Heroin addiction and oral opiate addiction are a serious problem today.
   **C.** Regulation of opium as a controlled substance in the nineteenth century would have prevented our present problem with heroin addiction.
   **D.** Poorly trained physicians of the nineteenth century are largely responsible for the present-day problem with heroin addiction.

**51.** The success of patent medicines at the turn of the century was due to all of the following factors EXCEPT that:

   **A.** physicians were unwilling to prescribe opiates as a form of treatment.
   **B.** the medical community could not provide appropriate service to the population.
   **C.** patent medicines were affordable to the average person.
   **D.** the average person believed that patent medicines offered a quick cure.

**52.** All of the following are supported by information in the passage EXCEPT:

   **A.** Alcohol strengthens the pharmacologic effect of medications that contain opiates.
   **B.** Consumers of patent-medicine opiates were often unaware of the opium content of the patent medicines.
   **C.** Oral opiates are seldom associated with viral hepatitis or AIDS.
   **D.** The number of opiate addicts in the US at least quadrupled between 1840 and 1890.

**53.** The passage indicates that one of the advantages of taking opiates orally rather than intravenously was that:

   **A.** opiates taken orally would provide long-term medicinal effects.
   **B.** oral opiate users were less likely to experience mood swings.
   **C.** intravenous opiate users were less prone to violence.
   **D.** intravenous users of opiates were less likely to become addicted.

---

## END OF TEST 2

# ANSWER KEY — TEST 2

| Passage I | Passage II | Passage III | Passage IV | Passage V | Passage VI | Passage VII | Passage VIII | Passage IX |
|---|---|---|---|---|---|---|---|---|
| 1.  A | 7.  C | 13.  A | 20.  B | 26.  B | 32.  C | 38.  C | 43.  D | 48.  D |
| 2.  B | 8.  D | 14.  D | 21.  A | 27.  B | 33.  A | 39.  C | 44.  C | 49.  D |
| 3.  D | 9.  B | 15.  A | 22.  C | 28.  D | 34.  B | 40.  D | 45.  C | 50.  A |
| 4.  B | 10.  C | 16.  C | 23.  B | 29.  D | 35.  D | 41.  D | 46.  B | 51.  A |
| 5.  A | 11.  A | 17.  A | 24.  D | 30.  C | 36.  B | 42.  C | 47.  C | 52.  D |
| 6.  A | 12.  D | 18.  B | 25.  C | 31.  C | 37.  B | | | 53.  B |
| | | 19.  C | | | | | | |

© TPR Education IP Holdings, LLC

# Test Assessment Log

Use this Log to evaluate your performance on this CARS Practice Test. Diagnose what led you to select (or seriously consider) wrong answers, or to spend more time than necessary to identify the correct answer.

Approximate the time you spent on the Now passages and on the Later passages. Consider if you are spending the time needed on easier passages to get most of those questions right, or, if you are spending more time than necessary and not getting to as many questions as you could while still maintaining good accuracy. If you find that you are spending most of your 90 minutes on harder passages with a low level of accuracy, consider how best to reapportion your time on your next practice test. Finally, evaluate your ranking; are you choosing the right passages and doing them at roughly the right time within the section?

## Now Passages

| Now Passage # | Q # and Type (for questions you got wrong) | Attractors (for wrong answers you picked or seriously considered) | What did you do wrong? |
|---|---|---|---|
| | | | |
| | | | |
| | | | |
| | | | |
| | | | |
| | | | |

Approximate time spent on Now passages _____

Total Now passages attempted _____

Total # of Q's on Now passages attempted _____

Total # of Now Q's correct _____

% correct of Now Q's attempted _____

## Later Passages

| Later Passage # | Q # and Type (for questions you got wrong) | Attractors (for wrong answers you picked or seriously considered) | What did you do wrong? |
|---|---|---|---|
| | | | |
| | | | |
| | | | |
| | | | |
| | | | |
| | | | |

Approximate time spent on Later passages _____

Total Later passages attempted _____

Total # of Q's on Later passages attempted _____

Total # of Later Q's correct _____

% correct of Later Q's attempted _____

# Final Analysis

Total # of passages attempted (including partially completed) _____

Total # of questions attempted _____

Total # of correct answers _____

Total % correct of attempted questions _____

## Revised Strategy

| | |
|---|---|
| **Pacing** | |
| **Passage choice/ranking** | |
| **Working the Passage** | |
| **Attacking the Questions** | |

MCAT
Critical Analysis and
Reasoning Skills

Practice Test 2
Solutions

# TEST 2 SOLUTIONS

## Passage I
This is a Now passage.

**Bottom Line:** Characteristics of minority include unequal resources and treatment, as well as group identity.

1.  A      This is an Inference/Roman numeral question.
    I:      **True. "The existence of a minority in a society implies the existence of a corresponding dominant group with higher social status and greater privileges" (paragraph 1). The status and privileges mentioned are distinct advantages.**
    II:      False. The word "sacrifices" is too strong. The passage offers no evidence that social equality is a zero-sum game, i.e., that additional benefits for one group can come only at a cost to some other group. Be careful not to use outside knowledge based on discussions you may have heard in the real world on this topic.
    II:      False. Wagley and Harris's observation (about minority group solidarity) is more recent than Wirth's work (paragraph 1), but that doesn't mean that the behavior they describe is recent. Nothing in the passage suggests that members of the majority have changed their views.

2.  B      This is a Main Idea question.
    A:      No. No causal connection is drawn between how minorities are defined by sociologists and how they are treated in society.
    B:      **Yes. The focus is on the many ramifications of belonging to a minority. This choice can encompass all the major themes of the passage.**
    C:      No. This point is made only in the last paragraph; it is too narrow to be the answer to a main idea question. It is also too positive in tone to account for the passage's focus on disadvantages faced by minorities.
    D:      No. The author never addresses morality. This statement is too extreme for the mildly critical tone of the passage.

3.  D      This is an Inference question.
    A:      No. The author never alludes to religious conviction.
    B:      No. The author defines ideology as a set of ideas, not laws.
    C:      No. Nothing in the passage suggests that ideology is formulaic, or that it focuses particularly on what is moral.
    D:      **Yes. Ideology is "a set of ideas which the majority uses to justify and to defend its interests and actions" (paragraph 4). This answer is the best paraphrase of the relevant information from the passage.**

4.  B   This is an Inference/NOT question.

        Note: The credited response will be the statement that CANNOT be inferred to be part of Wirth's characterization. Recognizing the passage's structure allows you to see that all paragraphs save the final one discuss Wirth's definition. It is a common trick from the question writers to test your ability to differentiate between the ideas credited to different authorities in a given passage.

    A:  No. This statement can be inferred from paragraph 1.

    **B:  Yes. This is part of Wagley and Harris's theory (paragraph 5); Wirth never refers to this aspect of minority experience.**

    C:  No. See the last sentence of the first paragraph. This statement is supported by the passage.

    D:  No. This answer choice is implied by the first point in the third paragraph ("...whatever its numerical size..."). Clearly, the size of the minority can be smaller, or greater, than the size of the majority.

5.  A   This is a Tone/Attitude question.

    **A:  Yes. Think about the use of "disturbingly" in the first sentence of paragraph 4 and "difficult and unfair" in the last sentence of the passage. The author expresses disapproval, albeit very mildly.**

    B:  No. There might be a bit of positivity in the final paragraph, but the author does not direct it toward the overall treatment of minorities; it is directed, rather, to the collective identity of minority groups.

    C:  No. The author uses language, however subtly, to criticize discriminatory treatment of minorities. In paragraph 4, the author writes, "Most disturbingly, members of a minority are denied equal treatment." In paragraph 5, the author describes the position of minorities as "difficult and unfair." Detachment would require neutrality.

    D:  No. This language is too extreme; while you could say that the author is disapproving, he is not resigned to or scornful of the situation. Be suspicious of very strongly negative or otherwise unusual tone descriptions in answer choices; they are not always, but usually, incorrect.

6.  A   This is an Inference question.

    **A:  Yes. You can infer this answer from the remarks about "passing" in paragraph 2.**

    B:  No. This choice is too extreme. The author never indicates that the majority has no opinion about or reaction to attempts by minority members to "pass."

    C:  No. The only positive aspect of minority experience is that which comes from group solidarity, not from any interaction with the majority. This choice takes lines in the last paragraph out of context. Such "Words Out of Context" (Decoy) Attractors are often a trap for test takers who resist returning to the passage.

    D:  No. This goes beyond the information given in the passage. The author does not suggest that those who attempt to "pass" are less able to participate in majority culture. This is an Out of Scope Attractor.

## Passage II

This is a Killer passage.

**Bottom Line:** Parallels exist between modernity and schizophrenia that may provide insight into both conditions.

7.  C     This is a Main Idea question.

    A:    No. This choice is too narrow. The author does refute Sullivan on this basis (paragraph 3), but this is only one point made within the passage, not the main point of the entire passage.

    B:    No. This choice is too broad. The passage specifically explores how schizophrenia may relate to and reflect modernity, not how societal characteristics are *often* reflected in the thought processes of the mentally ill.

    **C:    Yes. Throughout the passage the author considers qualities of modernism and the peculiar characteristics of schizophrenic thought, and speculates at the end about what each may indicate about the other.**

    D:    No. This choice misses the issue of the passage. The author concerns himself not with biological or environmental causes of illness, but with similarities and affinities between schizophrenic and modernist thought.

8.  D     This is a Retrieval question.

    A:    No. It was Aragon, not Duchamp, who employed radical reversals (paragraph 1). Furthermore, the author rejects Sullivan's description of schizophrenic thought as regressive or childlike (paragraph 3). He states that schizophrenic cognition is in many ways similar to Duchamp's perspective (paragraph 2), thus Duchamp's imagery would not be characterized as regressive by the author.

    B:    No. Duchamp does not illustrate standard beliefs, but instead contemptuously rejects them (paragraph 1).

    C:    No. This choice takes words from the passage out of context. First, there is no discussion of subcategories in the text provided. Secondly, Duchamp's category includes not actual "physical phenomena," but rather skewed perspectives on physical realities.

    **D:    Yes. See paragraphs 1 and 2.**

9.  B     This is an Inference question.

    A:    No. The author never suggests that more people suffer from the disease than in the past, nor does he propose complexity or disorder of the world as an actual cause of schizophrenia. This would be a misinterpretation and overly literal reading of his discussion of the affinities between schizophrenic and modernist thought.

    **B:    Yes. Through his discussion of the modern awareness of multiple points of view (paragraph 4) and of how parallels between schizophrenia and modernism may indicate something about the modern sensibility (paragraph 5), the author indicates that the modern world and sensibility have become more complex and alienated than in the past.**

    C:    No. The wording in this choice is too extreme. The author poses the question of whether this might be the case (paragraph 5), but never definitively answers the question. This paragraph tells us that the author is considering various interpretations, not proposing clear and definitive answers.

    D:    No. This choice takes the author's reference to "homelessness of mind" (paragraph 3) too literally. The passage never suggests practical social conditions or problems as causal factors in schizophrenia.

10. C  This is an Inference question.

A:  No. Representation of "the object in the subject" (the object as perceived by the poet) arises *from* the poet's self-reflection and self-consciousness. "Object" in this context does not mean objective or purpose; the phrase refers to what the poet does, not Schiller's purpose in depicting the poet.

B:  No. This choice takes the words "object" and "subject" out of context. The object is not a subcategory within a larger category or subject. Rather, the object is the thing perceived and represented by the subject or poet.

**C:  Yes. According to the passage, the poet's self-consciousness (middle of paragraph 4) creates awareness of the multiple perspectives or ways of seeing things existing within himself ("self-divided"). This awareness leads him describe the character of things as something filtered or mediated through his own perceptions or point of view.**

D:  No. Self-awareness leads to the modernist's presentation of the object in the subject (the object as the poet perceives it—see paragraph 4). Thus the poet's (and in general the modernist's) work is *characterized* by self-awareness; the passage never indicates that his work focuses on self-awareness as a topic or "subject."

11. A  This is a Weaken question.

**A:  Yes. The author refutes Sullivan's claim that schizophrenia represents a regressed or developmentally primitive state (paragraph 3), and argues that it suggests an alienated (isolated from reality), not childlike, condition. If it were to be shown that the disease in fact corresponded to a form of arrested development, it would undermine the author's position.**

B:  No. "Primitive" in the context of the passage means a regressed or childlike personality (beginning of paragraph 3). The author never argues that schizophrenia is unique to advanced or modern societies. Therefore this finding would not undermine the author's position.

C:  No. This claim is entirely consistent with the author's depiction of the schizophrenic mind as "homeless," slipping from one curious perspective to another (paragraphs 2 and 3).

D:  No. The author describes the affinities or similarities he sees between modern culture and schizophrenia, but does not claim that modern culture or environment causes the illness. Thus the existence of biological causes or preconditions would not be inconsistent with his position on Sullivan's work.

12.　D　This is an Analogy question.

A:　No. Based on the context of the passage, and specifically on the author's point of disagreement with Sullivan (paragraphs 3 and 6), "unintelligible" suggests our inability to understand or share in the schizophrenic's peculiar perspective on reality (see example in paragraph 2). "Unintelligent" corresponds to Sullivan's claim that schizophrenic thought arises from failure or lack of "higher referential processes" (childlike, in the author's terms). While "foreign" could correspond to strangeness or unintelligibility, "unconventional" does not correspond to Sullivan's view of schizophrenic thought. This choice is only half right, and so is incorrect.

B:　No. See discussion for A. "Unnatural" does not correspond to the author's use of "unintelligible," not does "unknown" connect to Sullivan's "primitivity hypothesis" (paragraph 3).

C:　No. See discussion for A. The author describes how multiplicity (and oddness) of perspective characterizes schizophrenic thought (beginning of paragraph 2). Thus "multiperspectival" would correspond to "unintelligible" (the author's view), not "unintelligent" (Sullivan). "Singular" corresponds to neither.

**D:　Yes. See discussion for A. Something that is illegible cannot easily be understood, and yet may have value or interest to us if we could in fact decipher it. This is similar to the author's consideration of what schizophrenia may be able to tell us about the modern mind and condition (beginning of paragraph 5). Something that is illogical lacks rationality— it is defined negatively by what it is missing, i.e., reason. This corresponds to Sullivan's depiction of schizophrenics as regressed and childlike, a characterization that the author rejects in the beginning of paragraph 6, and earlier at the end of paragraph 3.**

## Passage III

This is a Now passage.

**Bottom Line:** Therapists and law makers have increasingly recognized the legitimacy of limiting confidentiality when necessary to protect the public.

13.　A　This is an Inference question.

**A:　Yes. In paragraphs 4 and 6, the author discusses how psychotherapists are increasingly accepting of such policies.**

B:　No. This contradicts the author's statements in the fourth and sixth paragraphs. The movement is in the opposite direction.

C:　No. The author indicates that psychotherapists believe there is a need for increased protection of the public (paragraph 4). However, there is no suggestion in the passage of a connection to civil liability in this context. This is an Out of Scope Attractor.

D:　No. While psychotherapists initially reacted with dismay to the California ruling, that dismay has changed to qualified acceptance of legal intervention in the their profession (paragraph 4). Thus no increased hostility toward the legal system is indicated. Be careful not to make assumptions about how psychotherapists could react and instead focus on how the passage says they have reacted.

14.  D    This is an Inference question.

A:    No. The passage indicates just the opposite. The California case served as a precedent for similar limitations on confidentiality in other states (paragraph 5), suggesting that lawmakers reacted positively, not negatively.

B:    No. This choice is too extreme. The passage describes certain limitations placed on confidentiality in other states (paragraph 5). However, "determination to prevent violent crime" goes too far past the measures described.

C:    No. The author never suggests that lawmakers were unaware of the potential problem before the California case, only that the first laws intended to address the problem were passed after the case.

D:    **Yes. The author presents the California case as a turning point between previous protection of patient-therapist privilege (paragraph 1) and post-1974 legal limitations placed on that privilege (paragraphs 4 and 5).**

15.  A    This is an Inference question.

A:    **Yes. The passage describes a trend toward an increasing acceptance of limitations on patient-therapist privilege (paragraphs 2 and 5). Therefore it is possible to infer based on the passage that if the safety and welfare of the public were at stake, more states would enact further limitations on the rights of therapists to remain silent in such cases.**

B:    No. The passage suggests just the opposite. It displays a trend toward greater, not lesser limitation on patient-therapist privilege when the safety of others is at issue.

C:    No. This choice is not supported by the passage. While therapists may be held more responsible for providing information and testimony when their patients endanger others, there is no indication that this will lead to more testimony by therapists specifically in civil trials.

D:    No. While involuntary hospitalization is one method by which therapists may protect the public from dangerous patients (paragraph 4), the author does not give evidence that this will occur in the absence of any mental illness. The choice is too extreme.

16.  C    This is an Inference/Roman numeral question.

I:    **True. The author indicates that therapists are not entirely comfortable with these laws (paragraph 6), even though they have come to accept them.**

II:   False. This choice is too strong. The passage suggests some discomfort and eventual acceptance, not fundamental opposition.

III:  **True. Therapists have come to accept that they should in some cases take action to prevent harm to others (paragraph 4) and that this may involve legal limitations on confidentiality (paragraph 6).**

17.  A    This is an Inference/Roman numeral question.

I:    **True. This possibility is attested to in the final sentence of paragraph 6.**

II:   False. The author says in the final sentence of paragraph 6 that patients may well know of the new laws.

III:  False. In paragraphs 4 and 5, the author describes therapists as relatively accepting of the new laws and willing to comply with them.

18.  B     This is an Inference question.
     A:    No. This choice is too extreme. The fact that a therapist is absolved of liability when he
           or she notifies the police (paragraph 5) doesn't mean that he or she is held liable in *all*
           situations when no notification is given. Compare this answer with choice B.
     **B:    Yes. The passage states that the Colorado law provides that the therapist take action
           when a threat exists. If the police are notified, the therapist is absolved of responsibility
           (paragraph 5), indicating that if no notification is given the therapist may in fact be held
           liable. Notice that this choice is a less extreme version of choice A, which makes choice B
           a more suitable answer.**
     C:    No. While the therapist may be held liable (paragraph 5), the author never says that he or
           she will be considered to be an accessory.
     D:    No. This choice is too extreme. While the therapist may be held liable (paragraph 5),
           the author does not say that he or she will be considered to be just as guilty as the actual
           perpetrator.

19.  C     This is an Inference question.
     A:    No. The privilege is weaker, not stronger (paragraph 2).
     B:    No. While recognition is relatively new (paragraph 1), we are not told how new in such
           specific terms.
     **C:    Yes. The author states that the privilege is comparatively new (paragraph 1).**
     D:    No. This choice is too extreme. The privilege is more limited than in certain times in the past.
           However, the author indicates that it still has meaning for psychotherapists (paragraph 6).

## Passage IV

This is a Later passage.

**Bottom Line:** Theatre of the Absurd confronts loss of old way of understanding reality by portraying new
tragic yet comic reality.

20.  B     This is a Main Idea question.
     A:    No. While the Theater of the Absurd has become something of a religious quest (para-
           graph 4), religious beliefs that the playwrights might hold are not discussed, beyond the
           fact that they believe that there is no God (paragraphs 2, 3, and 4).
     **B:    Yes. The first four paragraphs describe how the Theater of the Absurd arose out of the
           modern belief that God does not exist and the resulting need to find some ultimate
           reality. The last four paragraphs discuss the role or purpose served by the Theater
           through presenting its version of reality to the audience.**
     C:    No. There is one reference to Greek tragedy (beginning of paragraph 6). However, the
           passage as a whole is about Theater of the Absurd.
     D:    No. While the Theater of the Absurd's belief in the absurdity of the human condition is
           discussed, the passage as a whole is structured around the description of different aspects
           of the Theater, not around progressive stages of absurdity in our condition.

21.   A   This is an Inference question.

   **A:**   **Yes. Beginning in paragraph 2, the author posits that it was the belief that God does not exist, and the search for some other form of ultimate reality, that inspired the Theater of the Absurd.**

   B:   No. Nietzsche's *Zarathustra* expresses the belief that God is dead; neither the character nor the work, however, is presented as a direct inspiration for the Theater of the Absurd.

   C:   No. The Theater of the Absurd arose from a disbelief in the existence of God, and a search for an alternate form of ultimate reality (paragraphs 4 and 6).

   D:   No. The Theater portrays people entangled in illusion as a way of showing the audience how precarious and mysterious our existence is. However, the Theater itself was inspired by a search for an ultimate reality that exists beneath or beyond our illusions (paragraphs 3, 4, and 5).

22.   C   This is an Inference question.

      Note: The credited response will be inconsistent with the author's description of Theater of the Absurd.

   A:   No. See paragraph 4: "Theatre of the Absurd attempts to shock its audience out of an existence that has become trite...." Also see paragraph 7: "The subject matter of most plays that are considered Absurdist is somber, violent, and bitter."

   B:   No. See the second sentence of paragraph 5: "In one way it castigates, satirically, the absurdity of lives lived unaware of ultimate realities."

   **C:**   **Yes. The author states that audiences laugh at the characters because they do not identify with them. Therefore, when they laugh they are not laughing at themselves (paragraph 7).**

   D:   No. See the end of paragraph 7: "That is why the Theatre of the Absurd transcends the categories of comedy and tragedy."

23.   B   This is an Inference question.

   A:   No. While Absurdist theater at times uses disturbing imagery and subject matter to portray the human condition (paragraph 7), the author does not describe the writers themselves as angry about that condition.

   **B:**   **Yes. According to the passage, the most essential goal of the Absurdist writers was to display the absurdity of the "human condition" (paragraph 5). This is described as paradoxical by the author (beginning of paragraph 4). Finally, the writers "combine laughter with horror" (paragraph 7) in part to show the contradictions inherent in the human condition.**

   C:   No. While Theater of the Absurd does express the "tragic loss" of the ultimate certainty formerly to be found in God (paragraph 3), the Absurdist writers are not, as described, sad about the nature of human existence. In fact, they use comedy and laughter as a technique to portray the human condition to audiences (paragraph 7).

   D:   No. While the Absurdist writers do not believe in God (paragraph 2), the author makes no mention of criticism of those who do believe.

24. **D** This is a Weaken question.
  A: The correct answer will be a statement that is inconsistent with the passage. The author suggests that the original function of theater, represented by the ancient Greeks, was to make audiences aware of the position of humanity in the universe. The claim that the Greeks were concerned with the meaning of life does not contradict this description.
  B: No. Nothing in the passage equates similarity with the past with a lack of modernity.
  C: No. Absurdist theater looks for meaning with the assumption that God does not exist, and attempts to communicate that meaning to audiences. The Greeks looked for and communicated meaning in the context of different religious or philosophical beliefs. The similarity drawn by the author is in the act of communication of meaning to the audience, not in the particular nature of the beliefs involved.
  **D: Yes. This assumption is inconsistent with the author's position that the Absurdists, like the ancient Greeks, attempted to make the audience "aware of the...position of human beings in the universe" (beginning of paragraph 6).**

25. **C** This is an Inference question.
  A: No. This choice is too extreme. It is only those who believe God is dead for whom the continuation of certain standards is invalid (beginning of paragraph 3).
  B: No. Neither artificiality nor constraint is at issue here. The question at hand is whether the certainties expressed by the standards still exist.
  **C: Yes. The wording in paragraph 3 ("For those for whom the world has lost...") indicates that for some, the world still has a central explanation. For those people, the standards would still be valid.**
  D: No. This choice is too extreme. While for some the standards may still be valid, we do not know that the standards are, for those people, the *only* means of accepting art.

## Passage V
This is a Now passage.

**Bottom Line:** Political leaders confronted threat to parliamentary democracy in 1936 Spain.

26. **B** This is an Inference question.
  Note: A passage like this looks intimidating because of its potentially unfamiliar language and subject matter. However, if you keep your attention on answering the questions (most of which give you lead words from the passage) and don't try to get a deep understanding of the events being described, it isn't as challenging as it might seem at first glance.
  A: No. Critical here means "important." The beginning of the passage describes how the Cortes today is used only for occasional ceremonies. This is an Opposite (Decoy) Attractor.
  **B: Yes. In paragraph 1, the author describes how, in contrast with the past, the Cortes is now used "only occasionally, when a few honorific dignitaries give formal assent to decrees...."**
  C: No. "Anachronistic" means out of date or out of one's historical time. While the political function of the Cortes may have changed or decreased, to call it anachronistic is too extreme.
  D: No. The modern Cortes serves a ceremonial, not an administrative function (paragraph 1).

27.  B   This is a Retrieval question.
     A:  No. The later period (1931–1936) was marked by parliamentary activity. The earlier peri-
         od (1923–1931) covered the eight years of dictatorship mentioned in paragraph 1. This is
         a Reversal (Decoy) Attractor.
     **B:  Yes. 1931–1936 covers the five years of parliamentary activity that followed the eight
         years of dictatorship (1923–1931) under General Primo de Rivera (paragraph 1).**
     C:  No. The author does not describe the period of parliamentary rule as more stable than
         dictatorship. Significant political change came at the end of each period; in that sense,
         the two periods were equally unstable. This is a Not the Issue (Out of Scope) Attractor.
     D:  No. The author does not describe one period as being more or less unstable than the
         other. This is a Not the Issue (Out of Scope) Attractor.

28.  D   This is an Inference question.
     A:  No. Holding of political office has no direct relevance to political ideology. This is a Not
         the Issue (Out of Scope) Attractor.
     B:  No. It was Robles' party, the CEDA, that contained those described as "almost fascists"
         (paragraph 3). This is a Reversal (Decoy) Attractor; it is also too extreme.
     C:  No. Level of public support does not indicate ideology. Also, the author never writes that
         Casares had the support of the majority. This is both Out of Scope and too extreme.
     **D:  Yes. Casares' alliance, the Popular Front, represented working class groups (paragraph
         4). This alliance is contrasted by the author with Robles' National Front, which includ-
         ed monarchists, agrarians, etc., described as representing the forces of old Spain.**

29.  D   This is an Inference question.
     A:  No. The author does not state that Casares had majority support. Neither is he described
         as having a firm grasp on his supporters (paragraph 4). This is an Absolute (Too Extreme)
         Attractor.
     B:  No. The author describes their control over their respective factions as precarious, not
         firm (paragraph 4). This is an Opposite (Decoy) Attractor.
     C:  No. While they are the only two leaders mentioned by name in the passage, this does
         not support an inference that no other popular leaders existed. This is an Absolute (Too
         Extreme) Attractor.
     **D:  Yes. The passage describes Casares as part of a group of middle-class liberals anxious
         about the threat to parliamentary life (paragraph 1). The passage later depicts Robles's
         concern over what he saw as a state of crisis and anarchy (paragraph 3).**

30.  C   This is a Tone/Attitude question.
     A:  No. The author does not express nostalgia or a sentimental longing for any of the histori-
         cal events or periods he describes.
     B:  No. The passage is written in neutral, descriptive language, and is entirely about the past,
         with no predictions for the future. This is a Crystal ball (Out of Scope) Attractor.
     **C:  Yes. The author describes the events from the position of a neutral or disinterested observer.**
     D:  No. The author describes the anxieties and disappointments of others, but never indicates
         that he or she shares them. This is a Words Out of Context (Decoy) Attractor.

31.   C      This is an Inference question.

A:     No. The passage never indicates how long CEDA had been in existence.

B:     No. In paragraphs 1 and 2, the author describes how the liberalism of men like Casares was modeled on the ways of Britain, France, and America. Robles, however, is not described as a liberal (paragraph 3), and no connection is made between the origin of CEDA as a party and other European governments.

C:     **Yes. In paragraph 2, the author writes that Casares called for home rule in his province. Thus you can infer that he did not believe that all power should be held by the central government of Spain.**

D:     No. You do know that both parties were "prominent in the history of the Second Republic" (paragraph 4). However, that is not enough information from which to infer that they had been present "for some time." The answer choice goes beyond what can be supported by the passage and is therefore Out of Scope.

# Passage VI

This is a Now/Later passage.

**Bottom Line:** Confronting our responsibilities to the environment is complicated, as shown by application of Clean Water Act.

32.   C      This is an Inference question.

A:     No. There has actually been a general improvement in water quality (paragraph 8).

B:     No. The writer, though not overly optimistic, seems convinced that progress has been made (paragraph 8).

C:     **Yes. See the end of paragraph 8.**

D:     No. "Open sewers" still exist, in spite of progress (paragraph 8).

33.   A      This is an Inference question.

A:     **Yes. Read the end of paragraph 5 carefully; the entire sentence refers to a single "best usage" category. The sentence reads "permits all uses included within that "best usage" category," not "permits uses in all categories below the best usage." Remember not to eliminate answers simply because they employ extreme words; here, the "only" is not too extreme in the context of the passage.**

B:     No. This is a misreading of paragraph 5. The statement in this choice indicates that water with the highest classification AA could also be used for boating, for example.

C:     No. Each "best usage" designation includes a set of criteria, but there is no one standard that must be met by all bodies of water.

D:     No. The word "ideal" is too strong; it brings in a standard of evaluation that is beyond the scope of the language used in the passage. For example, it may be "ideal" that all water is so clean that it could be used for drinking, but that in reality some water is too polluted to serve that purpose. Best usage indicates the best use to which a particular body of water can be put. It may be the case that some water is so polluted that best that can be done with it is to boat on it (and pray that you don't fall in)—hardly an ideal.

34. B     This is an Inference question.

Note: Remember that whenever a question stem gives you a quotation or paragraph reference, the best approach is to go back to the passage before reading the answer choices.

A: No. This is mentioned earlier in the passage but is irrelevant to the "problem" mentioned in paragraph 3.

**B: Yes. The problem is that the intended purpose changes by area (see paragraph 3). The phrase "this problem" in the relevant part of the passage indicates that the answer to this question will paraphrase information in the preceding sentences of the passage (which describe the problem).**

C: No. The passage never suggests that in some areas the "intended use" is more difficult to determine. Rather, it states that the difficulty arises because the "intended use" in some areas (for example, of a river) may be defined differently than in others.

D: No. Political lobbying is mentioned in paragraph 7, and is part of the discussion of the development of standards. It is supposed to "throw light on" (paragraph 3) the problem—it does not in itself constitute the problem. This is a Decoy Attractor.

35. D     This is an Inference question.

A: No. The author does not compare the severity of different environmental issues. The word "most" makes this choice too extreme. Beware of superlatives in answer choices unless the text supports them. You cannot infer that because the author focuses on water in this particular passage that he considers it to be most important of all environmental issues.

B: No. This is inconsistent with paragraph 1, where the author specifically states that man has been forced to recognize his responsibility to the environment.

C: No. The author does not suggest that industrial development is "recent," nor does he imply that contemporary pollution has dramatically changed the relationship: "man has always had problems with his environment" (paragraph 1). It's just that now we have been forced to recognize the problem.

**D: Yes. One can infer this from the author's statement that people have "always" had problems with their environment (first sentence). Effective highlighting helps you to catch these sorts of words, so that you are less likely to eliminate good answers simply because they contain words that could, out of context, be considered too extreme.**

36. B     This is a New Information question.

A: No. Although a change in the classification system is theoretically possible, no such information is provided in the passage.

**B: Yes. The objectives of the Act are to improve water quality, and not to degrade it. In the case described in the question stem, the water could be degraded by people swimming (class B) in water that was suitable for human consumption in its natural state (class AA).**

C: No. The question asks us to consider what must be true, not what could be true. There is nothing in the passage or the question stem to suggest that the classification would be accurate for some parts of the body of water but not others.

D: No. Lobbyists have influenced the classification system within the government, but no information is provided as to lobbyists' efforts on specific bodies of water.

37.  B       This is a Tone/Attitude question.

             Note: Effective annotation – highlighting as well as summarizing – is extremely helpful on these types of questions. If you are looking for the tone indicators while working the passage, you will get to the answer much more efficiently

     A:      No. The author expresses some misgivings about the nature of classification (paragraph 3), so this answer choice, with the phrase "wholeheartedly support," is too strongly positive.

     **B:      Yes. Despite the problems the author notes with classification, the author does conclude that "the result of all this work has been a general improvement of fresh water quality" (paragraph 8). We can thus infer that he might be favorably disposed toward more such efforts, although with some reservations.**

     C:      No. The author seems to have qualms about the current classification system and points out some of its inadequacies, but ultimately he praises some of the system's accomplishments. Therefore, he is not "indifferent" to the issue and he would probably favor further attempts to classify bodies of water.

     D:      No. Although the author states that classifications are far from clear, he also points out that the whole classification effort has resulted in improved water quality (paragraph 8).

## Passage VII

This is a Later passage.

**Bottom Line:** Author experiences each story as unique at the time, but patterns and connections to her life emerge in retrospect.

38.  C       This is a Retrieval question.

     A:      No. Meaning found by readers in a story is never discussed. The passage is about how authors create stories and find meaning in their own creations.

     B:      No. Meaning rises up behind the story, in retrospect (paragraph 1). It is not available before the fact as a guide to the story.

     **C:      Yes. According to the author, meaning arises in retrospect or hindsight, emerging for the author only after the writing is done (paragraph 1).**

     D:      No. Meaning comes in part out of the recognition of recurring characters (paragraph 3). Meaning is not described as something that overshadows character development.

39.  C       This is an Inference question.

     A:      No. Themes and patterns emerge for the writer only in retrospect; her stories "begin with the particular, never the general" (paragraph 2).

     B:      No. This choice is too extreme. The author states that there are in fact hidden patterns and commonalities (paragraphs 1, 2, and 3). She refers to these patterns as a way of discovering "sequence in experience" (beginning of paragraph 1).

     **C:      Yes. The author describes the "freedom ahead" at the start of each new story (paragraph 2). Patterns and themes are not imposed on the story from the beginning; they only appear in hindsight.**

     D:      No. While the author does suggest that she learns life lessons through her writing (paragraphs 1 and 2), she does not suggest that the progression of one matches the other.

40. D      This is a Retrieval/EXCEPT question.
           Note: The credited response will NOT have been described as a factor in creating a true work of fiction.

   A:      No. Memory is discussed in paragraph 4 as a contributing factor.

   B:      No. Experience is discussed in the same context as memory, as something that the author draws upon to create fiction (paragraph 4).

   C:      No. The author states that she invents her characters, for example, rather than copying them from real people (paragraph 4). This suggests the use of imagination.

   **D:     Yes. The author does use bits and pieces of her own experiences in her work (paragraph 4). However, "autobiography" indicates that the author writes fiction as an account or mirror of her own life, an undertaking rejected by this author. In particular, she refuses to turn real people she has known well into characters in her stories.**

41. D      This is a Retrieval/Roman numeral question.

   **I:      True. In paragraphs 1 and 2, the author states that patterns in her work repeat themselves in a way visible only in hindsight**

   **II:     True. One repeated pattern is the reappearance of characters from other stories (paragraph 3).**

   III:    True. In the beginning of the passage, the author describes writing as a way of uncovering the action of cause and effect in one's life.

42. C      This is a Retrieval/EXCEPT question.
           Note: The credited response will NOT be described in the passage as contributing to the development of a character.

   A:      No. Personal experiences do in fact contribute to character development, as attested to in paragraph 4.

   B:      No. Luck, while not the primary factor, does at times play a role in creating a character (paragraph 4).

   **C:     Yes. This is the factor which, according to the author, does not play a role in character development. The author claims that when while writing one story, no other stories "exist," and that each writer must find meaning for him or herself (paragraph 2).**

   D:      No. The author refers to the plot as a contributing factor in the sentence, "Characters I invent along with the story that carries them" (paragraph 4).

## Passage VIII

This is a Now passage.

**Bottom Line:** Term limits increasingly popular but unlikely to survive.

43. D     This is a Retrieval question.

    A:     No. According to the passage, the idea originated during the first Congress of the United States (first sentence). It was over 150 years later that the idea was revived by Republican Conventions (paragraph 2). This is the only mention made in the passage of major political parties.

    B:     No. Term limits were first proposed during the first Congress (first sentence). State constitutional conventions are not mentioned in this context.

    C:     No. The author does state that voters today support term limits (paragraph 2). However, the idea originated over 150 years before 1943 (paragraph 1) and citizen-driven referenda are not mentioned as a factor in those times.

    **D:     Yes. The passage states that support for term limits first appeared during the first Congress (first sentence).**

44. C     This is a General Structure question.

    A:     No. Compare this choice piece by piece to the passage, and to choice C. The passage ends with a prediction that the states' attempts to evade the issue of constitutionality will fail. It does not end with opposition to the likelihood that the courts or Congress will negate state-based term limits.

    B:     No. There is no qualification at the end of the passage to the prediction that state-level term limits will fail. Instead, the passage closes with the claim that only limits imposed through a (national) Constitutional amendment could survive.

    **C:     Yes. The author describes current enthusiasm for term limits in paragraphs 1 and 2. At the end of paragraph 2, the author predicts that limitations based on amendments to state constitutions will fail. Next, the author gives reasons why he or she believes this prediction to be accurate (paragraphs 3 and 4). In paragraph 5, the author describes how states have attempted to avoid negation of their term limits by the courts and Congress. Finally, in paragraph 6, the author reasserts his or her claim that term limits not based on an amendment to the federal Constitution will be overruled.**

    D:     No. The author never revises his or her prediction (it is reasserted in the last paragraph). The author also does not return at the end of the passage to a contrast between past and present.

45. C     This is a Structure question.

    A:     No. The Supreme Court case is cited to illustrate a case made against term limits (paragraph 4), not to argue for the wisdom of limits.

    B:     No. The *Powell v. McCormack* decision is not presented as flawed or mistaken.

    **C:     Yes. The case is cited by opponents of term limits in order to argue that Article 1 of the Constitution does not allow for additional requirements for office-holding (paragraph 4).**

    D:     No. The Court in this case ruled that term limits were unconstitutional (paragraph 4).

46.    B       This is a Structure/EXCEPT question.
               Note: The credited response will NOT be given as evidence in support of the idea that
               support for term limits is growing.

       A:      No. The Republican Conventions are presented as evidence that the idea of limits is "hot-
               ter than ever" (paragraph 2).

       **B:    Yes. This contradicts the passage, which states that Congress is likely to negate any
               state laws imposing limits (paragraph 6).**

       C:      No. Voter support for term limits is mentioned in paragraph 2.

       D:      No. State legislation limiting successive terms is mentioned in paragraph 2.

47.    C       This is a Primary Purpose question.

       A:      No. The author argues that term limits that are not supported by an amendment to the Con-
               stitution (that is, those imposed by the states), not *all* term limits, will fail (paragraph 6).

       B:      No. This choice is too narrow. It only describes the purpose of the fifth paragraph.

       **C:    Yes. Throughout the passage, the author explains why term limits not based on a Con-
               stitutional amendment will fail.**

       D:      No. While the author argues that some term limits may currently be unconstitutional,
               the passage does not indicate that the author opposes an amendment to the Constitution
               that would allow term limits.

# Passage IX

This is a Now passage.

**Bottom Line:** Opium consumption through medication and opiate addiction high in 19th century, but not as
harmful as modern heroin use.

48.    D       This is a New Information/Roman numeral question.

       **I:    True. The combination of opium and alcohol guaranteed "a genuine pharmacologic
               effect" that convinced consumers that the medicines were effective for a wide variety of
               illnesses (paragraph 3). This effect would likely be used in any sales pitch.**

       II:     False. Opium taken orally does not produce sudden rushes of euphoria (paragraph 5).
               Thus, it would not be marketed on that basis.

       **III:  True. The passage explicitly states that patent medicines were sold as cures for opium
               addiction (paragraph 2).**

49.    D       This is a Retrieval/LEAST question.

       A:      No. The correct answer will list an unlikely characteristic of modern opiate addicts. In
               paragraph 6, the author refers to many reported cases of opiate addiction among mod-
               ern-day physicians. No reason is given in the passage to exclude European physicians.

       B:      No. In paragraph 6, the author suggests that opiate addiction is not uncommon among
               physicians.

       C:      No. In paragraphs 5 and 6, the author suggests that the typical modern opiate addict is
               an intravenous heroin user.

       **D:    Yes. The average housewife fits the turn-of-the-century profile (paragraph 5), not the
               modern pattern of opiate addiction.**

50.    A     This is an Inference question.

        A:    **Yes. In the fifth and sixth paragraphs the author argues that in the nineteenth century, opiate addiction usually did not interfere in daily life, and did not involve physical danger. This contrasts sharply with the dangers of modern heroin addiction.**

        B:    No. Addiction to oral opiates is not described as a modern-day problem.

        C:    No. Oral opium and heroin are portrayed as being significantly different in both their physical and social effects. There is no suggestion in the passage that lack of nineteenth-century regulation contributed to modern problems with heroin.

        D:    No. Poor training of nineteenth-century doctors did contribute to the popularity of opiate-containing patent medicines in the 1800s (paragraph 1). However, no connection is made by the author to modern problems with heroin addiction.

51.    A     This is an Inference/EXCEPT question.

             Note: The credited response will describe a factor that did NOT, as far as we know from the passage, contribute to the success of patent medicines.

        A:    **Yes. The author argues that the cost of prescription medication played a role, but never suggests that physicians were unwilling to prescribe opiates.**

        B:    No. Lack of access to professional medical care and medication is given in the passage as a significant factor (paragraph 1).

        C:    No. The author does in fact describe patent medicine as cheaper than prescription medications (paragraph 1).

        D:    No. The author indicates in paragraph 3 that people commonly believed the patent medicines to be effective and rapid cures. The large number of people using medications containing opium in the nineteenth century (paragraph 4) provides further evidence of how common this belief was.

52.    D     This is an Inference/EXCEPT question.

             Note: The correct choice will be a statement that would NOT be supported by the passage.

        A:    No. In paragraph 3 the author suggests that the addition of alcohol to opium ensured that there would be a noticeable pharmacologic effect.

        B:    No. Because labeling of patent medicines was not required, patients had no way of knowing what the opium content was (paragraph 2).

        C:    No. The author sharply contrasts addiction to oral opiates on one hand, and to heroin on the other. Heroin is closely associated with AIDS and hepatitis (paragraph 6). From this we can infer that oral opiate use is not, according to the passage.

        D:    **Yes. This number corresponds to the per-capita importation of crude opium (paragraph 4), not to the number of opiate addicts.**

53.    B     This is an Inference question.

        A:    No. The passage never suggests that opiates in any form have true medicinal effects.

        B:    **Yes. This is one of the contrasts drawn between oral and intravenous opiates (paragraph 5). "Euphoria" in the passage corresponds to "mood swings" in the answer choice.**

        C:    No. The passage suggests just the opposite—that oral opiate users are less vulnerable to violence than intravenous users (paragraph 6).

        D:    No. Neither oral nor intravenous opiates are claimed to be less addictive.

# MCAT
## Critical Analysis and Reasoning Skills

## Practice Test 3

## Passage I (Questions 1-5)

Global strategies to control infectious disease have historically included the erection of barriers to international travel and immigration. Keeping people with infectious diseases outside national borders has reemerged as an important public health policy in the human immunodeficiency virus (HIV) epidemic. Between 29 and 50 countries are reported to have introduced border restrictions on HIV-positive foreigners, usually those planning an extended stay in the country, such as students, workers, or seamen.

Travel restrictions have been established primarily by countries in the western Pacific and Mediterranean regions, where HIV seroprevalence is relatively low. However, the country with the broadest policy of testing and excluding foreigners is the United States. From December 1, 1987, when HIV infection was first classified in the United States as a contagious disease, through September 30, 1989, more than 3 million people seeking permanent residence in this country were tested for HIV antibodies. The U.S. policy has been sharply criticized by national and international organizations as being contrary to public health goals and human-rights principles. Many of these organizations are boycotting international meetings in the United States that are vital for the study of prevention, education, and treatment of HIV infection.

The Immigration and Nationality Act requires the Public Health Service to list "dangerous contagious diseases" for which aliens can be excluded from the United States. By 1987 there were seven designated diseases—five of them sexually transmitted (chancroid, gonorrhea, granuloma inguinale, lymphogranuloma venereum, and infectious syphilis) and two non-venereal (active tuberculosis and infectious leprosy). On June 8, 1987, in response to a Congressional direction in the Helms Amendment, the Public Health Service added HIV infection to the list of dangerous contagious diseases.

A just and efficacious travel and immigration policy would not exclude people because of their serologic status unless they posed a danger to the community through casual transmission. U.S. regulations should list only active tuberculosis as a contagious infectious disease. We support well-funded programs to protect the health of travelers infected with HIV through appropriate immunizations and prophylactic treatment and to reduce behaviors that may transmit infection.

We recognize that treating patients infected with HIV who immigrate to the United States will incur costs for the public sector. It is inequitable, however, to use cost as a reason to exclude people infected with HIV, for there are no similar exclusionary policies for those with other costly chronic diseases, such as heart disease or cancer.

Rather than arbitrarily restrict the movement of a subgroup of infected people, we must dedicate ourselves to the principles of justice, scientific cooperation, and a global response to the HIV pandemic.

Adapted from *New England Journal of Medicine*, "Screening Immigrants and International Travelers for the Human Immuno-deficiency Virus," © 1990 *New England Journal of Medicine*.

1. The passage indicates that countries in the western Pacific have:

   A. a very high frequency of HIV-positive immigrants and thus a greater reason to be concerned over this issue than other countries.
   B. opposed efforts on the part of the United States to establish travel restrictions on HIV-positive foreigners.
   C. established travel restrictions on HIV-positive foreigners in an effort to maintain the relatively low HIV seroprevalence in those countries.
   D. continued to obstruct efforts to unify policy concerning immigrant screening.

2. With which of the following conclusions would the authors most likely agree?

   A. It is unjust to exclude people based on their serological status without determining whether such people pose a threat to the health of the general public.
   B. US regulations should require more stringent testing to be implemented at all major border crossings.
   C. It is the responsibility of the public sector to absorb the costs incurred by treatment of immigrants infected with HIV.
   D. The HIV pandemic is overstated and screening immigrants is not indicated.

3. With regard to travel restrictions placed on HIV-positive individuals, it can be inferred from the passage that:

   A. countries with low seroprevalence have a disproportionate and unjustified concern over the spread of AIDS by immigration.
   B. the United States' policy may have an unintended negative impact on research related to HIV.
   C. current law is sufficient for prudent handling of a potentially hazardous international issue.
   D. actions by western Pacific and Mediterranean countries to prevent the transmission of disease by restriction of the flow of travel are ineffective.

4. As it is used in the passage, the expression "casual transmission" (paragraph 4) most likely refers in part to:

   A. non-sexual transmission of infection.
   B. transmission of infection through casual sexual and non-sexual relationships.
   C. frequent transmission of infection.
   D. transmission of infection based on intimate physical contact alone.

5. The author explains that "the country with the broadest policy of testing and excluding foreigners is the United States," a country in which the seroprevalence of HIV is markedly higher than other countries with such stringent restrictions. Which of the following, if true, would most justify this US policy?

   A. The US spends more money on AIDS research than any other country.
   B. The individual immigration policies of a given country are not an issue when dealing with a global affliction such as HIV.
   C. The US has a low rate of chronic diseases in comparison with most other countries.
   D. US citizens on average tend to engage in practices that easily transmit HIV more than do citizens of other countries.

## Passage II (Questions 6-10)

The religious group known as the Shakers made a number of important contributions to American culture. They were descended from a small English sect that appeared in the early to middle eighteenth century. The English Shakers were radical millenialists; they believed the second coming of Christ was going to occur momentarily. In America, the mother colony was established at New Lebanon, New York. By the 1830s, twenty settlements in seven states had a combined membership of approximately six thousand.

Beginning in 1837, religious services in the Shaker communities became wildly ecstatic. Relatively formalized proceedings were replaced by spontaneous and violent "shaking and turning." In almost every service, members fell into trances and spoke in strange languages, which were believed by the Shakers to convey messages from the spirit world.

The Shakers had many unique features as a religious group that separated them from other sects; they largely banned sexual intercourse among themselves, and to enforce the policy they segregated men and women in most economic and social activities. Some schools of psychology might attribute the frenzy of the Shaker ceremonies to repressed sexuality. Professor Applebaum, for example, known for his in-depth studies of the psychological nature of religion and religious feeling, has said that when deeply religious people begin to throw themselves about physically, they are manifesting an understandable desire for direct physical communion with their peers, for whom they naturally feel affection. Chastity was, by and large, the rule among Shakers and with their ecstatic dancing, the Shakers may have been expressing for each other that which less restricted peoples express in more direct fashion.

That Shaker ceremonies should have become highly charged with energy during the 1830s may, on the other hand, need no such elaborate explanation, since that period was a time in which religious revivalism swept the country at large. The Shakers might simply have been affected by the broader national trend, their outburst of enthusiasm showing, perhaps, that they were not, as many believed, totally separated from the rest of the world. Since Shakers were already intensely devout, their revivals were even more frantic than those taking place within other faiths.

The Shakers valued simplicity in all things, and this ideal became the basis for much creative achievement. The Shakers believed in function, not extravagance. They believed in use, not show. Shaker artisans designed buildings and furnishings without ornamentation. Their art and architecture is characterized by spareness and economy.

In the eyes of modern art critics and historians, Shaker handiwork achieved an elegance and purity of form that ranks their handiwork among the best loved in America. Great art created by a people or by an individual, of course, is usually a product of some deep and abiding faith, and commentators observe that the power of the Shaker faith is manifest in the clarity and ease of the Shaker work. The Shakers do not, however, represent the only instance of this general principle. Witness, for example, Michelangelo's work on the Sistine Chapel.

6. Why did Shaker architecture and furniture lack ornamentation?

   A. Shakers were skilled at creating great art with limited resources.
   B. Shakers placed a high value on cleanliness and order.
   C. Shakers believed simplicity was more decorative than elaborate design.
   D. The Shakers believed that objects should serve a practical purpose and should not be decorative.

7. Which of the following, if true, would *least weaken* Applebaum's interpretation of the Shakers' religious ceremonies?

   A. The Shakers had a relatively high degree of contact and communication with other religious sects.
   B. The English Shakers, before migrating to America, did not enforce a strict separation of the sexes.
   C. While chastity was a fundamental aspect of Shaker faith in theory, there was little compliance with that dogma in practice.
   D. Shakers were known to be cold and unaffectionate people.

8. Assume that a piece of Shaker furniture is on display at a metropolitan museum. On the basis of information contained in the passage, the piece would most likely be characterized by:

   A. religious figurines and illustrations.
   B. impractical design.
   C. absence of ornate features.
   D. suitability for a single purpose only.

9. According to the passage, the great art of the Shakers arose from their deep faith. What evidence is given that this is true in other cases as well?

   A. Michelangelo's painting of the Sistine Chapel
   B. The claim that great art is characterized by simplicity
   C. Ecstatic Shakers' religious services
   D. The highly valued art of devout Shakers

10. Given the author's statements, if a team of archeologists found a number of great and elaborate works of art on a previously unexplored site, the find would most likely indicate that the people who had occupied the site:

   A. held deep religious beliefs.
   B. were enthusiastic and energetic.
   C. were relatively sophisticated.
   D. did not believe in ornamentation.

## Passage III (Questions 11-17)

There is one thing a professor can be absolutely certain of: almost every student entering the university believes, or says he believes, that truth is relative. If this belief is put to the test, one can count on the students' reaction: they will be uncomprehending. They are unified only in their relativism and in their allegiance to equality. The relativity of truth is not a theoretical insight but a moral postulate, the condition of a free society, or so they see it. They have all been equipped with this framework early on, and it is the modern replacement for the inalienable natural rights that used to be the traditional American grounds for a free society. Relativism is necessary to openness; and this is the virtue, the only virtue, which all primary education for more than fifty years has dedicated itself to inculcating. Openness is the great insight of our times. Now, the true believer is seen as the real danger. The study of history and culture now teaches that all the world was mad in the past; men always thought they were right, and that led to wars, persecutions, slavery, xenophobia, racism, and chauvinism. The point is not to correct the mistakes and really be right; rather it is not to think you are right at all.

Every educational system has a moral goal that it tries to attain and that informs its curriculum. It wants to produce a certain kind of human being. We began with the model of the rational and industrious man, who was honest, respected the laws, and was dedicated to the family. Above all he was to know the rights doctrine; the Constitution, which embodied it; and American history, which presented and celebrated the founding of a nation "conceived in liberty and dedicated to the proposition that all men are created equal." A powerful attachment to the letter and the spirit of the Declaration of Independence gently conveyed, appealing to each man's reason, was the goal of the education of democratic man. This called for something very different from the kinds of attachment required for traditional communities where myth and passion as well as severe discipline, authority, and the extended family produced an instinctive, unqualified, even frantic patriotism, unlike the reflected, rational, calm, even self-interested loyalty—not so much to the country but to the form of government and its rational principles—required in the United States. This was an entirely new experiment in politics, and with it came a new education. This education has now evolved in the last half-century from the education of democratic man to the education of the democratic personality.

The recent education of openness pays no attention to natural rights or the historical origins of our regime, which are now thought to have been essentially flawed and regressive. It does not demand fundamental agreement or the abandonment of old or new beliefs in favor of the natural ones. But when there are no shared goals or vision of the public good, is the social contract any longer possible?

The reason for ethnocentrism is clear. Men must love and be loyal to their families and their peoples in order to preserve them. Only if they think their own things are good can they rest content with them. A very great narrowness is not incompatible with the health of an individual or a people, whereas with great openness it is hard to avoid decomposition.

Adapted from A. Bloom, *The Closing of the American Mind*, © 1987 Simon & Schuster.

11. What is the central thesis of the passage?

   A. Every educational system has as its goal the formation of a certain kind of character, and the creation of a particular kind of citizen.
   B. The prioritization of openness and relativism is one of the primary moral insights of our time.
   C. The moral standards that structure a society are often intertwined with the character of that society's educational system.
   D. The American educational system has developed in a way that may be destructive to the health of the nation as a whole.

12. The author indicates which of the following to be true of the modern university?

   A. All university students today, as they begin their college education, accept and/or profess a belief in the relative nature of truth.
   B. The university today is an arena for a debate between those who believe in a single standard that defines what is right and good, and those who believe that we must accept as legitimate a variety of moral systems.
   C. Few students question the validity of the value of openness that they were taught as children.
   D. No virtue but the value of openness has been taught in any primary school for the last fifty years.

13. In another part of the essay not included here, the author of the passage writes, "...tradition does provide a counterpoise to and a repair from the merely current, and contains the petrified remains of old wisdom (along with much that is not wisdom). The active presence of a tradition in a man's soul gives him a resource against the ephemeral, the kind of resource that only the wise can find simply within themselves." This statement is most likely to be:

    A. an extension of the author's arguments concerning the potentially corrosive effects of the education of the democratic personality.

    B. a description of a position posited by the author's opponents, who claim that an excessive respect for tradition perpetuates anachronistic beliefs that are no longer appropriate to today's modern world.

    C. a further illustration of the author's nostalgia for traditional communities structured around the extended family and based on clear systems of authority.

    D. a discussion of the importance of remaining open to and respectful of all ideas and beliefs, including those handed down to us from the founding fathers and our familial ancestors.

14. One point of contention between Northern and Southern states during the Constitutional Convention in 1787 was resolved by the agreement to count a slave as three-fifths of a person. Suppose that a historian were to convincingly demonstrate that this and other similar agreements show that the Constitution essentially represents not a shared vision of equality and liberty, but a practical political compromise. What effect would this have on the author's argument in the second paragraph of the passage?

    A. It would weaken his claim that ethnocentrism (loyalty to one's one family and people) is a necessary element in the construction and maintenance of a strong and unified nation.

    B. It would weaken his argument that Americans in earlier historical periods came to some fundamental agreement on basic beliefs and principles.

    C. It would strengthen his depiction of America as a nation historically committed to respecting and tolerating a diversity of beliefs and opinions.

    D. It would strengthen his claim that the educational system of today seeks to inculcate different ideas and virtues than did the schools of 100 years ago.

15. By "social contract" (paragraph 3), the author most probably means:

    A. the explicit laws and regulations which together constitute the legal code of a society.

    B. the belief that a free society cannot exist without true equality.

    C. the Constitution of the United States.

    D. general acceptance of the necessity of a certain level of ideological compromise for the well-being of the nation.

16. The author's discussion of the "democratic man" and the "democratic personality" (paragraph 2) suggests which of the following distinctions or contrasts?

    A. The democratic man was formed by his dedication to a particular political party, while the democratic personality is formed by dedication to particular political ideas.

    B. The democratic man was a true believer in the value of a particular type of political system, while the democratic personality believes that political systems should not value one belief more highly than another.

    C. The democratic man valued hard workers and rational thinkers most highly, while the democratic personality believes in the equality of all people.

    D. The democratic man was formed in the context of a traditional community characterized by passionate patriotism and devotion to the nation, while the democratic personality believes that such patriotism often leads to wars and persecution of others.

17. The passage suggests which of the following to be true about the relevance of history to the modern age?

    A. To make the national culture of today as strong as possible, it is important not to discuss mistakes that may have been made in the past.

    B. The unity of any national community is best maintained through identification with foundational documents similar to the Declaration of Independence and the US Constitution.

    C. To best preserve the unity of the nation and preserve the public good, we should both identify with and learn lessons from the history of our country.

    D. True believers present a danger to national security; radical or fanatical beliefs have often led to violence and destruction in the past.

## Passage IV (Questions 18-23)

The influence of external forces is obviously a crucial aspect of any analysis of the Peruvian military government during the 1968–1978 period. In spite of, or perhaps because of, the importance of the actions by foreign corporations and foreign governments, there is little consensus on how to interpret them. Were they a key determinant in the downfall of Velasco and the increasingly conservative policies of his successor or was foreign impact marginal, of little consequence in shaping the course of events in Peru? Did the military government's policies complement or contradict the interests of foreign capital?

At the risk of oversimplification, three major positions on these questions can be described: (1) government reforms were positive for international capitalists, and the capitalist response to the reforms was positive or at least neutral; (2) the reforms were negative, and the response was negative; and (3) the foreign sector was not particularly relevant—domestic factors provided the key to understanding the process.

Aníbal Quijano's early and influential study, *Nationalism and Capitalism in Peru*, directly challenged the widely held belief that the Peruvian generals were initiating a process that contradicted the [imperialist] interests of [foreign capital and governments]. Writing in 1970, Quijano argued that the reforms being made represented a change in the *form* of imperialist control rather than its elimination. He writes, "If this policy follows the same lines in the future, the result may well bring Peru a new mode of operating within the imperialist system, and an economic structure that is dependent in a new way."

A quite different approach is offered by Laura Guasti. Guasti emphasizes the negative aspects of the military government's policies toward foreign corporations. In her view, at the same time the corporations' interests were being challenged, the government was also pursuing an industrialization policy that required their help:

> Therefore the military government was challenging the basic motivations and interest of international corporations at the same time that it created a large requirement for precisely those resources most concentrated in the hands of international corporate groups. International corporations were thereby placed in strong positions to affect the achievement of industrialization goals and to pressure against the autonomy-producing policies.

A third position tends implicitly to relegate the foreign sector to a minor role by virtually ignoring it in discussions of the origins of Peru's political-economic crisis. Overwhelming emphasis is placed on internal factors as determinants of the process.

Aspects of each of these three positions are useful in trying to analyze the role of international capitalist forces vis-à-vis the Peruvian regime, but none of the three alone is satisfactory. I argue that the main influence of foreign capital on Peru came through the historical structuring of the socioeconomic system; short-term influences were of minimal importance. With respect to the effects of Peru's reforms on foreign capital, I see them as beneficial for maintaining a capitalist mode of production in the long run though harming various individual firms in the process.

Adapted from B. Stallings, "International Capitalism and the Peruvian Military Government," in *The Peruvian Experiment Reconsidered,* C. McClintock and A. F. Lowenthal, eds., © 1983 Princeton University Press.

18. The author's primary purpose in the passage is to:

    A. suggest that methodologies traditionally used to analyze political change are incomplete or inaccurate, and so cannot adequately capture the true causes and character of all political transformation.
    B. take issue with the claim that military governments in developing nations tend to act in the interests of foreign capital rather than to provide benefits to domestic populations.
    C. present and critique standard interpretations of a particular case, and argue for a more complex analytical approach.
    D. reject current explanations of a specific sequence of events, and propose a new and fundamentally distinct methodological framework.

19. The passage implies which of the following to be true about the author of *Nationalism and Capitalism in Peru*?

    A. He participated in the formation and implementation of Peruvian economic policy during the 1968–1978 period.
    B. He criticized the Peruvian generals' reforms on the basis that they did not sufficiently resist or weaken imperialist domination.
    C. He argued against majority opinion regarding the true effect of the military government's policies on Peruvian autonomy.
    D. He directly considered the question of whether or not the generals' policy vis-à-vis imperialist forces contributed to the regime's downfall.

20. Which of the following can be inferred regarding the nature of the economic reforms instituted by the Peruvian military regime, based on the author's analysis presented in the passage?

    A. They attempted to eliminate foreign influence over the Peruvian economy, and so contributed to the political autonomy of the nation.
    B. They negatively affected a certain number of foreign corporations who had economic interests in Peru.
    C. They had no real effect on the foreign sector and its activities in Peru, although a few firms may have suffered damages in the short run.
    D. They provided significant benefits to the domestic population, while at the same time disadvantaging certain foreign capitalist forces.

21. Which of the following statements best summarizes the main idea of the passage?

    A. Quijano and Guasti's approaches to explaining the causal role of foreign actors in the events of 1968–1978 in Peru are incomplete; other factors must also be taken into account.
    B. Scholars have provided useful models of the role of foreign actors in the sequence of events in Peru between 1968 and 1978; however, one must also take into account different actors and time frames.
    C. Any analysis of the success or failure of a regime must include both domestic and international forces; an exclusive focus on one or the other leads to an overly simplistic model that lacks true explanatory power.
    D. Despite some theorists' claims to the contrary, the Peruvian government's reforms between 1968 and 1978 in fact supported the long-term interests of foreign capital.

22. Based on the author's discussion in paragraph 6, which of the following scholars would be committing the same kind of error as those who advocate the third approach to explaining events as they unfolded in Peru?

    A. A psychologist who explains individual behavior without taking into account how that behavior is shaped by the social context and life history of that person
    B. An anthropologist who studies an isolated community without considering how his or her own presence affects the activities being observed
    C. A sociobiologist who publicly presents a theory of evolution without considering the ethical ramifications of his or her work
    D. A political scientist who argues that imperialist domination often has a long-term destructive effect on the development and stability of Third World nations

23. The author indicates that which of the following is not highly relevant to a consideration of the evolution and eventual fate of the Peruvian military regime?

    A. The perceptions of the participants
    B. The time at which reforms were implemented
    C. The socioeconomic history of the nation
    D. The immediate effects of the actions of foreign corporations

## Passage V (Questions 24-29)

A friend comes with poems to be criticized. "Be brutal," he says. "Be ruthless. Tear them apart." You smile and take the poems in your hand. Be brutal? Somehow you never feel brutal toward a poem, even when it obviously deserves brutality. Toward a human being, perhaps, now and then, but not toward a poem. You know that whatever else it may be, a poem itself is blameless for its content and usually represents its author's pride.... It lies there on the page so helpless to defend itself, at your mercy.

No, you could never really be brutal with a poem. And you suspect he knows you couldn't. What he really wants and hopes is that you will love his poems and recite their virtues. Ideally he himself would like to be brutal while you triumphantly defended his poems.

I have no love for the indecipherable poem, but for the indecipherable poet I often have a warm, friendly feeling. The indecipherable poet is usually a bright chap, someone worth knowing and worth watching. He is also often a college undergraduate majoring in English and in love with writing.

Consider the undergraduate's literature and writing courses. It is taken for granted that the significant poets are the difficult ones. So, what less can an undergraduate poet do than be difficult himself?

Difficulty, of course, is not the only virtue of great poets. They [must] give us passion, vision, [and] originality. None of these the undergraduate poet probably has, but he can be difficult, for difficulty is relatively easy to achieve. He can be as difficult as he wants to be. He need only give the words he uses a private set of meanings.

What I mean is, a poem that is very difficult to read may not have been difficult to write. If its young author feels pleased with himself, how can we blame him? He has produced something as difficult as anything by Ezra Pound. Why shouldn't he be pleased?

The young poet generally believes that poetic license privileges him to set forth any and every sort of linguistic construction he fancies. If his teacher ventures to criticize a phrase or a line, the author can say that the passage is exactly the way he wants it. Is it awkward? Well, he intended it to be awkward since awkwardness was needed at that point. This would be clear, he murmurs, to anyone who understood the poem.

Nobody can touch him. Nobody at all. He is safe. In an ever-threatening world full of old perils and new, such security is to be envied. To be able to sit tight and pretty on top of your poem, impregnable like a little castle perched on a steep rock....

I knew a poet once who defended poetry. Actually, he did more than defend poetry, he defended individual poems. Thus he went beyond Shelley and Sidney who were content to defend poetry in general and in the abstract. One might almost say there never was a poem this poet wouldn't defend. It must be frailty rather than beauty that arouses such pronounced devotion to the defense of an art. Yet I would say that a poem worth defending needs no defense, and a poem needing defense is not worth defending.

Adapted from R. Francis, "The Satirical Rogue" in *The Massachusetts Review*, Vol. 6 #3 © 1965.

24. Based on the passage, if one were to attempt to describe the sort of poet and the sort of poem that the author admires, what qualities would they most likely possess?

    A. The poet would be a defender of poetry and the poem would be largely indefensible.
    B. The poet would be enamored of writing and the poem would offer emotion and insight.
    C. The poet would be unwilling to discuss his poetry and the poem would be largely incomprehensible to anyone but the poet himself.
    D. The poet would be older and relatively mature and the poem would evidence youthfulness and optimism.

25. A psychological experiment found that relatively inexperienced poets who submit their work to more experienced poets and ask for comment generally become angry when the more experienced poet shows clear understanding of the poem and offers insightful critical comment. Based on the information provided by the author, this reaction is best explained by the fact that:

    A. poets dislike thoughtful criticism.
    B. poets tend to feel secure when they are young, but later realize that their poetry needs defense.
    C. young poets are especially likely to take criticism as a personal attack and to react defensively.
    D. inexperienced poets equate indecipherability with greatness; the comments of the critic would call into question the value and quality of the inexperienced poet's work.

26. Referring to younger poets, the author states, "He can be as difficult as he wants to be. He need only give the words he uses a private set of meanings" (paragraph 5). Which of the following situations would be most analogous to the situation described by the author?

    A. A young woman who cannot read Braille is puzzled by the patterns of its raised dots.
    B. A court stenographer uses her own eccentric abbreviations to record the proceedings.
    C. A mathematics student copies from a book countless formulas he does not understand.
    D. A lighthouse that warns passing ships of the impending, dangerous shoreline.

27. Among the following insights, which would most *weaken* the assertion that great poems always express passion?

    A. A great many art forms other than poetry evoke passion from those who experience them.
    B. There is no known physiological association between the ability to write poetry and the capacity to experience passion.
    C. Many passionate people neither write nor appreciate poetry.
    D. Ezra Pound's poems are most admired for their steely precision and dispassionate logic.

28. The passage indicates that the novice who writes poetry believes his work to be immune to attack. Which of the author's statements best explains this phenomenon?

    A. It must be frailty rather than beauty that arouses such pronounced devotion to the defense of an art.
    B. The young poet often regards poetic license as the privilege to set forth any sort of linguistic construction he may fancy.
    C. The indecipherable poet is usually a bright chap, someone worth knowing and worth watching.
    D. Ideally he himself would like to be brutal while you triumphantly defended his poems.

29. The author implies that poems are usually a manifestation of:

    A. defensiveness.
    B. innocence.
    C. pride.
    D. brutality.

_____

## Passage VI (Questions 30-36)

The capacity to deal effectively with syphilis and tuberculosis represents a milestone in human endeavor, even though full use of this potential has not yet been made. And there are, of course, other examples: the treatment of endocrinological disorders with appropriate hormones, the prevention of various nutritional disorders, and perhaps just around the corner the management of Parkinsonism and sickle-cell anemia. There are other examples, but the truth is that there are nothing like as many as the public has been led to believe.

The point to be made about this kind of technology—the real high technology of medicine—is that it comes as the result of a genuine understanding of disease mechanisms, and when it becomes available, it is relatively inexpensive, and relatively easy to deliver.

Offhand, I cannot think of any important human disease for which medicine possesses the outright capacity to prevent or cure where the cost of the technology is itself a major problem. The price is never as high as the cost of managing the same diseases during the earlier stages of no-technology or halfway technology. If a case of typhoid fever had to be managed today by the best methods of 1935, it would run to a staggering expense. At, say, around fifty days of hospitalization, requiring the most demanding kind of nursing care, I should think $10,000 would be a conservative estimate for the illness, as contrasted with today's cost of a bottle of chloramphenicol and a day or two of fever. The halfway technology that was evolving for poliomyelitis in the early 1950s, just before the emergence of the basic research that made the vaccine possible, provides another illustration of the point. Do you remember Sister Kenny, and the cost of those institutes for rehabilitation, with all those ceremonially applied hot fomentations, and the debates about whether the affected limbs should be totally immobilized or kept in passive motion as frequently as possible, and the masses of statistically tormented data mobilized to support one view or the other? It is the cost of that kind of technology, and its relative effectiveness, that must be compared with the cost and effectiveness of the vaccine.

Pulmonary tuberculosis had similar episodes in its history. There was a sudden enthusiasm for the surgical removal of infected lung tissue in the early 1950s, and elaborate plans were being made for new and expensive installations for major pulmonary surgery in tuberculosis hospitals, and then INH and streptomycin came along and the hospitals themselves were closed up.

It is when physicians are bogged down by their incomplete technologies, by the innumerable things they are obliged to do in medicine when they lack a clear understanding of disease mechanisms, that the deficiencies of the health-care system are most conspicuous. If I were a policy-maker, interested in saving money for health care over the long haul, I would regard it as an act of high prudence to give high priority to a lot more basic research in biologic science. This is the only way to get the full mileage that biology owes to the science of medicine, even though it seems, as used to be said in the days when the phrase still had some meaning, like asking for the moon.

Adapted from L. Thomas, *The Lives of a Cell,* © 1974 The Viking Press.

**30.** Which of the following would most *challenge* the veracity of the author's argument?

A. Very costly germ-free "isolation houses" are found to indefinitely prevent HIV-positive patients from dying of full-blown AIDS.

B. Heart disease is preventable to a greater extent by non-medical means, such as dietary change, than by medical means.

C. A custom-designed, genetically-engineered interferon molecule can be formed at great expense to cure certain bronchial diseases.

D. Public health measures such as sewage treatment are claimed by some to have been more instrumental than medical science in extending longevity.

**31.** What can be inferred from the passage about examples of "the real high technology of medicine" (paragraph 2)?

A. They are actually inexpensive and do not utilize technology.

B. They include treatment of tuberculosis, Parkinsonism, and sickle-cell anemia.

C. The ways in which they have been publicized may have been misleading.

D. They are more costly than less effective treatments.

**32.** Which of the following controversial medical issues or procedures would the author most likely NOT support?

A. Legislation allowing voluntary, patient-directed euthanasia

B. Increasing the national budget for human genome/genetic mapping research

C. Providing expensive treatment to people currently suffering from Parkinsonism

D. Increasing the percentage of research dollars spent on finding better ways to lessen the severity of sickle-cell anemia symptoms

**33.** By claiming that asking for more basic research is like "asking for the moon" (paragraph 5), the author most likely suggests that:

A. there is less money than there used to be for basic medical research.

B. it is likely that health care policy-makers would be reluctant to spend money on basic research rather than on clinical applications.

C. medical breakthroughs are very difficult to achieve without basic research.

D. finding cures for many diseases seems as far away as getting to the moon once did.

**34.** The passage suggests which of the following about the relation between basic research and clinical medicine?

A. Although clinical application is the true fruit of medical science, from a funding point of view we must focus more on its roots in basic research.

B. Although basic research is the high technology of medical science, we must keep the practical goal of treatment in mind.

C. Supportive therapy is an unacceptable societal expenditure of money that should go to basic research.

D. Basic science research, though desirable, is less cost-effective than clinical medicine and thus funding of research should be scrutinized carefully.

**35.** According to the passage, each of the following diseases is or once was very costly to treat EXCEPT:

A. sickle-cell anemia.

B. poliomyelitis.

C. tuberculosis.

D. typhoid.

**36.** The author uses the example of Sister Kenny in order to suggest that:

A. medical treatment is better applied by trained doctors than by caregivers who are not physicians.

B. a lack of true knowledge can make the cost of medical care very high.

C. some medical treatments are expensive because they do much more than is necessary.

D. medical caregivers who fail to provide the best available treatments should be reprimanded.

## Passage VII (Questions 37-42)

A growing taste for shark steaks and shark-fin soup has for the first time in 400 million years put the scourge of the sea at the wrong end of the food chain. Commercial landings of this toothsome fish have doubled every year since 1986, and shark populations are plunging.

It is hardly a case of good riddance. Sharks do for gentler fish what lions do for the wildebeest: they check populations by feeding on the weak. Also, sharks apparently do not get cancer and may therefore harbor clues to the nature of that disease.

Finally, there is the issue of motherhood. Sharks are viviparous. That is, they bear their young alive and swimming (not sealed in eggs) after gestation periods lasting from nine months to two years. Shark mothers generally give birth to litters of from eight to 12 pups and bear only one litter every other year.

That is why sharks have one of the lowest fecundity rates in the ocean. The female cod, for example, spawns annually and lays a few million eggs at a time. If three quarters of the cod were to be fished this year, they could be back in full force in a few years. But if humans took that big a bite out of the sharks, the population would not recover for 15 years.

So, late this summer, if all goes according to plan, the shark will join the bald eagle and the buffalo on the list of managed species. The federal government will cap the US commercial catch at 5,800 metric tons, about half of the 1989 level, and limit sportsmen to two sharks per boat. Another provision discourages finning, the harvesting of shark fins alone, by limiting the weight of fins to 7 percent of that of all the carcasses.

Finning got under the skin of environmentalists, and the resulting anger helped to mobilize support for the new regulations. Finning itself is a fairly recent innovation. Shark fins contain noodle-like cartilaginous tissues that Chinese chefs have traditionally used to thicken and flavor soup. Over the past few years rising demand in Hong Kong has made the fins as valuable as the rest of the fish. Long strands are prized, so unusually large fins can be worth considerably more to the fisherman than the average price of about $10 a pound.

But can US quotas save shark species that wander the whole Atlantic? The blue shark, for example, migrates into the waters of something like 23 countries. John G. Casey, a biologist with the National Marine Fisheries Service Research Center in Narragansett, R.I., admits that international coordination will eventually be necessary. But he supports US quotas as a first step in mobilizing other nations. Meanwhile the commercial fishermen are not waiting for the new rules to take effect. "There's a pre-quota rush on sharks," Casey says, "and it's going on as we speak."

Adapted from *Scientific American,* "Man Bites Shark," © 1990 Scientific American.

37. According to the passage, shark populations are at greater risk than cod populations because:

    A. sharks are now being eaten more than cod.
    B. the shark reproductive rate is lower than that of the cod.
    C. sharks are quickly becoming fewer in number.
    D. sharks are now as scarce as bald eagles and buffalo.

38. According to the passage, a sizable decrease in shark populations:

    I. might cause some fish populations to go unchecked.
    II. would significantly hamper cancer research.
    III. might take decades to recover from.

    A. I only
    B. II and III only
    C. I and III only
    D. I, II, and III

39. The passage implies that the commercial catch of sharks before the proposed federal government cap was approximately:

    A. 5,800 metric tons.
    B. more than two sharks per boat.
    C. almost three quarters of the shark population.
    D. 11,600 metric tons.

40. The passage suggests that commercial shark fishing has had which of the following effects?

    A. Sharks will soon be placed on the endangered species list.
    B. US quotas on shark fishing will not be effective in protecting certain species of shark.
    C. Some practices of Chinese chefs have angered environmentalists.
    D. Several countries have agreed to coordinate their efforts to protect shark populations.

41. The announcement of US quotas on shark fishing has led to which of the following results?

    A. The quotas will have a negative impact on cancer research in the US
    B. Sharks are again becoming far more dangerous to other fish than we are to them.
    C. More chefs are now using the cartilaginous tissues found in shark fins.
    D. The number of sharks killed after the announcement, but before the quotas take effect, has increased.

42. Based on the information in the passage, which of the following seems to be a characteristic of sharks that makes it more difficult to save them?

    A. Their predatory habits
    B. Their migratory habits
    C. Their large fins
    D. Their ability to bear live young

## Passage VIII (Questions 43-47)

Linguistics is the science of language, and the word *science* is significant in this context. A scientific description is one that is carried out systematically, on the basis of objectively verifiable observations and within the framework of some general theory. This modern view of the study of language began to develop in opposition to the earlier investigations which were largely subjective, speculative, and unsystematic.

Traditional grammar originated in Greece in the fifth century B.C. Since its beginnings, it has been intimately connected with philosophy and literary criticism. At various times, either the literary or the philosophical influence has been predominant. Together, they have shaped the attitudes with which scholars have approached the study of language. When modern linguists claim autonomy for their subject, they ask to be allowed to take an objective look at language. The Bloomfieldian school of linguistics, dominant in the United States following the Second World War, was in part a vehement expression of linguistic innovation. It rejected traditional grammar as a basis for the study of language.

Early Western grammarians were mainly concerned with the texts of classical Greek writers. These scholars thus concentrated on the written language, which they believed to be of prime importance. Speech was regarded as an imperfect copy of the written language. In contrast, most linguists of today take it as axiomatic that speech is primary and that the written word is secondary. The range of sounds that can be produced by the "speech organs" is the medium in which language is embodied. Every known language existed first in spoken form, whereas thousands of languages have never, or at least not until recent times, been committed to writing. Without any training, children acquire the spoken language before they learn to read and write. Indeed, previous acquisition of the spoken language seems to be a necessary basis for successful instruction in the written language.

Modern linguists do not, however, contend that written language is wholly derived from the spoken. The conditions in which written language is used are different from the conditions in which the spoken language is used. For example, there is no face-to-face engagement of the reader and writer. Information that is normally carried by gestures and facial expressions accompanying speech must be conveyed in writing, and conventions of punctuation, for example, have been developed to answer the purpose.

The primacy of the spoken language over the written is further evidenced by the fact that all human beings utilize the "speech organs" for language production in a way that is as natural as breathing or walking. Although the lungs are used in respiration, the teeth in mastication, and so on, an evolutionary event, remote in human development, made possible the collective functioning of these structures and the vocal cords for spoken communication. It has been theorized that there is genetic programming influencing the coordination of various biological components into the "speech organs."

Common to all human languages is the capacity of the speaker to generate an infinite number of sentences he or she may never have heard before. This creative ability is called "open-endedness." It gives evidence of the superiority of human language over the languages of other animals and undoubtedly contributes to humankind's position on the earth.

**43.** According to the passage, early and modern grammarians would most likely *disagree* over which of the following statements?

- **A.** Every known language first appeared in written form.
- **B.** Grammar is associated with philosophy and/or literary criticism.
- **C.** The Bloomfieldian school of linguistics rejected traditional grammar.
- **D.** It is just as important to study gestures as to study punctuation.

**44.** It can most readily be inferred from the passage that speech is now regarded as the fundamental form of language because:

- **A.** people speak before they write.
- **B.** expression can be conveyed without punctuation.
- **C.** written grammar is less precise than spoken grammar.
- **D.** speech made a significant contribution to literature.

**45.** Implied in the passage is the assumption that:

- **A.** human beings cannot communicate with animals.
- **B.** no animal can truly communicate.
- **C.** animals have less need for communication than do human beings.
- **D.** human beings have a higher position on the earth than do animals.

**46.** In paragraph 3, the word axiomatic most nearly means:

- **A.** the rule.
- **B.** the exception.
- **C.** perfect truth.
- **D.** cutting-edge.

**47.** The author asserts that punctuation marks were developed, in part, because written communication offers no opportunity for:

- I. inflection.
- II. tone.
- III. face-to-face engagement.

- **A.** III only
- **B.** I and II only
- **C.** I and III only
- **D.** II and III only

## Passage IX (Questions 48-53)

Public opinion has pushed Isadora Duncan forward as the progenitor of modern American dance largely because of her strong impact upon the development of modern ballet via Fokine and other innovative Russian choreographers. Her work, however, does not truly represent all aspects of American modern dance. "If it had remained her exclusive responsibility," said John Martin, former *New York Times* dance critic, "there would be no American dance today." He nominates Denishawn, the company and school founded by Ruth St. Denis and Ted Shawn, as the "parent organization of the American dance." These two innovators sought inspiration for dance through the physical and spiritual exercises of both Eastern and Western cultures. From the East, St. Denis incorporated philosophies and practices, like yoga, from such distant lands as East India and Japan. Western influences included a more relaxed version of classical ballet as well as theories of expression developed by Delsarte. Denishawn was as eclectic as America itself. According to critic Walter Terry, the fifteen years of Denishawn's existence were extremely rich, busy, and successful. Most subsequent modern dance companies have, often somewhat unconsciously, modeled themselves after this organization.

Although conceding that modern dance originated with Denishawn, critic Walter Sorrell finds that "the spiritual rebellion that followed was more important." He considers the children of Denishawn to be the real pioneers of modern dance. This second generation boasted such illustrious members as Martha Graham, Louis Horst, Doris Humphrey, and Charles Weidman. These names may be more familiar than Ruth St. Denis and Ted Shawn in contemporary society. Indeed, Marcia Segal reinforces the relative unimportance of the founders of Denishawn in her belief that neither St. Denis nor Shawn was an outstanding choreographer. Of course, even upon the point of choreographic competence, dissenters glow in favor of St. Denis pieces such as "Radha" as one of the greatest works of this century.

It is hard to view the developments of Denishawn's descendants as a rebellion. One of the major premises expressed by Ted Shawn was a need for development of each talent individually. Accepting all styles, both from abroad and from within as a basis for creativity, Denishawn nurtured its heirs. Almost every major choreographer in modern dance today has roots in the Denishawn tradition through at least one of many routes. In fact, looking at revivals of Denishawn works, it is clear how strong an influence this lineage had on the succeeding generations. Those who underestimate these compositions have probably never witnessed them performed.

The mystical and exotic as well as the dramatic in St. Denis' works, some interesting in their own right, have been expanded upon by Martha Graham. Short and intense, this great dancer energized her movement with a strongly percussive attack alien to St. Denis' smooth quality. She also sought to internalize the dramatic in a more symbolic than literal context. Considered by many to be the most influential choreographer of our time, Martha Graham created a technique integrating the personal and the dramatic. Although she herself has denied any choreographic debt to Denishawn, anyone viewing "Serenata Morisca," a Ted Shawn solo she performed countless times, will witness Graham's strong ties to her dance heritage.

48. The primary purpose of the author of the passage is to discuss:

   A. the cultural influences of Eastern vs. Western dance movements.
   B. a debate over the role of Denishawn in the development of modern dance.
   C. the chronological progression of traditional dance forms.
   D. events in the lives of various choreographers.

49. On the basis of the information supplied in the passage, one can best conclude that American modern dance derives from:

   A. the Denishawn company.
   B. Eastern philosophies and practices.
   C. the insights and innovative works of Isadora Duncan.
   D. American eclecticism.

50. It can most readily be inferred from the passage that when critic Walter Sorrell states "the spiritual rebellion that followed was more important," he is referring to:

   A. the mystical approach to dance formulated by St. Denis.
   B. the work of Martha Graham, Charles Weidman and others.
   C. St. Denis's introduction of the science of yoga to the art of dance.
   D. Martha Graham's performance of "Serenata Morisca."

51. From the information contained in the passage, which of the following indicates that the Denishawn school affected even the greatest dancers?

   I. Martha Graham's performance of "Serenata Morisca"
   II. The development of modern ballet
   III. The claim that Isadora Duncan was not in fact the progenitor of modern dance

   A. I only
   B. II only
   C. I and II only
   D. I and III only

52. One can sensibly infer from the passage that Ted Shawn's philosophy of dance, as discussed in the third paragraph, included:

   A. the use of idealistic interpretation.
   B. innovative choreography that de-emphasized the individual dancer.
   C. the acceptance of many styles of dance.
   D. an attitude of rebellion.

53. The fact that public opinion recognizes Isadora Duncan as the progenitor of modern American dance would cast the most doubt on a claim that:

   A. Russian choreographers have had no influence on modern American dance.
   B. John Martin is a competent dance critic.
   C. the public is well informed about the origins of modern American dance.
   D. the work of Martha Graham reflects qualities of modern American dance.

## END OF TEST 3

# ANSWER KEY — TEST 3

| Passage I | Passage II | Passage III | Passage IV | Passage V | Passage VI | Passage VII | Passage VIII | Passage IX |
|---|---|---|---|---|---|---|---|---|
| 1. C | 6. D | 11. D | 18. C | 24. B | 30. C | 37. B | 43. D | 48. B |
| 2. A | 7. B | 12. C | 19. C | 25. D | 31. C | 38. C | 44. A | 49. A |
| 3. B | 8. C | 13. A | 20. B | 26. B | 32. D | 39. D | 45. D | 50. B |
| 4. A | 9. A | 14. B | 21. B | 27. D | 33. B | 40. B | 46. A | 51. A |
| 5. D | 10. A | 15. D | 22. A | 28. B | 34. A | 41. D | 47. A | 52. C |
|  |  | 16. B | 23. D | 29. C | 35. A | 42. B |  | 53. C |
|  |  | 17. C |  |  | 36. B |  |  |  |

# Test Assessment Log

Use this Log to evaluate your performance on this CARS Practice Test. Diagnose what led you to select (or seriously consider) wrong answers, or to spend more time than necessary to identify the correct answer.

Approximate the time you spent on the Now passages and on the Later passages. Consider if you are spending the time needed on easier passages to get most of those questions right, or, if you are spending more time than necessary and not getting to as many questions as you could while still maintaining good accuracy. If you find that you are spending most of your 90 minutes on harder passages with a low level of accuracy, consider how best to reapportion your time on your next practice test. Finally, evaluate your ranking; are you choosing the right passages and doing them at roughly the right time within the section?

## Now Passages

| Now Passage # | Q # and Type (for questions you got wrong) | Attractors (for wrong answers you picked or seriously considered) | What did you do wrong? |
|---|---|---|---|
| | | | |
| | | | |
| | | | |
| | | | |
| | | | |
| | | | |

Approximate time spent on Now passages _____

Total Now passages attempted _____

Total # of Q's on Now passages attempted _____

Total # of Now Q's correct _____

% correct of Now Q's attempted _____

## Later Passages

| Later Passage # | Q # and Type (for questions you got wrong) | Attractors (for wrong answers you picked or seriously considered) | What did you do wrong? |
|---|---|---|---|
| | | | |
| | | | |
| | | | |
| | | | |
| | | | |
| | | | |

Approximate time spent on Later passages _____

Total Later passages attempted _____

Total # of Q's on Later passages attempted _____

Total # of Later Q's correct _____

% correct of Later Q's attempted _____

# Final Analysis

Total # of passages attempted (including partially completed) _____

Total # of questions attempted _____

Total # of correct answers _____

Total % correct of attempted questions _____

## Revised Strategy

| | |
|---|---|
| **Pacing** | |
| **Passage choice/ranking** | |
| **Working the Passage** | |
| **Attacking the Questions** | |

# MCAT
# Critical Analysis and Reasoning Skills

# Practice Test 3
# Solutions

# TEST 3 SOLUTIONS

## Passage I
This is a Now passage.

**Bottom Line:** Rather than excluding those infected with HIV, the US should cooperate in global response to the disease.

1.  C      This is an Inference question.
    - A:    No. Countries in the western Pacific have a relatively low incidence of HIV infection (paragraph 2).
    - B:    No. The US has been criticized by national and international organizations (paragraph 2); the nations of the western Pacific are not mentioned in this context.
    - **C:    Yes. See paragraph 2.**
    - D:    No. Obstructionist efforts are not mentioned in the passage.

2.  A      This is an Inference question.
    - **A:    Yes. See paragraph 4.**
    - B:    No. The authors argue that even the existing restrictions are unnecessary and unfair.
    - C:    No. The authors admit that medical costs will be incurred by the public sector, but they do not argue that it is the responsibility of the public sector to pay.
    - D:    No. The authors never claim that the pandemic has been "overstated."

3.  B      This is an Inference question.
    - A:    No. This is too extreme. The authors do claim that travel restrictions exist primarily in the western Pacific and the Mediterranean, and that those regions have relatively low HIV seroprevalence, but they never comment on the severity of the restrictions in those countries in general. Therefore they do not imply that those restrictions are "disproportionate."
    - **B:    Yes. The authors state that US policy has been criticized by organizations who are "boycotting international meetings...vital for the study of prevention, education, and treatment of HIV..." (paragraph 2). These indirect consequences of US policy may negatively affect progress in HIV research.**
    - C:    No. The authors' references to "inequitable" exclusion and to "arbitrary" restriction of movement (paragraphs 5 and 6) contradict the assertion of "prudent handling."
    - D:    No. The authors never address the issue of the effectiveness of other countries' measures.

4.  A      This is an Inference question.
    - **A:    Yes. Such an interpretation would justify the authors' claim that all of the sexually transmitted diseases should be removed from the list.**
    - B:    No. The authors never mention relationships, casual or otherwise—and if this were their criterion, there would be no reason to exclude gonorrhea, for example, from the list.
    - C:    No. The authors never mention frequency.
    - D:    No. "Intimate physical contact" is not considered casual by the author.

5.  D    This is a Strengthen question.
    A:    No. In order to justify the US policy, a situation in which the US requires such stringent restrictions must be established. The amount of money the US spends on AIDS research does not accomplish this.
    B:    No. This does not address the subject at hand, it simply dismisses the issue.
    C:    No. Chronic diseases are out of the scope of the passage.
    **D:    Yes. If this were true, the US population would be at greater risk of a widespread HIV epidemic than would be other countries. Hence, stringent policies would be more justified.**

## Passage II
This is a Now passage.

**Bottom Line:** The Shakers had unique characteristics; belief in simplicity and deep religious faith led them to create great art.

6.  D    This is an Inference question.
    A:    No. The author never indicates that the Shakers had limited resources with which to work. They avoided ornamentation out of a belief in simplicity, not out of necessity.
    B:    No. Shakers valued order at one time but not at all times in their history (paragraph 2), and order is not presented by the author as a reason for the simplicity of Shaker works. Furthermore, cleanliness is never mentioned.
    C:    No. Shakers believed in absence of decoration (paragraph 5), not that simplicity was more decorative.
    **D:    Yes. The Shakers believed in "function, not extravagance" (paragraph 5).**

7.  B    This is a LEAST Weaken question.
          Note: The credited response will NOT weaken Applebaum's explanation.
    A:    No. This would weaken Applebaum's claims by suggesting that the real reason for the Shakers' ecstatic ceremonies may have been the influence of a "broader national trend" of revivalism (see paragraph 4), not repressed sexuality.
    **B:    Yes. This claim would be consistent with Applebaum's argument that repressed sexuality was the cause. A correlation between increased separation of the sexes (if the English Shakers did not segregate the sexes but the American Shakers did) and the changes in Shaker ceremonies (after they migrated) would strengthen, not weaken, his interpretation.**
    C:    No. If the Shakers in reality were not especially chaste, there would be no reason to believe that their sexuality was unusually repressed (paragraph 3).
    D:    No. Applebaum argues that ecstatic dancing may have been a way in which the sexually repressed Shakers expressed the affection for each other that "less restricted people express in a more direct fashion" (paragraph 3). However, if the Shakers were unaffectionate by nature, it would undermine this interpretation.

8.  C    This is a New Information question.
    A:    No. Shaker furniture was characterized by a lack of ornamentation. Therefore, one would not expect illustrations and figurines on such a piece.
    B:    No. Shaker furniture was built to be functional (paragraph 5), which would entail a practical design.
    **C:    Yes. Shaker furniture was designed "without ornamentation" (paragraph 5).**
    D:    No. The issue of multiple uses for single pieces is never discussed.

9.  A     This is a Structure question.
    A:    **Yes. Michelangelo's painting is offered as evidence that the relationship between great art and faith acts as a general principle, and that it is not limited to the Shakers (paragraph 6).**
    B:    No. The author never claims that all great art is characterized by simplicity, nor does he or she connect simplicity to deep faith in general terms.
    C:    No. The correct answer will go beyond the particular case of the Shakers and their art.
    D:    No. The correct response will show how the relationship between great art and deep faith exists in cases other than that of the Shakers.

10. A     This is a New Information question.
    A:    **Yes. The author states that great art is usually produced by people who have a deep faith (paragraph 6). Thus these works would likely have been produced by people with great faith. The fact that they are elaborate is irrelevant; the author does not argue that great art must always be simple.**
    B:    No. The Shakers were energetic, but the author does not argue that energy and enthusiasm give rise to great art.
    C:    No. The Shakers were not especially sophisticated, and they produced great art. The author makes no causal connection between great art and sophistication.
    D:    No. This is a characteristic specific to the Shakers. The author proposes deep faith, not simplicity, as a generator of great art (paragraph 6).

# Passage III

This is a Later/Killer passage.

**Bottom Line:** Unfortunately the US educational system has shifted from commitment to shared ideals to commitment to openness to all ideas.

11. D     This is a Main Idea question.
    A:    No. This choice is too narrow. It is directly supported by the passage in the beginning of paragraph 2, but represents only one piece of the author's overall argument.
    B:    No. This choice is not consistent with the passage. The author asserts that openness and relativism are taken as "moral postulates" (not theoretical insights) by the students (paragraph 1). The author himself does not accept those beliefs as morally insightful.
    C:    No. This choice is too broad. While the author does posit this interrelationship as a general rule (paragraph 2), the passage as a whole explores its meaning for one particular case—the United States.
    D:    **Yes. The first two paragraphs describe why and how the educational system has come to inculcate relativism in its students, and the final two paragraphs indicate how this could be destructive to the social contract and national cohesion.**

12. C   This is an Inference question.
   A:   No. The word "all" makes this choice too extreme. According to the passage, this is true of "almost every student" (first sentence).
   B:   No. The author identifies an almost unanimous belief in relativism (as opposed to belief that a particular truth stands above all others) on today's campuses. The students are not debating the issue; they for the most part accept it as true without question (first half of the first paragraph).
   **C:   Yes. See the first half of the first paragraph. According to the author, students have all been educated in the "moral postulates" of relativity of truth and of openness. Most accept it without question, often without an understanding that it could even be open to question.**
   D:   No. The author states that openness is the only virtue that *all* early education teaches, not that it is the only virtue taught in any school (paragraph 1).


13. A   This is a New Information question.
   **A:   Yes. The passage claims that the historical origins of the United States and the belief in natural rights bound up with those origins are neither taught nor respected within the education of the "democratic personality" (second half of the second paragraph). The quote provided in the question suggests that this disappearance of traditional beliefs (such as those described in paragraph 2) may entail the loss of a source of individual strength of character.**
   B:   No. This choice takes the word "petrified" out of context. The quote uses the word to communicate the idea that bits of wisdom from the past have hardened into lasting and "active" beliefs, carried on through the generations. This answer choice is inconsistent with the quote's portrayal of those beliefs as active, alive, and useful today. Don't be misled by the word "tradition"—while the author argues in the passage that the moral standards of "traditional communities" may not be relevant to a modern democratic state (paragraph 2), this does not apply to all traditions or ideas from the past.
   C:   No. See the middle of paragraph 2. The author has no nostalgia for traditional communities, which are based on ideas and beliefs quite different from those of the "democratic man." Rather, he regrets the waning of the tradition of natural rights as it is expressed in the Constitution and Declaration of Independence.
   D:   No. The author criticizes relativism, or the belief that one must remain open to and accepting of all ideas and values held by others.

14.   B   This is a New Information question.

A:   No. A demonstration that the Constitution did not truly represent a shared belief in equality and liberty would not, by itself, significantly undermine the author's claim that such shared visions are generally necessary for national unity.

B:   **Yes. The author argues that the education of the "democratic man" was founded on belief in and attachment to basic principles (the rights doctrine) embodied in the Constitution (middle of paragraph 2). If the Constitution did not in fact embody some shared vision of rights and liberty, it would undermine the author's claim that this education involved a coming together in the belief in certain basic truths to be held above all others.**

C:   No. This choice misrepresents the author's views. He argues that Americans in the past were committed to certain *particular* beliefs, rather to a belief in openness (relativism) to all points of view (middle of paragraph 2).

D:   No. The new information in the question stem is inconsistent with the author's argument that the Constitution represents ideals that were in the past commonly held and defended. Therefore, it would undermine rather than strengthen the author's argument about changes in education.

15.   D   This is an Inference question.

A:   No. The author makes no reference to explicit legal codes as constituting the social contract.

B:   No. This choice takes words out of context of the passage. The American social contract is (or was) based in part in a coming together in the belief that we are all created equal (paragraph 2), but the contract itself is not reducible to a belief in equality.

C:   No. The social contract is based on belief in the ideas expressed in the Constitution. The contract is not the actual document itself.

D:   **Yes. The author fears that relativism, or lack of agreement on certain fundamental truths, will weaken or destroy the social contract (paragraphs 3 and 4). The social contract is not a written code or document, but a willingness to compromise some of one's individual beliefs in the service of a "shared goal or vision of the public good" (end of paragraph 3).**

16.   B   This is an Inference question.

A:   No. The democratic man was formed by dedication to "a form of government and its rational principles" (second half of paragraph 2), not to a particular political party.

B:   **Yes. The democratic man was educated to believe in the natural rights and principles embodied in the Constitution, the Declaration of Independence, and in the history of the United States (paragraph 2). The democratic personality is educated in relativism, the belief that no one belief is more "true" than another (middle of paragraph 1).**

C:   No. The democratic man believes that "all men are created equal" (middle of paragraph 2). This is not a distinction between the two. The point of contrast is that the democratic man does not accept that all beliefs or principles are created equal.

D:   No. The democratic man was formed with an attachment to the "letter and spirit of the Declaration of Independence," that is, with loyalty to certain ideas and to a *type* of government (paragraph 2). The author contrasts this education with "the kinds of attachment required for traditional communities," which include passionate patriotism and unthinking loyalty to a particular country.

17.    C      This is an Inference question.

      A:      No. This statement is too extreme. The author suggests (through his discussion of the relativist view of the past at the end of paragraph 1) that he believes we should correct our historical mistakes and "really be right." He clearly wishes to celebrate the historical origins of the nation (paragraph 3), but never suggests that past mistakes should be hidden or forgotten.

      B:      No. He identifies the ideas in these documents as a source of the American social contract and national unity (paragraphs 3 and 4). He does not, however, indicate that *all* national communities should be defined through *similar* foundational documents.

      **C:      Yes. The author views our history as a source of identity and unity (first half of paragraph 2), and indicates that we should also learn from it in order to correct our mistakes and "really be right." This is in contrast to the relativists who, according to the author, wish to disassociate from our past. In the author's view, relativism teaches that we should not hold or defend true beliefs in the first place, as opposed to implementing our true beliefs by learning from and correcting our mistakes.**

      D:      No. This choice presents the author's depiction of relativist beliefs, not the ideas held by the author himself (end of paragraph 1).

# Passage IV

This is a Later passage.

**Bottom Line:** Relationship of foreign actors to Peruvian military gov't not purely positive, negative, or neutral —have to consider more complex factors.

18.    C      This is a Primary Purpose question.

      A:      No. This choice is too broad. The passage critiques the three major approaches to explaining events in Peru, not traditional methodological approaches to explaining political change in general.

      B:      No. This choice is also too vague, and it takes words out of context from the passage. The actions and fate of the Peruvian military government, not military governments in developing nations in general, is at issue, and comparative provision of benefits to the Peruvian domestic population is never directly discussed.

      **C:      Yes. The author describes three major positions on the Peruvian case, indicates shortcomings of those positions, and advocates a different, more complex approach.**

      D:      No. This choice is too extreme. The author states that parts of each of the three approaches are useful, but that no one of these approaches by itself is sufficient (paragraph 6). The author accepts and incorporates aspects of each of the three in her own analysis. Thus her analysis is different and more complex, but not so different as to qualify as a "fundamentally distinct methodological framework."

19. C   This is an Inference question.
   - A: No. While Quijano did write during the time that the military regime was still in power, neither the quote from his work nor the rest of the passage gives evidence that he participated in policy making.
   - B: No. Quijano argues that the reforms redefined imperialist domination of Peru rather than eliminating it, but the quote presented in the passage offers no opinion about or criticism of the regime.
   - **C: Yes. In paragraph 3, the author states that Quijano's work "directly challenged… widely held belief." As with all Inference questions that indicate where in the passage to find the answer, going back to the passage here allows you to get to the credited response efficiently.**
   - D: No. Quijano wrote in 1970 (paragraph 3), while the regime fell in 1978 (paragraph 1). It would have been impossible for Quijano to analyze the actual ouster of the regime from power, and the quote offers no evidence that he expected or predicted the regime's failure.

20. B   This is an Inference question.
   - A: No. This choice is too extreme. While the author indicates that the reforms may have been intended to promote some level of increased Peruvian autonomy vis-à-vis foreign corporations (the extent to which they did so is one of the questions at issue in the passage), the passage does not suggest that they attempted to eliminate foreign influence altogether.
   - **B: Yes. The author asserts that the reforms "harmed various individual [foreign] firms" (paragraph 6).**
   - C: No. This choice is only partially correct (therefore, all wrong). The author argues that the reforms had a beneficial effect on foreign capital in the long run by "maintaining a capitalist mode of production" (paragraph 6) even though they worked against the short-term interests of some individual companies.
   - D: No. No benefit to the domestic population is discussed.

21. B   This is a Main Idea question.
   - A: No. This choice is too narrow. The author considers and critiques three different positions; Guasti and Quijano are given as examples of the first two.
   - **B: Yes. The passage presents the three positions and asserts that while each makes some valuable points, none accurately capture the role and influence of foreign actors. The author suggests a variety of other factors that must be considered (paragraph 6).**
   - C: No. This choice is too broad to be the main idea of this passage. While the author does argue that both domestic and foreign forces played a role in Peru, she does not generalize her discussion to include or apply to all regimes.
   - D: No. This choice is too narrow. While the author does claim that the reforms aided foreign firms in the long run by "maintaining a capitalist mode of production" (paragraph 6), this is only one of many issues discussed in the passage.

22.   A      This is an Analogy question.
             Note: The error committed by the cited scholars is their focus on internal domestic fac-
             tors without sufficient consideration of the influences of foreign actors on the "historical
             structuring of the socioeconomic system" of Peru (paragraph 6).

      **A:**     **Yes. The psychologist attempts to explain individual behavior (analogous to events with-
             in Peru) without reference to the person's life history and the part played in it by the larg-
             er society and other participants in that society. Thus he explains internal events without
             considering the role played by other actors or factors in a larger historical context.**

      B:      No. The potential effect of the presence of an observer on the thing being observed is not a
             relevant issue to this passage in general, nor does it play a role in the third standard explanation.

      C:      No. The author does not argue that those following the third model should have consid-
             ered the ethical nature of their work.

      D:      No. Those advocating the third position pay little or no attention to the potential role
             or influence of foreign actors. Thus an argument about the destructive impact of foreign
             powers on a nation would not be at all analogous to their methodological approach.


23.   D      This is an Inference question.

      A:      No. The correct answer will list a factor that the author sees as being essentially irrelevant
             to the rise and fall of the regime. The author never suggests that the perception of partici-
             pants was irrelevant.

      B:      No. While the author never directly discusses timing, she does suggest that historical
             context was important, which would be relevant to timing. Therefore, we cannot infer
             that she sees timing as unimportant.

      C:      No. The author refers to the importance of the historical structuring of the socioeco-
             nomic system in lines paragraph 6. Therefore, you can infer that she sees socioeconomic
             history as a relevant factor.

      **D:**     **Yes. In paragraph 6 the author states that "short-term influences [of foreign capital]
             were of minimal importance." Therefore, you can infer that she believes the immediate
             effects of the actions of foreign firms to be of little relevance.**


## Passage V
This is a Later passage.

**Bottom Line:** Value of poem not determined by difficulty, despite what young poets may think.

24.   B      This is an Inference question.

      A:      No. The author of the passage claims that poems need no defending (paragraph 9), and
             expresses no particular affection for indefensible poems.

      **B:**     **Yes. The author has warm feelings for young poets, in part because they are in love
             with writing (paragraph 3). As for the poem, the author indicates that great poems
             communicate passion and vision (paragraph 5).**

      C:      No. The author uses a critical tone in describing poets who are unwilling to discuss or
             explain their work (paragraph 7), and directly states that he or she dislikes indecipherable
             poetry (paragraph 3).

      D:      No. The author expresses warmth towards young (indecipherable) poets (paragraph 3),
             while never discussing feelings about mature poets. As for the poem itself, the author says
             nothing to suggest that he or she particularly values youthful and optimistic poetry.

25.   D      This is a New Information question.
      A:     No. While the second paragraph indicates that poets hope to be praised, it would be too extreme to infer from this that poets as a rule dislike thoughtful criticism once it is given. The passage even suggests that young poets may take criticism as a sign of the difficulty and therefore the value of their poetry.
      B:     No. If young and inexperienced poets tend to feel secure, then there is no particular reason they should react with anger when their work is critiqued.
      C:     No. The author never describes young or inexperienced poets as being especially liable to take critiques personally. If anything, they are portrayed as relatively thick-skinned in the face of criticism, in most situations (paragraph 7).
      **D:     Yes. According to the passage, inexperienced poets believe that if their poetry is difficult to understand, it approaches greatness (paragraphs 5 and 6). If a critic were able to understand the poem, the work may not be quite as difficult as intended and so not as great. Thus the author specifically suggests indecipherability or lack thereof as a potential sore point for inexperienced writers.**


26.   B      This is an Analogy question.
      A:     No. The correct answer will present a situation in which a person makes communication impossible through the use of some form of private language. Braille is a public language—just because the young woman has not learned it does not mean that the language itself is indecipherable.
      **B:     Yes. The stenographer takes what is usually a form of communication, and renders it indecipherable to others through the use of abbreviations only she could understand.**
      C:     No. The individual student's lack of comprehension does not constitute evidence that the formulas are fundamentally incomprehensible to others.
      D:     No. This is an example of clear communication, not of indecipherability.


27.   D      This is a Weaken question.
      A:     No. The author does not claim that only great poems arise from or communicate passion.
      B:     No. The author's claim does not depend on there being a physiological connection.
      C:     No. The author does not argue that passion always produces great poetry; the claim is that great poetry always evokes passion.
      **D:     Yes. The passage suggests that Pound is a great poet (paragraph 6). If his poetry fails to express passion, this would weaken the author's assertion that passion is necessary for great poetry.**

28.   B      This is a Structure question.

   A:   No. This statement is made as part of the author's discussion of the defense of poems later in the passage (paragraph 9). Frailty has no direct connection to the novice's belief in his or her own immunity.

   **B:   Yes. Paragraph 7 illustrates the circularity in the logic of young poets. If their poems are criticized, that is simply an indication of lack of understanding on the part of the critic. After all, if they understood the poem, they would not criticize it. With this kind of logic in hand, the poet can write anything, no matter how obscure or awkward, and claim that it is just as it should be.**

   C:   No. The intelligence and likeability of the novice poet (paragraph 3) does not explain why he or she sees their work as impregnable.

   D:   No. The author makes this statement to illustrate the yearning for praise that underlies a poet's plea for brutal critique (paragraph 2). It is not directly relevant to the illusions of invulnerability attributed to young poets in paragraph 7.

29.   C      This is an Inference question.

   A:   No. While the author's description of young poets suggests that some may be insecure, the passage does not suggest that poetry arises from or is shaped by insecurity.

   B:   No. A poem may be innocent or "blameless for its content" (paragraph 1), but this is a characteristic, not a cause, of poetry.

   **C:   Yes. In paragraph 1 the author states that a poem "usually represents its author's pride."**

   D:   No. The critic never feels brutal towards a poem (paragraph 1), but doesn't describe poetry that itself manifests or is created by brutality.

# Passage VI

This is a Now passage.

**Bottom Line:** Real cure/prevention is cheaper—should increase basic research to improve understanding.

30.   C      This is a Weaken question.
              Note: The main idea of the passage is that true prevention and cures are relatively inexpensive and easy to deliver.

   A:   No. This is neither prevention nor cure of a disease, but only an expensive "halfway technology" (paragraph 3) meant to manage the symptoms. The availability of such a therapy would not challenge the author's argument about the characteristics and advantages of "real high technology" (paragraph 2).

   B:   No. Non-medical strategies are not relevant to the passage, which focuses on the "real high technology of medicine" (paragraph 2).

   **C:   Yes. The existence of an expensive cure undermines the main idea.**

   D:   No. This is a non-medical strategy—the author compares different medical strategies in the passage. Furthermore, the fact that some have claimed this to be true does not by itself make it true. The correct answer to a weaken question needs to be strong enough to undermine the passage.

31.   C      This is an Inference question.

      A:    No. They are inexpensive, but technology is definitely involved. This is a Half right/half wrong (Decoy) Atrractor.

      B:    No. This is incorrect because Parkinsonism and sickle-cell anemia cannot yet be prevented or cured (paragraph 1); the author suggests their management is "just around the corner."

      C:    **Yes. "The truth is that there are nothing like as many as the public has been led to believe" (paragraph 1).**

      D:    No. This is the opposite of what the author asserts: "when it becomes available, it is relatively inexpensive, and relatively easy to deliver" (paragraph 2).

32.   D      This is an Inference question.

             Note: While this looks like an Inference/NOT question (for which an answer where you just didn't know the author's opinion might be correct), the wording of this question requires you to find an answer that is explicitly inconsistent with the author's argument in the passage. That is, you have direct evidence that the author would reject the proposal.

      A:    No. Nothing in the passage indicates that the author would be against this kind of legislation; this choice is Out of Scope.

      B:    No. The author argues for increased "basic research in biological science" (paragraph 5).

      C:    No. The author does not argue against providing expensive "halfway" treatments when no "high-tech" therapy is available. The passage lists Parkinsonism as a disease for which we do not yet have a high technology, inexpensive cure (paragraph 1).

      D:    **Yes. The author argues that more basic research should be done, since "a clear understanding of disease mechanisms" is what allows us to replace "no-technology or halfway technology" measures with real cures or prevention (paragraphs 2 and 3). Therefore, out of these four choices, the author would most oppose increasing the percentage of the budget spent on managing diseases (rather than on eliminating them).**

33.   B      This is an Inference question.

      A:    No. The author never implies that basic research is less well funded than it used to be, just that it should be even better funded than it is (paragraph 5).

      B:    **Yes. You can infer that "it" (as in "it seems...like asking for the moon") refers to "this" (as in "this is the only way"), which in turn refers to giving high priority to—and spending money on—basic research. To ask for the moon is to ask for something that is out of reach; therefore this answer choice suggests that funding basic biological research is currently not adequately prioritized.**

      C:    No. Although this may be true based on the passage, this is not the point the author makes with "asking for the moon."

      D:    No. The author does not indicate how long it will take to cure a disease. Furthermore, the issue in the relevant part of the passage is money and policy priorities. Beware of answers that take an overly literal approach to the wording of the passage. This choice, for instance, mentions the moon but in the context of getting to it in the past, not "asking for" the moon itself.

34.    A    This is an Inference question.

      A:    **Yes. The author urges us to remember that basic science is the source of true medical effectiveness, and that without sufficient research, any attempt at clinical treatment is likely to be expensive and ineffective. Hence he "would regard it as an act of high prudence to give high priority to a lot more basic research in biologic science" (paragraph 5).**

      B:    No. This choice is inconsistent with the author's emphasis on the value of basic research.

      C:    No. The author deplores the expense of supportive treatment, but he also suggests that it is often the best available treatment at the time. Therefore, he would not argue that NO money should be spent on supportive therapy. This choice is too extreme.

      D:    No. The author argues the opposite in paragraphs 3 and 5.

35.    A    This is a Retrieval/EXCEPT question.

         Note: The wrong answers will be diseases that the author indicates are or were expensive to treat. The correct answer will be a disease that you either know from the passage was never expensive, or, a disease that you don't know to be or have ever been expensive.

      A:    **Yes. While we cannot yet prevent or cure sickle-cell anemia, the author never claims that its treatment is expensive.**

      B:    No. Polio is a disease that was once treated only by very expensive supportive therapies (paragraph 3).

      C:    No. Tuberculosis is the topic of the fourth paragraph. The author uses it as an example of a disease whose treatment was extremely costly.

      D:    No. See paragraph 3. This disease is used as an example, like polio, of a condition that was extremely costly to treat.

36.    B    This is a Structure question.

      A:    No. The author's point about Sister Kenny's treatments is that nothing better was available at the time; thus, having an MD apply treatment would not necessarily have been an improvement. This is an Out of Scope Attractor since the author does not mention a difference between medical professionals and non-professionals in this passage.

      B:    **Yes. Just prior to the Sister Kenny example, the author indicates it is "a halfway technology" that came "just before the emergence of basic research that made the vaccine possible." In this paragraph, he is arguing that once the technology is developed, treatment becomes less costly. Later in the passage, the author underscores the need for basic research. This answer choice is the best fit both with the paragraphs' main points and the Bottom Line of the Passage.**

      C:    No. This is the most tempting Attractor but it is not quite accurate to claim that Sister Kenny's methods went beyond what was necessary. A cure was not yet available (paragraph 3) and the author suggests that she was doing the best she could with what was available to her. This is a Judgments and Recommendations (Extreme) Attractor.

      D:    No. Sister Kenny was apparently providing the best care available at the time; this answer choice doesn't describe the situation accurately. The author makes no mention of reprimanding practitioners. The point of this paragraph is to illustrate how costly treatments can be before knowledge and technology are available to more efficiently treat diseases.

## Passage VII

This is a Now passage.

**Bottom Line:** Fishing practices are endangering sharks: difficult to protect.

37.  **B**    This is a Retrieval question.

    A:    No. There is no indication which fish is eaten more frequently or in greater volume.

    **B:**    **Yes. This is the point of paragraph 4, where the author states that the cod population can replenish itself much more quickly than the shark population can.**

    C:    No. This does not explain why sharks are at greater risk than are cod. While this is true in the context of the passage, it is a Right answer/wrong question Attractor.

    D:    No. This has nothing to do with shark survival relative to cod. Additionally, while the shark is about to join the bald eagle and buffalo on the list of managed species, it is unclear whether they are as scarce. We do not know the range encompassed by managed species.

38.  **C**    This is a Retrieval/Roman numeral question.

    **I:**    **True. This is supported by the analogy drawn between lions and sharks (paragraph 2).**

    II:    False. This is too strong an inference to draw from paragraph 2. The author does not imply that sharks are near extinction, only that their numbers are falling significantly. Furthermore, the passage does not indicate that cancer research based on sharks depends on having a large population of sharks in the wild. Finally, the author only says that sharks "may" offer some knowledge about the disease. While the disappearance of sharks might prevent one avenue of potential research, then, it would not "significantly hamper" cancer research as a whole.

    **III:**    **True. Given sharks' low fecundity, it is reasonable to infer that a dip in population might take a long time to correct; after all, we are told that a three-fourths' reduction in the population would take fifteen years to recover (paragraph 4).**

39.  **D**    This is an Inference question.

        Note: All of the Attractors, A, B, and C, are found in the passage, but not correct in this context. They are Words out of context (Decoy) Attractors.

    A:    No. 5,800 metric tons is the current cap, not the take previous to the cap (paragraph 5).

    B:    No. The two-sharks-per-boat limit refers to sport fishing, not the commercial catch (paragraph 5).

    C:    No. This figure is only an example, used in the discussion of the fecundity issue. It isn't given as an actual number of sharks caught.

    **D:**    **Yes. The author asserts that the quota cap (of 5,800 metric tons) constitutes about half of the take in the previous year, so we can infer that the pre-quota take was twice the cap, or 11,600 metric tons (paragraph 5). More support for this answer is in paragraph 1, where it states that the numbers double every year.**

40. B    This is an Inference question.
- A: No. Sharks will be placed on the list of managed, not endangered, species (paragraph 5).
- **B: Yes. Since some sharks migrate outside of US jurisdictions, they cannot be protected by US quotas (paragraph 7).**
- C: No. It is the practice of finning (which is done by fishermen), not cooking the fins (which is what the chefs do) that has angered environmentalists.
- D: No. Such coordination will eventually be necessary, but it has not yet taken place (see paragraph 7).

41. D    This is an Inference question.
- A: No. Paragraph 2 implies that sharks may be useful in cancer research, not that they are currently being used. Even if they were used for research, the quotas would have a positive impact due to more sharks being saved.
- B: No. The author does not mention this in the passage.
- C: No. The author does not state that more shark fins are being used because of the announcement of quotas. This choice is too specific to the practice of finning, rather than shark fishing in general.
- **D: Yes. Paragraph 7 implies that, knowing the quotas will take effect soon, commercial fishermen are currently attempting to catch as many sharks as possible. John G. Casey notes that there is a "pre-quota rush on sharks… as we speak."**

42. B    This is an Inference question.
- A: No. The author doesn't link predatory behavior with survival. In the first paragraph, he calls them the scourge of the sea, but explicitly references growing appetite for shark meat, not a fear of sharks, as the threat to their survival.
- **B: Yes. We can limit US fishing, but we can't monitor the fishing restrictions of the countries into whose territorial waters the sharks migrate (see the last paragraph).**
- C: No. Their fins are a motive to hunt them, but this does not affect how easy they are to save.
- D: No. It is the fact that females bear few young (paragraph 3), not that they bear live young, that hinders shark populations from replenishing themselves. This is the right answer to the wrong question.

## Passage VIII

This is a Later passage.

**Bottom Line:** Study of language evolved over time—now focuses on primacy of spoken language.

43  D  This is a Retrieval question.

A:  No. The correct answer will be a statement with which one group will agree, and the other will disagree. The author states that "every known language first appeared in spoken form" (paragraph 3), and gives no indication that the early grammarians would contest this fact. Thus it seems that both early and modern would disagree with *this statement*, not disagree with each other over it.

B:  No. The author states this in reference to the historical beginnings of traditional grammar. There is no evidence that either the early or modern grammarians would disagree with it.

C:  No. Again, this is part of the author's description of the history of the study of grammar. It is not presented as a point of debate between early and modern grammarians.

**D:  Yes. Early grammarians study written texts, and so would say that punctuation is more important than gesture. The modern grammarians, who focus on spoken language, would say yes, gesture is just as important (paragraph 3). Thus the early and modern would disagree over this statement.**

44.  A  This is an Inference question.

**A:  Yes. According to the modern or current view, this is true both of individuals (paragraph 3) and of languages themselves.**

B:  No. Expression in written speech requires punctuation (paragraph 4), and nothing about punctuation is given as a reason for the primacy of spoken language.

C:  No. Precision is not discussed in the passage.

D:  No. The contribution of speech to literature is never discussed.

45.  D  This is an Inference question.

A:  No. This choice is too extreme. People and animals speak different languages (paragraph 6), but that by itself is not enough evidence that we are completely unable to communicate in any form.

B:  No. Animals may speak inferior languages (paragraph 6), yet that does not mean that they cannot truly communicate with each other. This choice is too extreme.

C:  No. The languages of animals may be inferior to those of humans (paragraph 6), but this indicates nothing about their need to communicate.

**D:  Yes. The author argues that the "open-endedness" and thus the superiority of human languages contributes to our position on earth (paragraph 6). By those terms, if our language is superior, our position must also be superior.**

46.  A  This is an Inference question.

**A:  Yes. In the sentence cited, the author indicates that most modern linguists take it as true that speech is primary. Thus we can infer that "axiomatic" in this context means that they take or follow that belief as if it were a rule.**

B:   No. The passage indicates just the opposite. "Axiomatic" is used to indicate that modern linguists take primacy of speech to be a rule, not an exception to some other rule.

C:   No. This choice is too extreme. Most, not all linguists agree. Furthermore, some qualifications on the derivation of written from spoken language are discussed (paragraph 4). Thus the word "perfect" goes too far.

D:   No. The passage uses "axiomatic" to mean a point of agreement. The word itself indicates nothing about an innovative or cutting-edge quality of the belief in primacy of speech.

47.  A    This is a Retrieval/Roman numeral question.

I:   False. Inflection or lack thereof in written speech is never discussed in the passage. Be careful not to answer based on common sense or outside knowledge.

II:  False. The author never discusses lack of opportunity for tone in written speech.

III: **True. According to the passage, written punctuation takes the place of the gestures and facial expressions that carry meaning in face-to-face speech.**

# Passage IX

This is a Now passage.

**Bottom Line:** Denishawn played fundamental role in creation and development of modern dance.

48.  B    This is a Primary Purpose question.

A:   No. This choice is too specific. Eastern and Western influences are only mentioned in paragraph 1 (and the two influences are not contrasted with each other).

B:   **Yes. Each paragraph is geared towards an evaluation of the role of Denishawn in the creation of modern dance. In this context, the passage considers the genesis and character of the group itself as well as its influence on those who came after.**

C:   No. The passage discusses the founding and development of modern dance, not traditional dance forms.

D:   No. The passage discusses the work, not the personal lives, of various choreographers.

49.  A    This is an Inference question.

A:   **Yes. The author concludes that Denishawn founded modern dance (paragraphs 2 and 3).**

B:   No. Eastern beliefs and practices were but one influence on Denishawn (middle of paragraph 1).

C:   No. The author explains that while public opinion holds Duncan to be the progenitor or creator of modern dance, this belief is incorrect (beginning of paragraph 1).

D:   No. Denishawn was in fact as "eclectic as America itself" (second half of paragraph 1). However, modern dance derives specifically from Denishawn's work with all of its unique characteristics and influences, not from "American eclecticism" in general.

50.  B   This is an Inference question.

A:  No. Sorrell is referring to the supposed rebellion of the generation that followed Denishawn. St. Denis's work is described as having mystical elements (beginning of paragraph 4), but the quote by Sorrell cited in the question does not refer to qualities of St. Denis's work.

**B:  Yes. These are the "children of Denishawn" (paragraph 2). Sorrell makes this reference in the context of his argument that these "children" rebelled against Denishawn and so were the true pioneers.**

C:  No. Sorrell's reference is to the "children" or second generation (paragraph 2), not to St. Denis herself.

D:  No. Martha Graham is included in the group referred to as the "children of Denishawn" (paragraph 2). However, the "spiritual rebellion" is their supposed break as a whole with Denishawn's choreographic style, not the specific performance mentioned in paragraph 4 (which the author sees as connected to, not in opposition to, Denishawn's style).

51.  A   This is a Structure/Roman numeral question.

**I:  True. The author argues that this performance is clearly influenced by the heritage of Denishawn (paragraph 4).**

II:  False. It is Isadora Duncan, not Denishawn, who supposedly influenced modern ballet (beginning of paragraph 1).

III:  False. The claim that Duncan was not the creator of modern dance does not by itself support a claim about the influence or greatness of other *specific* choreographers.

52.  C   This is an Inference question.

A:  No. Neither idealism nor idealistic interpretation is mentioned.

B:  No. The role of individual dancers in Denishawn's choreography is never discussed. The author does say that Ted Shawn had just the opposite approach to the work of individual choreographers; their individualism was accepted and encouraged (paragraph 3).

**C:  Yes. In the beginning of paragraph 3 the author describes how Shawn accepted all styles "as a basis for creativity."**

D:  No. Shawn's attitude is not described as rebellious; also, the author argues that Denishawn's descendants were not rebellious (beginning of paragraph 3).

53.  C   This is a Weaken question.
    *Note:* The correct answer will be inconsistent with the public opinion described in the question stem. Keep in mind that the author disagrees with this belief.

A:  No. The correct answer will be inconsistent with the author's depiction of public opinion. The impact of Duncan on the Russians is mentioned (first sentence); lack of influence running in the other direction is not an issue in the passage.

B:  No. The author agrees with Martin and disagrees with public opinion (paragraphs 1 and 3). Therefore the author likely believes in Martin's competence.

**C:  Yes. The author argues that the true progenitors of modern dance were Shawn and St. Denis, suggesting that the public doesn't really know what it is talking about.**

D:  No. The qualities reflected in Graham's work have no direct relevance to public opinion about the role of Duncan as the originator of modern dance.

# MCAT
# Critical Analysis and Reasoning Skills

## Practice Test 4

## Passage I (Questions 1-6)

Over and over again the question arises as to why it is that so many music lovers feel disoriented when they listen to contemporary music. Why? Because they "just don't understand it."

In following a new work, the melodic content—or seeming lack of it—may be a source of confusion. You may very well miss hearing the straightforward tune that can be hummed. Melodies nowadays can be "unsingable," especially in instrumental writing, if only because they go far beyond the limitations of the human voice. Or it may be that they are too tortuous, or jagged, or fragmentary to have any immediacy of appeal. These are expressive attributes that may, temporarily, perplex the listener. But the modern composer, given the expanded scope of contemporary melodic invention, cannot return to the plain and sometimes obvious melody writing of an earlier day. Assuming a gifted composer, repeated hearings should make clear the long-range appeal of his more intricate line.

[Then] there is the reproach that is repeated more often than any other, namely, that today's music appears to avoid sentiment and feeling, that it is merely cerebral and clever rather than emotionally meaningful. If a contemporary composer's work strikes you as cold and intellectual, ask yourself if you are not using standards of comparison that really do not apply. Our audiences have come to identify nineteenth-century musical romanticism as analogous to the art of music itself. Because romanticism was, and still remains, so powerful an expression, they tend to forget that great music was written for hundreds of years before the romantics flourished.

The nineteenth century was the romantic century par excellence—a romanticism that found its most characteristic expression in the art of music. Perhaps that explains the continued reluctance of the music-loving public to admit that with the new century a different kind of music had to come into being. And yet their counterparts in the literary world do not expect André Gide or Thomas Mann or T.S. Eliot to emote with the accents of Victor Hugo or Sir Walter Scott. Why then should Bartók or Sessions be expected to sing with the voice of Brahms or Tchaikovsky? When a contemporary piece seems dry and cerebral to you, when it seems to be giving off little feeling or sentiment, there is a good chance that you are being insensitive to the characteristic musical speech of your own epoch.

To feel no need of involvement in the musical expression of one's own day is to shut oneself off from one of the most exciting experiences the art of music can provide. Contemporary music speaks to us as no other music can. It is the older music—the music of Buxtehude and Cherubini—that should seem distant and foreign to us, not that of Milhaud and William Schuman. But isn't music universal?

All depends on the angle of vision: what we see produces wider extremes of tension and release, a more vivid optimism, a grayer pessimism, climaxes of abandonment and explosive hysteria, coloristic variety—subtleties of light and dark. Various shades and gradations of these moods have their counterpart in older music, no doubt, but no sensitive listener would ever confuse the two. It is the uniqueness of any authentic art expression that makes even approximate duplication in any other period inconceivable. That is why the music lover who neglects contemporary music deprives himself of the enjoyment of an otherwise unobtainable aesthetic experience.

Adapted A. Copland, *What to Listen For in Music,* © 1988 McGraw-Hill.

1. According to the author, the most common problem associated with contemporary music is its apparent lack of:

   A. universality.
   B. sentiment and feeling.
   C. subtleties of light and dark.
   D. straightforward melodies.

2. If a modern composition contained many long and complicated melodies that are very difficult to follow, the author would most likely advise listeners to:

   A. listen to the composition repeatedly.
   B. disregard the composition and listen to a different piece by the same composer.
   C. disregard the composition and listen to a different piece by a different composer.
   D. the author does not give any advice for such a situation.

3. Suppose a musical composition is discovered which uses instrumentation, melodies, and harmonies typical of the sixteenth century. The discovery is accepted as authentic by musical scholars, but later laboratory analysis of its paper and ink prove conclusively that it is a contemporary counterfeit, an anonymous modern composition. This would most strongly *challenge* the author's assertion that:

   A. it is the older music that should seem foreign to us.
   B. most people seem to resent the controversial in music.
   C. when a contemporary piece seems dry and cerebral, there is a good chance you are being insensitive to the musical speech of your own epoch.
   D. the uniqueness of any authentic art expression makes even approximate duplication in any other period inconceivable.

4. One would NOT expect to find "climaxes of abandonment and explosive hysteria" (paragraph 6) in the music of:

   A. Milhaud and Schuman.
   B. Bartók.
   C. Sessions.
   D. Buxtehude and Cherubini.

5. The author mentions T.S. Eliot and Victor Hugo in order to:

   A. support his point of view that romantic music is not inferior to contemporary music.
   B. support his point that different musical periods should speak with different voices.
   C. dramatize the differences between literary and musical compositions.
   D. suggest that Eliot's works are dry and cerebral.

6. Which of the following, if true, would NOT *weaken* the author's contention that romantic standards of comparison do not apply to contemporary literary and musical compositions?

   A. Romantic standards may in some cases be appropriately applied by music critics when reviewing a twenty-first-century piece.
   B. The majority of contemporary readers prefer romantic-style novels to the intellectualism of T.S. Eliot or Thomas Mann.
   C. T.S. Eliot extensively studied the works of Victor Hugo, Sir Walter Scott, and other romantic writers.
   D. A new century does not necessarily demand a new musical language.

## Passage II (Questions 7-13)

Whether humans have obligations to other (lower) animals is intimately connected with our inquiry into the nature of these other animals. In general, in order for us to have a duty to a being, that being must satisfy certain conditions; in particular, the being must have certain capacities.

There are three capacities that have been thought by different thinkers to be such that, if a being lacked them, it would follow that we would not have any duties to it. The three are (1) *sentience*, or the capacity to experience pleasure and pain; (2) *rationality*, or the capacity to reason; and (3) *autonomy*, or the capacity to make free choices. Let us review the grounds and implications of each of these, beginning with rationality: A being must have the capacity to reason if we are to have any duties to it. This idea goes back to Aristotle, but was formulated more forcefully in the thirteenth century by the philosopher-theologian St. Thomas Aquinas.

In regard to animal sentience—their capacity to feel pain or pleasure—Aquinas, like Aristotle and unlike Descartes, believes that animals are sentient, and that because they have the capacity to feel pain it is possible to treat them cruelly—that is, to cause them unnecessary pain. Although Aquinas thinks it is *wrong* to treat them in this way, he does not think we have a duty to the lower animals to abstain from treating them cruelly. To understand this apparent contradiction requires some explanation.

The key to Aquinas's position is the idea that we can have duties only to those beings who have the capacity to reason. Thus, anytime it happens to be true that we have done something wrong, it will also be true that we have failed to fulfill a duty we have to ourselves, our neighbor, or God. Now, because lower animals cannot reason, according to Aquinas, we can no more have any duties to *them* than we can have duties to *things*. The only way we can do something wrong that involves doing something to lower animals is if our treatment of them leads us to sin against some *rational* being—either ourselves, our fellow man, or God.

Let us suppose that we do have obligations to animals—for example, the obligation not to treat them cruelly. Would it follow from this that animals have the *right* not to be treated cruelly? Some thinkers believe this would follow, because they accept the thesis that whenever one being has an obligation to another, that other being has a corresponding right, and vice versa. This is known as the *correlativity thesis*. If this thesis is accepted, then obviously if it is true that we have duties to animals, it must also be true that animals have corresponding rights.

But is the correlativity thesis true? Some philosophers think not. Some argue, for example, that it might be plausibly maintained that we have a duty to preserve great works of art, like the Pietà, as well as natural resources, such as the oceans or our woodlands. Yet these same thinkers contend that we do not suppose that the Pietà, the Atlantic Ocean, or our forests have rights. Thus, they think the correlativity thesis is false.

Proponents of the thesis, however, think this objection misses the mark. For they think the thesis applies only to cases of *direct* duty, while this objection appeals to cases in which our duties are indirect. To make this clearer, consider our supposed duty to take care of the Pietà. Now, preserving the Pietà is not something we owe it. Rather, preserving it is something we owe to future generations of *human beings*.

Adapted from T. Regan and P. Singer, eds., *Animal Rights and Human Obligations,* © 1976 Prentice-Hall.

7. Based on the information provided in the passage, the correlativity thesis:

   A. indicates that animals have the right not to be treated cruelly.
   B. has been questioned on the basis of the claim that it can apply only to cases of direct duties.
   C. is consistent with the author's own position on the question of animal rights.
   D. could indicate, dependent on other findings, that animals have certain rights.

8. Which of the following statements, if found to be attributable to St. Thomas Aquinas, would most *undermine* the author's depiction of Aquinas's beliefs regarding our duties towards animals?

    A. "It would seem that irrational creatures also ought to be loved out of charity. Now God loves irrational creatures out of charity, for He loves all things that are."

    B. "Murder is a sin because it deprives a man of life. Now life is common to all animals and plants. Hence for the same reason it is apparently a sin to slay dumb animals and plants."

    C. "According to the Divine ordinance the life of animals and plants, if it must be preserved, is preserved not for themselves, but for man."

    D. "Now irrational creatures can have no fellowship in human life which is regulated by reason. Hence friendship with irrational creatures is impossible, except metaphorically."

9. According to the passage, Aquinas and Descartes would disagree most over which one of the following statements?

    A. Humans have obligations to lower animals.

    B. Humans have duties only to creatures that have the capacity to reason.

    C. Animals can gain some measure of enjoyment from their daily existence.

    D. If one being has an obligation to another being, that other being has a corresponding right.

10. Suppose the author of the passage had, in the body of the essay, quoted the following statement from Jean-Paul Sartre: "There is no human nature.... Man first of all exists, encounters himself, surges up in the world, and defines himself afterwards. If man as the existentialist sees himself as not definable, it is because to begin with he is nothing. He will not be anything until later, and then he will be what he makes himself." These words would best illuminate the author's discussion of:

    A. sentience.
    B. correlativity.
    C. direct and indirect duties.
    D. autonomy.

11. The position of the proponents of the correlativity thesis would be most strengthened by which of the following statements?

    A. One species of animal has no greater right to life, or to humanitarian treatment, than any other animal species.

    B. We have a direct duty to the oceans and woodlands to protect them from destruction, so that future generations may use and enjoy them.

    C. We have an indirect duty to future generations to preserve great works of art.

    D. We have a direct duty to our descendants to preserve the overall health of the ecosystem.

12. The author discusses the capacities of sentience and rationality in order to:

    A. highlight the differences between St. Thomas Aquinas and Descartes.

    B. describe Aristotle's belief that these are sufficient conditions under which we would have duties to a being.

    C. support the claim that animals have certain rights to humanitarian treatment.

    D. describe the foundation for the claim that a being's lack of reason is sufficient cause to conclude that we have no duties towards that being.

13. Based on the information in the passage, we can infer that the author would most likely agree with which of the following statements?

    A. The only way our treatment of lower animals can be judged to be wrong is if those actions lead us to mistreat other human beings.

    B. Certain capacities exist which might obligate us to treat a being in a particular way.

    C. We have the obligation not to treat animals cruelly.

    D. We have a duty to preserve great works of art, such as the Pietà.

---

## Passage III (Questions 14-18)

In July 1982, I learned that I was suffering from abdominal mesothelioma, a rare and serious cancer usually associated with exposure to asbestos. When I revived after surgery, I asked my first question of my doctor and chemotherapist: "What is the best technical literature about mesothelioma?" She replied, with a touch of diplomacy (the only departure she has ever made from direct frankness), that the medical literature contained nothing really worth reading.

Of course as soon as I could walk I made a beeline for Harvard's Countway medical library and realized with a gulp why my doctor had offered that humane advice. The literature couldn't have been more brutally clear: Mesothelioma is incurable, with a median mortality of only eight months after discovery.

If a little learning could ever be a dangerous thing, I had encountered a classic example. Attitude clearly matters in fighting cancer. We don't know why (from my old-style materialistic perspective, I suspect that mental states feed back upon the immune system). I am, if anything, even-tempered and confident: a sanguine personality.

The problem may be briefly stated: What does "median mortality of eight months" signify in our vernacular? I suspect that most people, without training in statistics, would read such a statement as "I will probably be dead in eight months"—the very conclusion that must be avoided, both because this formulation is false, and because attitude matters so much.

We still carry the historical baggage of a Platonic heritage that seeks sharp essences and definite boundaries. This Platonic heritage, with its emphasis on clear distinctions and separated immutable entities, leads us to view means and medians as hard "realities."

But all evolutionary biologists know that variation itself is nature's only irreducible essence. Variation is the hard reality, not a set of imperfect measures for a central tendency. Therefore, I looked at the mesothelioma statistics quite differently. I had to place myself amidst the variation.

When I learned about the eight-month median, my first intellectual reaction was: Fine, half the people will live longer; now what are my chances of being in that half? A technical point added even more solace. I immediately recognized that the distribution of variation about the eight-month median would almost surely be…"right-skewed." (In a symmetrical distribution, the profile of variation to the left of a central tendency is a mirror image of variation to the right. Skewed distributions are asymmetrical, with variation stretching out more in one direction than the other—left skewed if extended to the left, right skewed if stretched out to the right.) The distribution of variation had to be right skewed, I reasoned. After all, the left of the distribution contains an irrevocable lower boundary of zero (since mesothelioma can only be identified at death or before). Thus, little space exists for the distribution's lower (or left) half—it must be scrunched up between zero and eight months. But the upper (or right) half can extend out like a tail for years and years, even if nobody ultimately survives. I saw no reason why I shouldn't be in that small tail, and I breathed a very long sigh of relief.

One final point about statistical distributions. They apply only to a prescribed set of circumstances—in this case to survival with mesothelioma under conventional modes of treatment. If circumstances change, the distribution may alter. I was placed on an experimental protocol of treatment and, if fortune holds, will be in the first cohort of a new distribution with a high median and a right tail extending to death by natural causes at advanced old age. So far, so good.

Adapted from S. J. Gould, "The Median Isn't the Message" in *Discover Magazine* © June 1985.

14. Progressive multifocal encephalopathy (PML), a degenerative and usually fatal disease of the central nervous system, presents with a sudden onset of mental status changes and has a median mortality of four to six months. From the information provided in the passage one could most reasonably conclude that:

    A. the mortality curve for PML is symmetrical.
    B. the mortality curve for PML is right skewed.
    C. the mortality curve for PML is left skewed.
    D. the median mortality must be greater than the mean mortality for PML.

15. Which of the following, if true, would most strengthen the claims made in the third paragraph?

    A. Some individuals with sanguine personalities never develop cancer.
    B. A new antidepressant is discovered which, when used in combination with hormone replacement therapy, significantly reduces the mortality of ovarian cancer.
    C. Most cancers are equally prevalent in the immunocompetent and the immunocompromised populations.
    D. Cancers of the brain are the least responsive to chemotherapy, and none are responsive to emotional status changes.

16. The passage suggests that when faced with statistics from the medical literature, the majority of patients diagnosed with mesothelioma:

    A. die within six months of diagnosis.
    B. irresponsibly interpret the medical literature.
    C. believe they have eight months or less to live.
    D. remodel their personalities and become more sanguine.

17. According to the passage, the author would most likely *disagree* with Platonic ideals in regards to:

    I. how to interpret statistical variations.
    II. the need to find a clear marker of when independent fetal life begins.
    III. what can be considered to be "reality."

    A. I and II only
    B. I and III only
    C. II and III only
    D. I, II, and III

18. The passage suggests which of the following about the relationship between attitude and health?

    A. Having a negative attitude may impair the functioning of a person's immune system.
    B. A strong positive attitude can cure a supposedly incurable disease.
    C. When a patient has a positive attitude, he or she may receive better care from physicians.
    D. The impact of a positive attitude on a person's immune system is one reason why the statistical distribution representing survival is right-skewed.

_____

# MCAT CARS Workbook

## Passage IV (Questions 19-24)

All of America's difficulties in the underdeveloped world came to a head in Cuba. In 1898 they drove the Spanish out and occupied it. After the Cubans wrote a constitution that gave the United States the right to intervene on the island whenever Washington felt it was necessary, the American troops left. Investors stayed behind. Three times after 1902 the United States intervened in Cuba to protect the investments.

Cuban life was controlled from Washington, for almost the only source of income was sugar, and by manipulating the amount of sugar allowed into the United States, Washington directed the economy. Fulgencio Batista was the Cuban dictator. He had come to power as a revolutionary but had adjusted to the realities of leading a small nation in which the United States had a large investment. Postponing land reform and other promising improvements, by the fifties he had become a fairly typical Latin ruler, with repressive policies. In January 1959, after a long struggle, Fidel Castro, who had placed himself at the head of the various anti-Batista guerrilla movements, drove Batista from power.

Within the American government, however, Castro did not receive an enthusiastic welcome. Allen Dulles told Ike [Eisenhower] that "Communists and other extreme radicals appear to have penetrated the Castro movement"; Dulles warned that the Communists would probably participate in the government. "Our only hope," Ike said, "lay with some kind of non-dictatorial 'third force,' neither Castroite nor Batistiano." The statement summed up the entire American relationship to the underdeveloped world—find a liberal who would not disturb the existing economic arrangements but who would rule in a democratic manner. It was a self-defeating program, for in Cuba—and elsewhere—there was little point to having a revolution if the basic economic structure were not changed, beginning with expropriation of foreign-owned property.

Castro…began an extensive land-reform program and a nationalization of American-owned property, without compensation. The United States turned down his requests for loans and relations steadily worsened. Cuban liberals began to flee the country; Cuban Communists rose to power under Castro. Khrushchev welcomed Castro as a new force in Latin America, pronounced the Monroe Doctrine dead, and in February 1960 signed a trade agreement to exchange Cuban sugar for Soviet oil and machinery. Four months later the United States eliminated the Cuban sugar quota; in the first days of 1961 Eisenhower formally severed diplomatic relations with Cuba.

In January 1961 Eisenhower delivered his farewell address. He was concerned about the internal cost of the Cold War. His ideals were those of small-town America. He was afraid that big government and the regimentation of private life were threatening the old American values. He pointed out that the "conjunction of an immense military establishment and a large arms industry,…new in American experience, exercised a total influence…felt in every city, every state house, every office of the federal government….In the councils of government we must guard against the acquisition of unwarranted influence, whether sought or unsought, by the military-industrial complex."

The Democrats paid no attention. In the campaign, and in his inaugural address, Kennedy emphasized that a new generation was coming to power in America. Hardened by the Cold War, it was prepared to deal with all the tough problems. He promised to replace Eisenhower's tired, bland leadership with new ideas and new approaches. Since these generalities were not reinforced by any specific suggestions, it was difficult to tell what the new direction would be. What was clear was that a forward-looking, offensive spirit had come to America. Action was about to replace inaction. Kennedy promised to get the country moving again. Where to, no one knew precisely.

Adapted from S.E. Ambrose, *Rise to Globalism: American Foreign Policy Since 1938*, © 1985 Penguin Books.

19. Elsewhere the author asserts that in regards to Korea, "Dulles's speeches, like Ike's, helped hide the fact that they did nothing about their promise to liberate the [economically] enslaved…" In this respect, according to the passage, United States policy towards Korea most closely resembled its approach towards:

    A. the Soviet Union.
    B. the military-industrial complex.
    C. Spain.
    D. Cuba.

20. According to the passage, which of the following can be assumed to be true of Cuba before 1898?

    I. The country was occupied by Spain.
    II. The American Ambassadorship reached the peak of its power in Cuba.
    III. American forces had intervened to protect investments.

    A. I only
    B. I and II only
    C. II and III only
    D. I, II, and III

21. According to the passage, President Kennedy and Allen Dulles would both most likely agree with which of the following?

    A. Action should be taken to limit Communist influence in Cuba.
    B. All foreign extremists pose a potentially serious threat to the United States.
    C. A new generation was coming to power in America.
    D. The Cuban economy would not require further US intervention.

22. Which of the following, if true, would most *weaken* the author's assertion that Castro seized American property in Cuba without offering compensation?

    A. New Cuban landowners, reluctant to pay damages, purposely had their property reassessed at lower values to reduce the amount of compensation that could be demanded by the original American owners.
    B. Batista had earlier been accused of similar transgressions and had been found by Congressional subcommittee to be entirely innocent.
    C. A Castro offer to recompensate Americans based on extremely underappraised land values was rejected by American investors as fraudulent.
    D. Castro offered to reinstate the Cuban sugar quota in return for United States military aid.

23. According to the last paragraph, the author's attitude towards Kennedy could best be described as:

    A. optimistic.
    B. ambivalent.
    C. antagonistic.
    D. condemnatory.

24. The author implies that the Democratic response towards the military-industrial complex would:

    A. be offensive and forward-looking.
    B. offer specific criticisms of big government.
    C. trample small-town American ideals.
    D. not fully address Eisenhower's concerns.

## Passage V (Questions 25-31)

Christmas consumes vast resources in the dubious and uncharitable activity of "forced giving." First, it is necessary to factor in all the time spent searching for "just the right gifts," writing and mailing cards to people one ignores the rest of the year, decorating trees, attending dreary holiday parties with highly fattening, cholesterol-rich eggnog drinks and false cheer, and returning presents. Assuming conservatively that each US adult spends an average of two days per year on Christmas activities, this represents an investment of nearly one million person-years per season. Just as important is the amount that Americans spend on gratuitous gifts each year—$40 billion to $50 billion, according to the US Commerce Department's monthly retail trade sales. Extra consumer spending is often considered beneficial because it stimulates the economy, but the massive yuletide spike creates numerous harmful externalities.

Mistargeted giving is one indication of this waste. According to New York department stores, each year about 15 percent of all retail dollar purchases at Christmas are returned. Allowing for the fact that many misdirected gifts are retained because people feel obliged to keep them (such as appliances, tablecloths, etc., which must be displayed when the relative who gave them to you comes for a visit), and allowing for the widespread inability of children to return gifts, this indicates that up to a third of purchases may be ill-suited to their recipients. Christmas is really a throwback to all the inefficiencies of the barter economy, in which people have to match other people's wants to their offerings. Of course, money was invented precisely to solve this "double coincidence of wants" problem. One solution would be to require people to give each other cash as presents, but that would quickly reveal the absurdity of the whole institution.

"Forced giving" also artificially pumps up consumption and reduces savings, since it is unlikely that all the silly and expensive presents given at Christmas would be given at other times of the year. One particularly noxious aspect of Christmas consumption is "conspicuous giving," which involves luxury gifts such as Tiffany eggs, crystal paperweights, and $15,000 watches that are designed precisely for those who are least in need of any present at all ("the person who has everything"). Most such high-priced gifts are given at Christmas; the fourth quarter, according to a sampling of New York department stores, provides more than half the year's diamond, watch, and fur sales.

Naturally, gratuitous spending delights retailers. Christmas accounts for more than a fifth of their sales and two-fifths of their profits, which suggests a Marxist explanation for the holiday—a powerful economic interest underlying the season's gift-centered ideology. But for the nation as a whole it increases the burden of consumer debt (almost a quarter of Christmas season sales are financed by credit cards or charge accounts, and January is the peak month for credit card delinquencies) and reduces our flagging savings rate (now below 5 percent of national income).

Adapted from J. Henry, "Why I Hate Christmas,"
© 1990 J. Henry. *The New Republic,* December 31 1990.

**25.** The central purpose of the passage is to:

**A.** establish an economic rationale for a strong critique of some Christmas traditions.

**B.** support a Marxist interpretation of Christmas.

**C.** argue for a return to a "bartering economy" at Christmas.

**D.** criticize the giving of luxury items as Christmas gifts.

**26.** As it is used in the passage, the word "gratuitous" (paragraph 1) most nearly means:

**A.** given in exchange for something.

**B.** unwanted.

**C.** extravagant.

**D.** wasteful.

**27.** The author would agree that all of the following are harmful externalities created by Christmas gift-giving EXCEPT:

**A.** a reduction in personal savings.

**B.** wasteful giving of inappropriate gifts.

**C.** a January slump in consumer spending.

**D.** an increase in credit card delinquencies.

**28.** We can infer from the statement "Christmas accounts for more than a fifth of their sales and two-fifths of their profits…" (paragraph 4) that merchants:

**A.** lose profits if they cut their prices at other times of the year.

**B.** charge higher prices for merchandise at Christmas than at other times of the year.

**C.** who desire profit have a vested interest in maintaining the Christmas giving tradition.

**D.** rely on the Christmas season in order to stay in business.

**29.** Which of the following inferences can most reasonably be drawn from the author's economic analysis of Christmas gift-giving?

**A.** The institution of Christmas exposes an inherent weakness in our capitalist economy.

**B.** The institution of Christmas undermines our economy by contributing to personal debt.

**C.** The Christmas season might eventually account for more than half of all consumer purchases.

**D.** The likely result of "forced giving" will be a glut in the market of "mistargeted goods."

**30.** Which one of the following would most *challenge* the author's assertion that large-scale spending at Christmastime causes harm to the economy?

**A.** The level of consumer debt in the fourth quarter of the year has been increasing at a rate of 3% over the past 25 years.

**B.** Economic recession in the early part of the year usually leads to reduced spending at Christmas.

**C.** Without the economic stimulus provided by increased consumer spending at Christmas, consumers are more likely to experience the effects of a recession in the early part of the following year.

**D.** Gift-buying for birthdays and other holidays, such as Mother's Day, also increases consumer debt.

**31.** According to the passage, the introduction of money solved the "double coincidence of wants" problem (paragraph 2) in which of the following ways?

**A.** Money solved the problem of transportation of goods so that buyers and sellers did not have to have in their immediate possession what was being bought or sold.

**B.** Money contributed to the solution by not requiring a seller's wants to match the buyer's offerings.

**C.** Money allowed a buyer to purchase goods on credit whenever the seller had something that the buyer wanted.

**D.** Money supplied a means for the seller to invest in industries and thus reap more profit from investments than he or she could in direct trade.

## Passage VI (Questions 32-36)

The women's movement of the [1960s] was born out of political movements, just as the previous feminist movements were born in the French Revolution and the Russian Revolution. Because they were born in politics, they had all the characteristics of a political movement in the full flush of its star—including intolerance of the past. They believed that they occurred for the first time in history. Sex began then too; as Larkin, the poet, said, "we invented sex in the sixties." Not only were these movements intolerant of the past; they were ignorant of the past. They wouldn't learn from history, and there was a great deal to learn from it. Also, all political groups and oppositions split endlessly. This of course is what has happened to the women's movement.

Another thing inseparable from political movements is rhetoric: that is, the use of sloganizing, oversimplifying ideas for the purpose of arousing people. One of the results of feminism being grounded in a political movement is that some of the attitudes go back to colonialism. Throughout this entire period, well-off and privileged white feminists have gone out to places like Zimbabwe to tell the local women what they should be doing and thinking.

Now, the first time I encountered this, I'd been on two trips around Zimbabwe on what they called the "grassroots" level. And I heard a couple of native women talking about some feminist from Europe who'd been there to tell them what to do. Some of these women bring up large families on as little as sixty, seventy, eighty dollars a month. They are unimaginably poor. They work so hard. Because in the past men were hunters and defended everyone and went to war, unless they happen to be in a structured job they tend not to do anything. The first thing you hear when you go to any third-world country is "the women do all the work." I heard women say at innumerable meetings, "We build the huts. We thatch the huts. We plaster the huts. We plant the grain, we weed it, we harvest it, we sell it. We bring up the children. We cook. And what are you doing, oh, my husband? You are sitting in the beer hall, drinking it away." They have these great ideological battles, but they are good-humored. Quite often, too, they will dance or sing their complaints about men.

When they are lectured by feminists that they should stand up to their husbands they are very funny about it. It is not lost on them that these feminists are—compared to themselves—unimaginably rich, privileged, protected. It is a pity ideologues cannot hear what is said about them when they have left. Or, often, what is acted and sung about them.

It's a Jellyby phenomenon. Do you remember Dickens' character, Mrs. Jellyby, who was always sending parcels to Nigeria or somewhere, while her children were unfed and unclothed? This Jellyby phenomenon is so rooted in all of us that again, it's very hard even to see it. I once went to talk to a group of German sixth graders near Munich. What they wanted to talk about was how they were supporting a group of children someplace in Africa. This was at a time when all the newspapers were full of the sufferings of their local Turkish workers. I suggested they do something about the wives and families of their local Turkish workers. It was so far from how they thought that I had to drop it. But why? It is because in Europe we all belong to ex-colonizing countries and we think in terms of going out and telling the natives how to live, and we don't seem to be able to stop doing it.

**32.** Based on the passage, which of the following people would be most likely to also exhibit the "Jellyby phenomenon"?

A. A policeman working an extra shift in an unfamiliar neighborhood
B. A psychiatrist who neglects his own psychological problems
C. A newspaper editor who focuses on world rather than local news
D. An employer who offers lavish vacation benefits for his employees

**33.** The author most likely uses the word *ideologues* (paragraph 4) to mean:

A. right-wing political movements.
B. European feminists.
C. women of Zimbabwe.
D. men of Zimbabwe.

**34.** Suppose that a large majority of feminists agreed to respect Zimbabwean cultural traditions, and to find a unified political agenda to follow in their own countries. This new information would most strongly *challenge* the author's claim that:

A. the Jellyby phenomenon is rooted in colonialism.
B. political movements are intolerant of the past.
C. political groups and oppositions split endlessly.
D. women in Zimbabwe see little value in feminist ideas.

**35.** The author quotes the poet Larkin in paragraph 1 in order to:

A. give a specific example of an intolerance of the past.
B. stress the groundbreaking accomplishments of the 1960s activists.
C. emphasize the openness and licentiousness of the 1960s.
D. illustrate the difference between right-wing and left-wing political viewpoints of the 1960s.

**36.** All of the following questions can be answered by information contained within the passage EXCEPT:

A. What is the average income of African families?
B. Does the political history of a nation affect that nation's citizens' perceptions?
C. Do the feminist movements of the 1960s and of the French Revolution have anything in common?
D. Are song and theater used as outlets of expression in Zimbabwe?

## Passage VII (Questions 37-41)

It is worth dwelling upon the complete parallel between the *theory of art* and the *theory of science*, for it reveals to us one of the most profound motifs in the entire intellectual movement of the Renaissance a new attitude towards the *problem of form*, and a new sensitivity to form. In this respect, poetry and the visual arts point to the same basic relationship.

Borinski has demonstrated the significance of *poetics* for the whole human and intellectual ideal of life in the Renaissance. "On the whole, the influence of antiquity on the Middle Ages was, as has been generally and accurately pointed out, an influence of *content*. And this 'antiquity of content' continued to exercise its influence on into the actual Renaissance period for a considerable time. A change in the attitude of the personality towards antiquity expressed itself in form—starting with the form of the individual in his feeling, thinking, and living, and going on to the renewal of ancient and classical forms in poetry and art, state and society."

The primacy of form in Renaissance life and thought is demonstrable in practically every intellectual field. Lyrical poetry leads the way by becoming the first and the most potent vehicle of the new will to form. In Dante's *Vita nuova* and in Petrarch's sonnets, the feeling for form is, as it were, advanced beyond the feeling for life; whereas the latter still seemed bound to medieval views and sentiments, the former became a truly liberating and redeeming force. The lyrical expression does not merely describe a complete inner reality that already has its own form; rather, it discovers and creates this reality itself.

We can understand the entire allegorical and conceptual language of this lyrical poetry and the content of its problems only if we derive them from their historical presuppositions—from the poetic tradition of the troubadours and from the scientific tradition of the Scholastics. But the new form into which this traditional content was poured was destined gradually to change the content.

In logic, too, the new Renaissance feeling for language, cultivated in humanistic circles, acted as a constant and direct incentive to thought. The striving for purity of language, for freedom from the "barbaric" deformities of Scholastic Latin, leads to a reform of dialectics. Valla's *Elegantiarum linguae latinae libri* have the same aim as his dialectical disputations: both strive for clarity, simplicity, and purification of the language, which, in turn, will immediately lead to neatness and purity of thought.

Clearly it was artistic sensibility that gave concrete determination to the *concept* of nature formulated by Renaissance science. Leonardo da Vinci's artistic work and his scientific achievement are joined not only in a kind of personal union by virtue of which he attains a new vision of "freedom" and "necessity," of "subject" and "object," of "genius" and "nature." It seemed as though the terms in each of these pairs were separated by an abyss, created apparently by the older art theory of Renaissance thinkers whose ideas Leonardo took up and developed further.

However, for Leonardo, the creative power of the artist is as certain as that of theoretical and scientific thought. Science is a second creation made with the understanding; painting is a second creation made with the imagination. But the value of both these creations consists not in their departure from nature and from the empirical truth of things, but precisely in their grasp and revelation of this truth.

Adapted from E. Cassirer, *The Individual and the Cosmos in Renaissance Philosophy*, © 1963 Barnes and Noble.

37. According to the information given in the passage, a common feature of antique, Middle Age, and Renaissance poetry was their similar use of:

    A. content.
    B. form.
    C. expression.
    D. lyrics.

38. The author most likely mentions Dante's *Vita nuova* in order to:

    A. contrast it with Petrarch's sonnets.
    B. emphasize the similarity of content shared between Dante and Petrarch.
    C. prove Dante's intellectual capacity.
    D. give an example of a redemptive poetic form.

39. Based on information in the passage, which of the following best represents the product of Renaissance humanistic teachings?

    A. Dante's *Vita nuova*
    B. Petrarch's sonnets
    C. Borinski's analysis of the significance of poetics
    D. Valla's *Elegantiarum linguae latinae libri*

40. It can be inferred from the passage that literature and art:

    A. were finally freed from the constraints of mirroring reality during the Renaissance.
    B. avoided most of the radical changes that the Renaissance's embrace of primacy of form brought to other fields.
    C. experienced changes during the Renaissance that were consistent with changes felt by scientific fields.
    D. have as their most respected Renaissance practitioners those who publicly eschewed traditional education and devoted themselves to the pure pursuit of abstract beauty.

41. According to the passage, all of the following pertain to form during the Renaissance era EXCEPT:

    A. traditional content was integrated with a new form.
    B. its primacy could be demonstrated in every intellectual field.
    C. it altered both poetry and visual arts.
    D. lyrical poetry was the most powerful expression of form.

## Passage VIII (Questions 42-47)

"Modernity," said Baudelaire, "is the transitory, the fugitive, the contingent, one half of art of which the other half is the eternal and the immutable." For this modern half, light is the vehicle and the resource. It was the Impressionists who made an art of the instantaneous, and Claude Monet (1840–1926) who showed how it could be done.

Monet was born in Paris in 1840 and as a child of five moved with his family to Le Havre on the Normandy coast. In the weather of Normandy, as generations of Channel passengers have painfully learned, the proverbially unpredictable sun, clouds, rain, and fog transform the sky and its sea reflections from moment to moment. Young Monet, impatient to flee the "prison" of school, eagerly explored beaches and cliffs.

At the age of eighteen his father sent him to Paris for advice from established artists and a tour of the salons where artists' reputations were made. He was fascinated by the artists' café world, by the debates between the romantic "nature painters" and the "realists" known for their still lifes.

By the summer of 1864, Monet had begun his staccato life of painting-excursions to the forests near Paris and the seacoasts of Normandy and elsewhere. It was during these twenty years that Monet developed as the Arch-Impressionist. Outside the familiar line of development of Western painting, with new ways of depicting the solid outer world, Monet instead aimed to report whatever the alert artist self could make of the moments of light that came to it.

On a visit to Le Havre in 1872 he painted a view of the harbor, *Impression: Sunrise*, which in 1874 was one of his twelve works (five oils, seven pastels) in a historic private group exhibit. The 165 works also included Degas, Pissarro, Cezanne, Manet, Renoir, Sisley, and Morisot, among others. Monet's painting became the eponym for the school and for a decisive movement in Western arts (not only painting). Monet's painting of Le Havre harbor viewed from his window showed a small brilliant red disk of a sun reflected in broken brushwork on the waters, with shadowy masts and hulls enveloped in damp vapors of a nebulous atmosphere. "I was asked to give a title for the catalogue; I couldn't very well call it a view of Le Havre. So I said, 'Put *Impression*.'" The Impressionist label stuck, and was adopted by the painters themselves. Every Impressionist painting was of a new "subject," which was the visual world of the artist at that evanescent moment.

The outdoor painter worked under stringent time limits. While the studio painter could take four years for a Sistine ceiling and another five to paint the wall behind the altar, an impression by Monet had to be painted with near-photographic speed. Monet sometimes painted for only fifteen minutes at a time on canvas. As Monet's biographer William C. Seitz puts it, he was "shucking off the image of the world perceived by memory in favor of a world perceived momentarily by the senses."

Though suspicious of all prescribed "forms," Monet did create a spectacular new form of painting. In the "series" he found a way to incorporate time in the artist's canvases by capturing a succession of elusive moments. Monet's series were his way of making peace between the laborious painter and the instant impression of the eye. In his early years Monet had sometimes painted more than one picture of the same scene, and so revealed the changing light and atmosphere. But now he planned extensive series of the same subject under variant light, season, and atmosphere. Here was a new use of time and atmosphere, a new epic form, in which the differences between paintings were part of the plot.

Monet's achievement was not in the durable but in the elusive moment. He conquered time by capturing light, the speediest messenger of the senses.

Adapted from D. Boorstin, *The Creators: A History of Heroes of the Imagination*, © 1993 Vintage Books.

42. The author uses the word *eponym* (paragraph 5) to mean:

    A. source
    B. namesake
    C. winner
    D. collective

43. Which of the following, if true, would do the most to *weaken* the author's argument in paragraph 7?

    A. Many Impressionists worked on the same painting from sunrise to sunset.
    B. Most of Monet's works took several days or weeks to finish.
    C. Monet was never able to finish a painting in fifteen minutes or less.
    D. Monet almost always painted from memory.

44. Suppose a new painting by Monet is discovered which closely resembles *Impression: Sunrise*, but which shows a smaller red disc of sun nearer the horizon, deeper shadows, and a darker atmosphere. Based on the passage, the new discovery would most likely:

    A. cause the art world to change to probable date of *Impression: Sunrise* from 1872 to 1895, when Monet was painting series.
    B. weaken the author's claim that the series was a new epic form.
    C. strengthen the author's claim that in his early years Monet had sometimes painted more than one picture of the same scene.
    D. discredit current conceptions about Monet's early years.

45. The author most likely discusses the weather of Normandy (paragraph 2) in order to:

    A. emphasize that young Monet was accustomed to the evanescent moments he would one day capture on canvas.
    B. highlight young Monet's impression of Normandy as a "prison."
    C. explain young Monet's paintings of harbor scenes.
    D. discredit the opinions of typical Channel passengers.

46. Elsewhere the author asserts: "the blurred image of photographed objects in motion had some effect on paintings like Monet's *Boulevard des Capucines* (1873)." Which of the following statements from the passage gives the *least* support to this statement?

    A. "He [Monet] was 'shucking off the image of the world perceived by memory in favor of a world perceived momentarily by the senses'" (paragraph 6).
    B. "Every Impressionist painting was of a new 'subject,' which was the visual world of the artist at that evanescent moment" (paragraph 5).
    C. "Monet's achievement was not in the durable but in the elusive moment. He conquered time by capturing light, the speediest messenger of the senses" (paragraph 8).
    D. "Here was a new use of time and atmosphere, a new epic form, in which the differences between paintings were part of the plot" (paragraph 7).

47. In his writings Monet compared himself to an animal that could not stop painting, for he was "a prisoner of his visual experiences." Based on the passage, this attitude can be most directly related to his:

    A. desire to make peace between the laborious painter and the instant impression of the eye.
    B. feeling of exclusion from the mainstream art world.
    C. reaction to the experiences of his early school days.
    D. impatience with the limitations created by the expectations of the public and other painters of what an "Impressionist" painting should look like.

## Passage IX (Questions 48-53)

In most cultures, there is no clear line separating myth from folk or fairy tale; all these together form the literature of preliterate societies. The Nordic languages have only one word for both: saga. German has retained the word *Sage* for myths, while fairy stories are called *Marchen*. It is unfortunate that both the English and French names for these stories emphasize the role of fairies in them—because in most, no fairies appear.

Myths and fairy tales alike attain a definite form only when they are committed to writing and are no longer subject to continuous change. Before being written down, these stories were either condensed or vastly elaborated in the retelling over the centuries; some stories merged with others. All became modified by what the teller thought was of greatest interest to his listeners, by what his concerns of the moment or the special problems of his era were.

Some fairy and folk stories evolved out of myths; others were incorporated into them. Both forms embodied the cumulative experience of a society as men wished to recall past wisdom for themselves and transmit it to future generations. These tales are the purveyors of deep insights that have sustained mankind through the long vicissitudes of its existence, a heritage that is not revealed in any other form as simply and directly, or as accessibly, to children.

Myths and fairy tales have much in common. But in myths, much more than in fairy stories, the culture hero is presented to the listener as a figure he ought to emulate in his own life, as far as possible.

A myth, like a fairy tale, may express an inner conflict in symbolic form and suggest how it may be solved—but this is not necessarily the myth's central concern. The myth presents its theme in a majestic way; it carries spiritual force; and the divine is present and is experienced in the form of superhuman heroes who make constant demands on mere mortals. Much as we, the mortals, may strive to be like these heroes, we will remain always and obviously inferior to them.

The figures and events of fairy tales also personify and illustrate inner conflicts, but they suggest ever so subtly how these conflicts may be solved, and what the next steps in the development toward a higher humanity might be. The fairy tale is presented in a simple, homely way; no demands are made on the listener. This prevents even the smallest child from feeling compelled to act in specific ways, and he is never made to feel inferior. Far from making demands, the fairy tale reassures, gives hope for the future, and holds out the promise of a happy ending. That is why Lewis Carroll called it a "love-gift"—a term hardly applicable to a myth.

Obviously, not every story contained in a collection called "Fairy Tales" meets these criteria. Many of these stories are simply diversions, cautionary tales or fables. If they are fables, they tell by means of words, actions, or events—fabulous though these may be—what one ought to do. Fables demand and threaten—they are moralistic—or they just entertain. To decide whether a story is a fairy tale or something entirely different, one might ask whether it could rightly be called a love-gift to a child. That is not a bad way to arrive at a classification.

Adapted from B. Bettelheim, *The Uses of Enchantment,*
© 1975 B. Bettelheim.

48. The main purpose of the passage is best summarized by which of the following?

    A. To explain the ways in which fables are related to fairy tales
    B. To promote the benefits of reading myths and fairy tales to children
    C. To elaborate on the similarities and differences between myths and fairy tales
    D. To explore the historical origins of myths

49. According to the author, fairy tales with which we are now familiar were:

    A. fashioned by generations of storytellers who may have known neither how to read nor how to write.
    B. originally written by gifted storytellers who knew what kind of stories would appeal to large audiences.
    C. first crafted as fables and gradually transformed into fairy tales.
    D. written first in German and only later translated into French or English.

50. Based on the passage, with which of the following would the author most likely agree regarding the virtues of fairy tales?

    A. They continue cultural traditions that children need and desire to be taught.
    B. They explain a culture's historical origins.
    C. They never fail to provide explicit behavioral standards.
    D. They help children understand how people manage to overcome obstacles faced in life.

51. The author suggests that each of the following is an important purpose of myth EXCEPT to:

    A. identify inner conflicts in people and to suggest how they may be solved.
    B. explain the natural phenomena that people observe every day.
    C. inspire ordinary people to emulate super-human heroes.
    D. transmit a society's cultural heritage.

52. The passage suggests which one of the following regarding fairy tales as they are thought of today?

    A. Their configuration is changeable, unless they have been written down.
    B. They evolved from myths, which were an earlier story form.
    C. They change over time to reflect moral conflicts faced by the audience.
    D. Most fairy tales represent real historical events.

53. The author's attitude towards fairy tales can best be described as:

    A. critical.
    B. patronizing.
    C. admiring.
    D. impartial.

## END OF TEST 4

© TPR Education IP Holdings, LLC | 243

# ANSWER KEY — TEST 4

| Passage I | Passage II | Passage III | Passage IV | Passage V | Passage VI | Passage VII | Passage VIII | Passage IX |
|---|---|---|---|---|---|---|---|---|
| 1.  B | 7.  D | 14.  B | 19.  D | 25.  A | 32.  B | 37.  A | 42.  B | 48.  C |
| 2.  A | 8.  B | 15.  B | 20.  A | 26.  D | 33.  B | 38.  D | 43.  D | 49.  A |
| 3.  D | 9.  C | 16.  C | 21.  A | 27.  C | 34.  C | 39.  D | 44.  C | 50.  D |
| 4.  D | 10.  D | 17.  D | 22.  C | 28.  C | 35.  A | 40.  C | 45.  A | 51.  B |
| 5.  B | 11.  D | 18.  A | 23.  B | 29.  B | 36.  A | 41.  B | 46.  D | 52.  A |
| 6.  C | 12.  D | | 24.  D | 30.  C | | | 47.  A | 53.  C |
| | 13.  B | | | 31.  B | | | | |

 © TPR Education IP Holdings, LLC

# Test Assessment Log

Use this Log to evaluate your performance on this CARS Practice Test. Diagnose what led you to select (or seriously consider) wrong answers, or to spend more time than necessary to identify the correct answer.

Approximate the time you spent on the Now passages and on the Later passages. Consider if you are spending the time needed on easier passages to get most of those questions right, or, if you are spending more time than necessary and not getting to as many questions as you could while still maintaining good accuracy. If you find that you are spending most of your 90 minutes on harder passages with a low level of accuracy, consider how best to reapportion your time on your next practice test. Finally, evaluate your ranking; are you choosing the right passages and doing them at roughly the right time within the section?

## Now Passages

| Now Passage # | Q # and Type (for questions you got wrong) | Attractors (for wrong answers you picked or seriously considered) | What did you do wrong? |
|---|---|---|---|
|  |  |  |  |
|  |  |  |  |
|  |  |  |  |
|  |  |  |  |
|  |  |  |  |
|  |  |  |  |

Approximate time spent on Now passages _____

Total Now passages attempted _____

Total # of Q's on Now passages attempted _____

Total # of Now Q's correct _____

% correct of Now Q's attempted _____

## Later Passages

| Later Passage # | Q # and Type (for questions you got wrong) | Attractors (for wrong answers you picked or seriously considered) | What did you do wrong? |
|---|---|---|---|
| | | | |
| | | | |
| | | | |
| | | | |
| | | | |
| | | | |

Approximate time spent on Later passages _____

Total Later passages attempted _____

Total # of Q's on Later passages attempted _____

Total # of Later Q's correct _____

% correct of Later Q's attempted _____

# Final Analysis

Total # of passages attempted (including partially completed) _____

Total # of questions attempted _____

Total # of correct answers _____

Total % correct of attempted questions _____

## Revised Strategy

| | |
|---|---|
| **Pacing** | |
| **Passage choice/ranking** | |
| **Working the Passage** | |
| **Attacking the Questions** | |

# MCAT
# Critical Analysis and Reasoning Skills

# Practice Test 4
# Solutions

# TEST 4 SOLUTIONS

## Passage I

This is a Later passage.

**Bottom Line:** Modern music should be appreciated, and on its own terms.

1.    B     This is a Retrieval question.
   - A:   No. The author specifies a variety of reasons that modern listeners may fail to appreciate contemporary music. Thus the passage suggests that people today criticize modern music for those specific characteristics, not because they believe it to be insufficiently universal. The author does use the word "universal" in paragraph 5, but in the context of the claim that contemporary music should be listened to because of its unique qualities.
   - **B:**   **Yes. In paragraph 3 the author says that avoidance of sentiment and feeling is the "reproach that is repeated more often than any other."**
   - C:   No. The author states that modern music does express subtleties of light and dark (paragraph 6).
   - D:   No. Lack of straightforward melody is one potential problem or source of confusion (paragraph 2), but it is not the *most* common problem. That problem would be the "reproach repeated more often than any other," the music's apparent lack of sentiment and feeling (paragraph 3).

2.    A     This is an Inference question.
   - **A:**   **Yes. The passage asserts that repeated hearings of intricate melodies will clarify their appeal (paragraph 2).**
   - B:   No. The author recommends listening repeatedly to the same piece (paragraph 2), not abandoning it for another piece.
   - C:   No. In paragraph 2 the author suggests listening to the piece again, not casting it aside for a different piece and different composer.
   - D:   No. The author gives explicit advice; listen to that piece repeatedly until it becomes clear.

3.    D     This is a New Information question.
   - A:   No. The correct answer will be a statement made by the author that is inconsistent with the scenario presented in the question. The author's assertion that older music should seem foreign to us has no direct relevance to the case of the counterfeit music.
   - B:   No. Controversy and resentment are not issues here.
   - C:   No. The scenario describes a piece in the style of the sixteenth century; it suggests nothing about sensitivity to contemporary music.
   - **D:**   **Yes. The question describes an exact duplication of the sixteenth-century mode of expression; the author claims in the statement cited in the answer choice that such duplication is impossible (paragraph 6).**

4. D    This is an Inference/NOT question.
   A:   No. We *would* expect to find such climaxes in modern music (paragraph 6). Milhaud and Schuman are presented as modern composers whose music should strike us as less foreign than that of the older (deceased) composers (paragraph 5).
   B:   No. We *would* expect to find abandonment and hysteria in modern composers such as Bartók (paragraph 4).
   C:   No. Sessions and Bartók are shown to be modern composers through the author's contrast between them and Brahms and Tchaikovsky (paragraph 4). Thus it would *not* be surprising to discover such climaxes and explosions in their work.
   **D:   Yes. Buxtehude and Cherubini are composers of the past (paragraph 5). Therefore it would be surprising to find climaxes of abandonment and explosive hysteria, characteristics of contemporary music, in their compositions (paragraph 6).**


5. B    This is a Structure question.
   A:   No. The author argues that modern music is or can be just as enjoyable as romantic compositions, not that romantic music is just as good as contemporary works.
   **B:   Yes. The author argues that we do not expect the modern Eliot to write with the voice of the romantics Hugo and Scott, and makes an analogy to what we should not expect of contemporary music (paragraph 4).**
   C:   No. The author mentions Eliot and Hugo to draw an analogy, not to dramatize differences between literature and music (paragraph 4).
   D:   No. The author suggests that Eliot's work is different from that of writers of the past, and so should be appreciated on its own terms. He uses this claim to make the point that listeners who complain that modern *music* is too dry and cerebral simply do not sufficiently appreciate the characteristic musical speech of their own time (paragraph 4).


6. C    This is a NOT Weaken question.
        Note: The credited response will be one that either strengthens or has no effect on the author's contention.
   A:   No. This choice would weaken the passage by indicating that romantic standards of comparison have relevance to contemporary music; the author himself recognizes a valid analogy between music and literature (paragraph 4).
   B:   No. This choice weakens the analogy made by the author between readers' appreciation of modern writing and the appreciation listeners should have for modern music (paragraph 4). If contemporary readers prefer romantic works, the author's contention (that those who fail to appreciate modern music are using inappropriate standards of comparison) becomes less convincing.
   **C:   Yes. This choice would have no effect on the author's contention. The fact that Eliot studied works from the past does not indicate that he followed their stylistic models or that contemporary literature does not have its own unique language.**
   D:   No. This choice directly contradicts the author's claims that each period has its own unique form of expression (paragraph 6), and that we cannot judge contemporary music and literature by romantic standards (paragraph 4).

## Passage II
This is a Later/Killer passage.

**Bottom Line:** Various views exist regarding rights of, and our duties to, animals.

7.    D        This is an Inference question.

A:    No. The correlativity thesis indicates that if we do show that we have obligations to animals, animals must have corresponding rights (paragraph 5). The author has us suppose that we have such obligations for the sake of explaining the thesis, but the passage never indicates that we do in fact have obligations to animals.

B:    No. The opponents of the thesis argue that it is invalid because objects and resources have no rights (paragraph 6). It is the proponents of the thesis who raise the issue of direct vs. indirect duties (paragraph 7).

C:    No. The author never states a personal position on the question of whether or not animals have rights.

**D:    Yes. If it were to be demonstrated that we have obligations to animals, and the thesis itself is accepted, it would be true that animals have rights (paragraph 5). Notice the moderate wording of this answer choice compared to choice A.**

8.    B        This is a Weaken question.

A:    No. The correct answer will be inconsistent with Aquinas's views as they are described in the passage. According to the author, Aquinas believes that we have no duties to animals; he never indicates that God does not love them.

**B:    Yes. Paragraph 3 tells us that Aquinas believes that we sin only when we fail to fulfill a duty to ourselves or to God, and that we have no duties to animals. The only way slaying of animals and plants would be a sin in these terms is if it leads us to sin against rational beings. The quote presents an analogy between humans on one hand and animals and plants on the other by claiming that taking the life of any plant or animal is a sin "for the same reason" (deprivation of life) that killing a human is a sin. This equivalence drawn between humans and animals is inconsistent with Aquinas's views as they are presented in the passage.**

C:    No. This statement is not inconsistent with Aquinas's view that our treatment of animals is to be judged by its effects on humans (paragraph 4).

D:    No. Aquinas agrees that animals are irrational (paragraph 4), and the passage never indicates that he supported human friendship with them. This choice is not inconsistent, and so does not undermine the author's depiction.

9.  C   This is an Inference question.

    A:  No. All we know of Descartes from the passage is that he believed (unlike Aquinas and Aristotle) that animals are not sentient (paragraph 3). Aquinas would disagree with the statement that we have obligations to animals, but we do not know Descartes' position on the subject.

    B:  No. As in choice A, we only know of Descartes' position on sentience. We cannot infer anything from that about his position on reason.

    **C:  Yes. The passage defines sentience as "the capacity to experience pleasure or pain" (paragraph 2). Thus Aquinas, who unlike Descartes believes animals are sentient (paragraph 3), would agree with the statement and Descartes would disagree.**

    D:  No. This answer choice applies to the discussion of correlativity in the final two paragraphs. No information is given in the passage to allow us to deduce the position of either Descartes or Aquinas on that issue.

10.  D   This is a New Information question.

    A:  No. The author defines sentience as "the capacity to experience pleasure and pain" (paragraph 2). The quote from Sartre entails how man acts to define or create himself in the world—there is no connection in the quote or in the passage between feelings and actions.

    B:  No. The correlativity thesis (if we have duties to others, they have corresponding rights (paragraph 5) has no direct relevance to this quote.

    C:  No. The issue of direct vs. indirect duties arises in the context of discussion of the correlativity thesis (paragraphs 5 and 7), which has no relevance to the Sartre quote.

    **D:  Yes. The author defines autonomy as "the capacity to make free choices" (paragraph 2). In the quote given in the question, Sartre describes how man makes and defines himself through his free will: "he will be what he makes himself" or what he chooses to be.**

11.  D   This is a Strengthen question.

    A:  No. The correlativity thesis, as described here, makes no claims or assumptions based on equal rights among animals or between animal species.

    B:  No. Proponents of the thesis argue that we have an indirect, not a direct duty to things such as oceans and woodlands—our direct duty is to future generations themselves (paragraph 7).

    C:  No. The proponents' position indicates that we have a direct duty to future generations (paragraph 7).

    **D:  Yes. Critics of the thesis claim that we have a duty not to destroy certain things that clearly do not have corresponding rights (paragraph 6). The proponents respond that we have only indirect duties to such things, and that the thesis applies only to cases of direct duty (paragraph 7). If we were to have a direct duty to future generations to preserve the ecosystem, it would support the distinction drawn by the proponents. It would also further undermine their critics' supposed counter example by showing that correlativity could explain our duty to preserve resources without claiming that those resources somehow themselves have rights.**

12.  D    This is a Structure question.

A:   No. Descartes is mentioned only in passing as someone who holds a different position on sentience (paragraph 3). The author does not dwell on or highlight this difference.

B:   No. The author does mention that the idea that a being must be able to reason in order to have rights goes back to Aristotle (paragraph 2). However, sentience and reason are discussed in the second paragraph in order to introduce the author's discussion of Aquinas's views, a discussion which continues on into the third and fourth paragraphs. Furthermore, sentience and reason are presented as necessary, not sufficient conditions. We have no duties towards beings that lack them (paragraph 2), yet the passage never indicates that we do have duties towards all beings that satisfy those conditions.

C:   No. The author never expresses a personal opinion on the issue of animal rights. Furthermore, sentience and rationality are part of the author's discussion of duties. His consideration of whether the existence of duties would entail the existence of rights comes later in the passage, in the final two paragraphs.

D:   **Yes. The author raises the issues of sentience and rationality in order to introduce the discussion of Aquinas's claim that we have no duties towards animals because they, while sentient, lack the capacity for reason (paragraph 2).**


13.  B    This is an Inference question.

A:   No. This statement is suggested as a belief held by Aquinas (paragraph 4). The author never indicates that he agrees with Aquinas on this point.

B:   **Yes. In the first paragraph the author states that the satisfaction of certain conditions may cause us to have duties towards beings, including animals. Note that the author never states his own opinion on whether or not those conditions are fulfilled by any non-human being.**

C:   No. This is taking the author's statement in the beginning of paragraph 5 too literally. The author has us suppose that we do have such an obligation in order to explain the correlativity thesis, not in order to indicate his own beliefs on the topic.

D:   No. The author describes others' beliefs that we have a duty to preserve great art (paragraph 6). However, we cannot infer that the author follows this belief. Note the wording used: "some argue" and "our supposed duty."

# Passage III

This is a Now passage.

**Bottom Line:** Positive attitude important in fight against cancer; requires in part correct understanding of mortality stats.

14.  B        This is a New Information question.

  A:    No. The author's description of the curve for mesothelioma in paragraph 7 would apply to PML as well. The mortality curve cannot be symmetrical. The lower boundary must be zero, as the disease could at the latest be discovered at or soon after death (paragraph 7). However, a few individuals might live for many years after diagnosis, thus skewing the curve to the right.

  **B:    Yes. See paragraph 7. The discovery of the disease begins the curve at zero. According to the author, one could die at the same time that the disease is discovered, but no earlier. However, while half those diagnosed would die before the median point and half after, some people may live much longer than four to six months after the median (that is, longer than eight to twelve months total). If one person, for example, lived for several years (a likely possibility), the curve would extend far to the right to include that individual. Thus the curve would be skewed to the right.**

  C:    No. The author states that disease is discovered at death or before (paragraph 7). Thus we cannot have a few individuals whose disease is "discovered" long after death pulling the curve to the left in the same way that at least a few long-term survivors are likely to pull it out to the right.

  D:    No. There is no evidence given in the question of the passage to indicate that the mean (average) mortality for PML will be lower than the median (the middle number in the series) length of survival.

15.  B        This is a Strengthen question.

  A:    No. This choice is too wishy-washy to significantly strengthen the author's claim. The third paragraph proposes a possible causal connection between attitude and ability to fight off cancer. The fact that not all people with sanguine or cheerful personalities get cancer does not show that their personality played any causal protective role.

  **B:    Yes. This indicates that when a person's attitude improves, they are less likely to die from ovarian cancer, thus supporting the existence of a causal connection. Notice the word "significantly," which makes this choice strong enough to bolster the author's claim.**

  C:    No. This statement would somewhat weaken, not strengthen the passage. The author argues in paragraph 3 that a positive attitude may boost the immune system and improve one's ability to fight cancer. This answer choice indicates that the immune system has little to do with whether or not we have cancer.

  D:    No. This statement would weaken, not strengthen the author's argument that a positive attitude or emotional status can help a person to resist cancer (paragraph 3).

16.   C       This is an Inference question.

A:     No. Mesothelioma has a median mortality of eight months (paragraph 2). A median is the midpoint in a series, meaning half the people die before eight months, and half after (paragraph 7). Therefore a majority will have died after eight months, not within six months.

B:     No. While the author suggests that most people would misunderstand or misinterpret the statistical information in the literature (paragraph 4), he does not suggest that misinterpretation of their own life expectancies constitutes irresponsibility.

C:     **Yes. In paragraph 4, the author claims that the majority of people faced with these statistics would (incorrectly) believe that they will die within eight months.**

D:     No. The author never suggests that people either can or will change their personality.

17.   D       This is an Inference/Roman numeral question.

I:     **True. The author states that Platonic logic sees means and medians as "hard 'realities'," yet that in fact variation is the true "reality" (paragraph 5).**

II:     **True. The author would reject a Platonic quest for a hard and clear marker of the boundary at which life begins (paragraph 5).**

III:     **True. Platonic thought holds that clear distinctions and categorizations define "reality," while the author believes reality lies in variation (paragraph 5).**

18.   A       This is an Inference question.

A:     **Yes. The author states in paragraph 3 that he believes that "Attitude clearly matters," and this is likely due to the effect of mental states on one's immune system. From this you can infer that a negative attitude would likely have a negative effect.**

B:     No. This choice is too extreme. The author only suggests that it can affect one's health, not that it can cure an incurable disease. Keep in mind that when the author discusses the possibility of beating his disease in the last paragraph, he is referring to the potential effect of experimental treatment, not the effect of attitude.

C:     No. Be careful not to use opinion or outside knowledge. The author never suggests that people with good attitudes might receive better health care.

D:     No. This is the right answer to the wrong question. In paragraph 7 the author lists a variety of reasons why this curve is right-skewed, but none of them relate to attitude.

# Passage IV

This is a Now passage.

**Bottom Line:** History of US/Cuba relations determined by economic and political concerns.

19. **D**     This is a New Information question.
    A:     No. The Soviet Union is only mentioned in paragraph 4 and only insofar as Cuban sugar was exchanged for Soviet oil. This is a Not the Issue (Out of Scope) Attractor.
    B:     No. The quote is relevant to the relationship between the US and underdeveloped countries (paragraph 3), not to relationships within the US's own political and economic system. (The military-industrial complex is mentioned in paragraph 5.).
    C:     No. The United States drove Spain out of Cuba (paragraph 1); no other relationship between the two countries is described in the passage.
    **D:**     **Yes. Dulles and Eisenhower wished to install a liberal democratic government in Cuba without transforming the economy in an equally democratic direction (paragraph 3).**

20. **A**     This is a Retrieval/Roman numeral question.
    I:     **True. The Spanish occupiers were driven out in 1898 (paragraph 1).**
    II:     False. There is no indication of any American role in Cuba before 1898. So, there is no evidence of any American power, including power held by the American Ambassadorship in Cuba before 1898.
    III:     False. According to the passage, American forces intervened to protect investments only after 1902 (paragraph 1).

21. **A**     This is a Retrieval question.
    Note: Before considering the answer choices, go back to paragraph 3 and 6 and read what each man is reported to have said; this makes it easier to eliminate wrong answers.
    **A:**     **Yes. Dulles was unenthusiastic about the coming to power of Castro, and warned Eisenhower of the likelihood that Communists would participate in the Cuban Government (paragraph 3). Eisenhower, under whom Dulles served, wished for some non-Castroite force to take control. The author indicates that Kennedy also had anti-Communist feelings engendered by the Cold War and that as President he wished to take decisive offensive action (in general terms) (paragraph 6). Thus both Dulles and Kennedy would likely agree with the statement.**
    B:     No. This choice is too extreme. While both would agree that Cuban extremists posed a danger, we have no evidence that both men had the same fears about all extremists.
    C:     No. Kennedy made such a claim (paragraph 6), but the passage gives no evidence that Dulles would agree.
    D:     No. The author indicates that both Dulles and Kennedy might be pro-intervention in the service of protecting United States' interests. The passage does not indicate that either believed that the need or opportunity to intervene in the Cuban economy would never arise again.

22.   C       This is a Weaken question.
              Note: The credited response will provide evidence that Castro did in fact offer some form of compensation.
      A:      No. While this answer choice indicates that new Cuban landowners *feared* that compensation would be offered, that is not enough evidence to show that it was actually offered. Remember that while wishy-washy answers are normally better supported than stronger answers, for "most strengthen" and "most weaken" questions they may not be strong enough to be good answers to the question. This is a Not strong enough Attractor.
      B:      Batista's actions in the past indicate nothing about Castro's actions during and after 1959. This answer choice is irrelevant to the question; it is a Not the Issue (Out of Scope) Attractor.
      C:      **Yes. This choice tells us that an offer of compensation, however low, was in fact given and then rejected.**
      D:      No. It was the US, not Castro who eliminated the sugar quota in the first place (paragraph 4), and the sugar quota has no direct relevance to showing whether or not compensation for seized property was offered. This is a Not the Issue (Out of Scope) Attractor.

23.   B       This is a Tone/Attitude question.
              Note: As with most questions, it is beneficial here to revisit the paragraph in question and formulate an answer before going through the answer choices. Define if 1) the tone is positive, negative, or neutral and 2) if positive or negative, how strongly. The Attractors that appear in these answer choices are all too extreme in one direction or another.
      A:      No. This choice is too strongly positive. The author describes Kennedy's promises for the future, yet indicates that it was unclear how or whether those promises would be fulfilled (paragraph 6).
      B:      **Yes. One is ambivalent when one has conflicting or differing feelings about a person or subject. The author presents Kennedy's promises in a positive light, and yet indicates doubt about how or whether they would be fulfilled (paragraph 6).**
      C:      No. This choice is too negative. The author uses a largely, though not completely positive tone in the sixth paragraph in describing Kennedy's ideas and approach.
      D:      No. Antithetical means in opposition. The passage does indicate some question or concern about the specific direction the Kennedy administration would take (paragraph 6). However, the author does not severely criticize Kennedy or his ideas.

24.   D       This is an Inference question.
      A:      No. The Democrats paid no attention to Eisenhower's concerns about the military-industrial complex (paragraph 6). This is a Right answer/wrong question (Decoy) Attractor.
      B:      No. The Democrats had no response towards the military-industrial complex (paragraph 6); their approach to governing, according to the author, lacked specificity.
      C:      No. This choice is too extreme. While the Democrats failed to respond to Eisenhower's concerns about protecting small-town ideals, the author does not suggest that their lack of response to the military-industrial complex itself trampled those ideals. Be careful not to use outside knowledge about antagonism between Republicans and Democrats to make too great of an inferential leap.
      D:      **Yes. The author indicates in paragraphs 5 and 6 that Eisenhower feared that the military-industrial complex and big government would trample small-town ideals, and that the Democrats paid no attention to these concerns.**

## Passage V

This is a Now passage.

**Bottom Line:** Forced giving of Christmas gifts has negative effect on economy.

25.  A    This is a Primary Purpose question.

    A:    **Yes. The author demonstrates the economic inefficiency of Christmas, and writes of the disastrous effect it has on consumer savings. According to the author, the entire institution is absurd (paragraph 2); piecemeal reforms or modifications are not a viable solution. Clearly, he is bah-humbugging Christmas. "Harsh critique" is strong language, but the passage itself is unrelentingly critical in its tone.**

    B:    No. The reference to a Marxist interpretation (paragraph 4) is only an aside; it is not the focus of the passage.

    C:    No. The author says exactly the opposite; in paragraph 2 he discusses the notable inefficiency of the barter system.

    D:    No. While the author does make this criticism (paragraph 3), it is only one part of the author's argument. This choice is too narrow. Be careful to look for and avoid overly specific Decoy answers on general questions.

26.  D    This is an Inference question.

    A:    No. The idea of exchange, or barter, comes later in the passage (paragraph 2) and is not connected by the author to gratuitous giving.

    B:    No. While the passage does state that some Christmas gifts are unwanted (paragraph 2), this is not the author's point in the first paragraph. This is the right answer to the wrong question.

    C:    No. Extravagant gifts ("for 'the person who has everything'") are discussed in the third paragraph, not here or in this context.

    D:    **Yes. Something that is gratuitous is unnecessary, or uncalled for. In the first paragraph the author discusses "forced giving" and "extra consumer spending" and characterizes it all as "waste."**

27.  C    This is an Inference/EXCEPT question.

    Note: The credited response will NOT be supported by the passage.

    A:    No. See paragraphs 3 and 4.

    B:    No. This is the main point of the second and third paragraphs.

    C:    **Yes. While the author points out that January is a peak month for credit card delinquencies, he does not claim that purchases fall off in that month. Be careful not to use outside knowledge, in this case to eliminate the choice thinking that it IS supported by the passage.**

    D:    No. See paragraph 4.

28.   C         This is an Inference question.
      A:        No. "...[O]ther times of the year..." are not discussed in the passage. Watch out for subtle changes in the scope of the answer as compared to the passage.
      B:        No. The pricing habits of retailers are not discussed in the passage.
      C:        **Yes. Although the author argues the trend does not serve consumers, retailers feel the economic benefit and share in the "economic interest."**
      D:        No. "...[T]o stay in business..." is too strong a statement, given the information found in the passage. Watch for conclusions that are too strong to be supported by the passage.

29.   B         This is an Inference question.
      A:        No. The author demonstrates only one flaw of capitalism: the way in which merchants can exploit a holiday and consequently waste some of our resources. He does not expose "an inherent weakness in the capitalist enterprise" as a whole; this answer choice goes too far.
      B:        **Yes. This can be inferred from paragraph 4, where the author claims that personal spending "increases the burden of consumer debt" not just on individuals but "for the nation as a whole."**
      C:        No. Only luxury goods (paragraph 3) currently fit this criterion. The author never implies that other categories of consumer goods will follow suit.
      D:        No. The statement makes a prediction that cannot be justified from the passage alone. This is a Crystal Ball (Out of Scope) Attractor.

30.   C         This is a Weaken question.
      A:        No. If consumer debt were steadily growing worse, then the author's assertions would be supported, not challenged.
      B:        No. This choice is irrelevant to the claims of the passage, which have to do with the effect of Christmas on the economy, not with the effects of the economy on Christmas. Be careful not to confuse the cause/effect relationship in the passage. This is a Reversal (Decoy) Attractor.
      C:        **Yes. This answer choice provides reason to believe that Christmas spending is beneficial to the economy, and that we would be worse off without it. This does weaken the author's claims.**
      D:        No. Just because other gift-buying occasions are bad for consumers doesn't mean that the author is wrong about Christmas; this statement does not address the question topic directly. This is a Not the Issue (Out of Scope) Attractor.

31.  B   This is a Retrieval question.
         Note: Whenever you find a paragraph reference or quotation in the question stem, return to the passage to establish your answer before reading your options. The problem of the barter system was the difficulty of ensuring that "people have to match other people's wants to their offerings" (paragraph 2). The author argues that this was the problem solved by money.

     A:  No. Transportation is not mentioned in the passage, and it is not the "double coincidence of wants" problem—the necessity of each person in the exchange having what the other wants.

     **B:  Yes. Thus, the seller gives the buyer what he or she wants, and the money that the seller receives can be used at any time to satisfy the seller's wants. Money eliminates the need for each to "match other people's wants to their offerings."**

     C:  No. Credit is not discussed in the context of the "double coincidence of wants" problem. The implication is that the buyer and seller make an immediate transaction of goods for money.

     D:  No. Investment is not discussed in the context of the "double coincidence of wants" problem.

# Passage VI

This is a Now/Later passage.

**Bottom Line:** Feminists, grounded in political movement, fail to understand the past and women in other countries.

32.  B   This is an Analogy question.

     A:  No. The Jellyby phenomenon occurs when people try to fix the problems of others while ignoring problems at home (paragraph 5). The policeman may be working to solve the problems of others, but there is no indication that he is failing to help people in his own neighborhood.

     **B:  Yes. A psychiatrist tries to help others, but at the same time this psychiatrist is ignoring his own problems. Out of these four choices, this one is the closest to the passage.**

     C:  No. Neither solving the problems of others nor ignoring one's own problems is involved in this example.

     D:  No. The employer is helping others in his own business, and there is no reason to conclude that he is ignoring problems in his own home.

33.  B   This is an Inference question.

     A:  No. "Ideologues" in this context refers to European feminists. The author does not suggest that these feminists are politically to the right.

     **B:  Yes. This paragraph continues the author's discussion of the irrelevance of European feminist ideas to Zimbabwean reality. The "ideologues" are the European feminists who are lecturing the African women.**

     C:  No. The ideologues are the European feminists who are being mocked or criticized by the Zimbabwean women.

     D:  No. The ideologues are Europeans, not Africans.

34.    C     This is a New Information question.
                 Note: The correct answer will be a statement that is inconsistent with the decisions described in the question.

         A:     No. Respecting Zimbabwean tradition is not inconsistent with focusing on the problems of others rather than the problems in one's own country. Furthermore, it doesn't undermine the author's claim that the phenomenon itself arises out of the colonial experience.

         B:     No. There is no reference to attitudes towards the past in the new scenario described in the question.

         C:     **Yes. If the majority of feminists agreed on a unified political agenda, it would undermine the author's claim that political groups are unable to work together (paragraph 1).**

         D:     No. Perhaps they might find something to value in the future if feminists do come to be more responsive to their concerns, but this does not mean that they currently see value in feminist ideas.

35.    A     This is a Structure question.

         A:     **Yes. Part of political movements' intolerance of the past is the belief that they are doing everything for the first time, even when this is clearly not the case (paragraph 1).**

         B:     No. This is taking Larkin's statement that "we invented sex" a bit too literally.

         C:     No. As in choice B, this takes Larkin's statement to mean that people in the '60s really did invent or transform sex in some fundamental way. The author intends the statement to indicate just the opposite. Despite the beliefs of many a political movement "in the full flush of its star" (paragraph 1), the author suggests that there is really nothing new under the sun.

         D:     No. The author never refers to left or right-wing movements.

36.    A     This is an Inference/EXCEPT question.
                 Note: The correct answer will be a question that cannot be answered by information provided in the passage.

         A:     **Yes. While the author tells us that some African women raise their families on between sixty and eighty dollars a month (paragraph 3), she never divulges the *average* income of African families.**

         B:     No. The author asserts that we "think in terms of going out and telling the neighbors how to live" because we (meaning Europeans) belong to "ex-colonizing countries" (paragraph 5). Therefore, this "Jellyby phenomenon" affects how we perceive the world and our actions within it. Therefore, political history (in this case colonialism) affects our perceptions.

         C:     No. In paragraph 1 the author states that the feminist movements of the '60s were born in politics, as were the feminist movements that arose from the French and Russian Revolutions. The rest of the first paragraph and the second paragraph go on to list a variety of characteristics that all political movements, including feminist movements, have in common.

         D:     No. This question is answered in the description of Zimbabwean women singing, dancing, and acting out their complaints and criticisms (paragraph 4).

# Passage VII

This is a Later/Killer passage.

**Bottom Line:** The shift to focus on form during Renaissance also affected ways of thinking.

37.    A     This is a Retrieval question.

       **A:**    **Yes. In paragraph 2 the author explains that the influence of content exerted by antiquity on the Middle Ages continued into the Renaissance.**

       B:    No. Use of, and importance placed on, form changed significantly in the Renaissance period (paragraph 2).

       C:    No. According to paragraph 2, the form of expression changed in the Renaissance; no similarities in other aspects of expression are mentioned.

       D:    No. "Lyrical poetry," as far as we know from the passage, is not the same thing as "lyrics," which are never mentioned by the author. The only reference to song comes in the mention of troubadours in paragraph 4. However, the passage never mentions a similarity in the lyrics of the songs of the troubadours in these two periods.

38.    D     This is a Structure question.

       A:    No. The author mentions both Dante's *Vita nuova* and Petrarch's sonnets as examples of the new primacy of form in the Renaissance (paragraph 3). No contrast between the two is given.

       B:    No. The author describes their similarity not in content, but in their "feeling for form" (paragraph 3).

       C:    No. The author refers to Dante to illustrate the primacy of form in "practically every intellectual field" (beginning of paragraph 3), not to demonstrate Dante's own intellectual capacity.

       **D:**    **Yes. Lyrical poetry, including *Vita nuova*, was the most powerful embodiment of this new "will to form." The passage calls this feeling for and transformation of form a "truly liberating and redeeming force" (second half of paragraph 3).**

39.    D     This is an Inference question.

       A:    No. Dante's *Vita nuova* represents the Renaissance feeling for form (paragraph 3), but the author doesn't directly connect it to humanism.

       B:    No. Petrarch's sonnets are mentioned in the same breath as Dante's *Vita nuova* in paragraph 3; neither is directly tied to humanistic teachings.

       C:    No. Borinski discusses the issue of form and content in the Middle Ages and the Renaissance (paragraph 2); the author does not indicate that Borinski himself was influenced by, or was a product of, humanism.

       **D:**    **Yes. Valla's work is cited as an example of the new Renaissance feeling for language (or form), which according to the passage was "cultivated in humanist circles" (paragraph 5).**

40. C    This is an Inference question.
    - A: No. Through the author's discussion of da Vinci, we see that art in the Renaissance attempted to better reflect the ultimate truth of nature (paragraph 7), not to divorce itself from reality.
    - B: No. The passage presents literature and art as powerful examples of the primacy of form in the Renaissance.
    - **C: Yes. In paragraph 6, the author mentions the influence of changes in artistic sensibility on Renaissance science.**
    - D: No. There is no mention of eschewing or rejecting traditional education. Furthermore, there is no direct connection made in the passage between purity of language and thought (paragraph 5), and the "pure pursuit of abstract beauty" cited in the question.

41. B    This is a Retrieval/EXCEPT question.
    Note: The correct answer will be a statement that does NOT pertain to the Renaissance conception of form.
    - A: No. In paragraph 2, the author describes how traditional content was expressed in a new form during the early part of the Renaissance era.
    - **B: Yes. The primacy of form could be demonstrated in *practically* every intellectual field (beginning of paragraph 3), not every field.**
    - C: No. The passage describes the effect of form on both poetry (paragraph 3) and painting (paragraphs 1 and 2).
    - D: No. The author describes lyrical poetry as "the most potent vehicle of the new will to form" (first half of paragraph 3).

# Passage VIII
This is a Later passage.

**Bottom Line:** Impressionists, epitomized by Monet, sought to capture fleeting moment.

42. B    This is an Inference question.
    - A: No. The painting's title was the inspiration for the name "Impressionism," not the source of the actual movement; the school or style of painting already existed.
    - **B: Yes. The name of the painting became the name of the school of painting (paragraph 5).**
    - C: No. There is no mention of winning or losing in this context.
    - D: No. If we substitute "collective" for "eponym," the sentence becomes nonsensical.

43. D    This is a Weaken question.
         Note: The correct answer will be inconsistent with the passage.
    A:   No. The seventh paragraph describes Monet's creation of the "series" as a way of portray-
         ing a "succession of elusive moments." We know from the previous paragraph that Monet
         himself sometimes only painted for fifteen minutes a day on a canvas. However, if some
         other Impressionists had a different approach, it would have no direct impact on the
         author's argument about Monet's series.
    B:   No. This is consistent with the author's description of the series as a way of reconciling
         the "laborious painter and the instant impression of the eye (paragraph 7).
    C:   No. The sixth paragraph states that he sometimes only painted for fifteen minutes at a
         time on a particular canvas. The statement that he never finished a painting in under
         fifteen minutes has no effect on the author's description of Monet's series in paragraph
         seven.
    **D:**   **Yes. The author claims that the series were a way of capturing the "instant impression
         of the eye" (paragraph 7). If Monet worked almost exclusively from memory, it would
         cast doubt on this point.**

44. C    This is a New Information question.
    A:   No. The passage states that Monet sometimes painted multiple pictures of the same scene
         even in his early years (paragraph 7).
    B:   No. The author mentions in paragraph 7 that Monet sometimes painted more than one
         version of a scene early in his career. The series were extensive collections of scenes of the
         same subject under a great variety of conditions. The discovery mentioned in the ques-
         tion would have no impact on the author's claim that the series was a new epic form.
    **C:**   **Yes. This would provide specific evidence supporting the author's statement in the
         middle of the seventh paragraph.**
    D:   No. This discovery would be entirely consistent with the author's conception (paragraph
         7), and no conflicting conceptions are mentioned.

45. A    This is a Structure question.
    **A:**   **Yes. The author writes that the "unpredictable sun, clouds, rain, and fog transform
         the sky at its sea reflections from moment to moment" (paragraph 2). This description
         mirrors the author's discussion of the key aspects of Monet's later work, including his
         desire to capture the world of the "evanescent moment" in changing states of water
         (paragraph 5).**
    B:   No. Monet appreciated the weather and attempted to capture it (paragraphs 5 and 7); he
         disliked school and wished to escape it (paragraph 2).
    C:   No. The author does not suggest that Monet chose harbor scenes as subjects later in life
         because of his exposure to the Normandy weather as a child.
    D:   No. Monet may have appreciated the weather, but the author does not suggest that the
         opinions of those who experience it as "painful" should be rejected.

46. D     This is a New Information question.

Note: The correct answer will be the choice that least supports and is least relevant to the statement in the question.

A:     No. A blurred photo of an object in motion captures a fleeting moment in time. This corresponds to Monet's quest to portray a momentary perception or visual sensation.

B:     No. The photograph captures a split-second in time, just as Monet wished to capture the evanescent moment.

C:     No. The blurred photo is created by a split-second impression of light on film; Monet attempted to capture a momentary impression of light on canvas.

D:     **Yes. Monet's series are inspired by his desire to portray a succession of moments through time rather than a single fleeting impression of light. This choice least supports the claim that photography affected Monet's work.**

47. A     This is a New Information question.

A:     **Yes. Monet was driven to capture the momentary impressions of light as experienced by the eye as best he could on the static surface of the canvas (paragraph 7).**

B:     No. The author gives no evidence that Monet felt excluded or isolated in any way.

C:     No. He saw school as a prison to be escaped; however, he wished to capture, not escape from his visual experiences. This is a too literal reading of the word "prisoner" in the question.

D:     No. No such impatience is described.

# Passage IX

This is a Now passage.

**Bottom Line:** Similarities and differences between myth and fairly tales; both embody cultural values and experience.

48. C     This is a Main Point question.

A:     No. Fables are related to fairy tales only in the last paragraph. This choice is too narrow to be the main purpose of the passage. Be careful not to fall for Decoy Attractors that tempt you based on echoing what you just read at the end of the passage; remember also to always summarize the passage's Bottom Line for yourself before starting the questions.

B:     No. This passage is descriptive, not persuasive. In any case, the sixth and seventh paragraphs indicate that the author favors fairy tales over myths, at least for children: the author is not specifically promoting reading myths to children.

C:     **Yes. The author begins in the first paragraph by discussing how some cultures equate them and others distinguish them from each other. The rest of the passage describes some ways in which fairy tales and myths are similar (for example, both take on definitive form only when written down, and both embody "the cumulative experience of a society) and other ways in which they are different (for example, myths are more likely to present a "culture hero," and fairy tales are more likely to suggest how conflicts might be resolved).**

D:     No. The passage is about fairy tales as well as myths. This answer choice is too narrow.

**266** | © TPR Education IP Holdings, LLC

49.   A      This is a Retrieval question.

      **A:**    **Yes. The author states that these stories "form the literature of preliterate societies"**
              **(paragraph 1), and that "before being written down [they] were elaborated...over the**
              **centuries" (paragraph 2). Be careful not to misinterpret paragraph 2 when it states**
              **that "myths and fairy tales alike attain a definite form only when they are committed**
              **to writing" to mean that they did not exist prior to being written down. Clearly, they**
              **must have already existed.**

      B:      No. The early stories were modified to suit their audiences, but the author states that they
              were first oral, not written (paragraph 2). This choice reverses that by stating that they
              were originally written rather than oral.

      C:      No. The author never identifies one form as always preceding the other.

      D:      No. The author mentions German, French, and English fairy tales, but does not suggest
              that they were all written first in German. Make sure to check back to the passage for
              details like this.


50.   D      This is an Inference question.

      A:      No. The author describes myths and fairy tales as "purveyors of deep insights that have
              sustained mankind" (paragraph 3), and writes that "men" (humanity) wish this wisdom
              to be passed on to future generations. However, no indication is ever made that children
              desire to attain this knowledge.

      B:      No. The author claims that the early tales might have reflected their eras (paragraph 2),
              but not that the current tales transmit knowledge about historical origins.

      C:      No. The author writes that fairy tales subtly "suggest" solutions to conflicts and human
              development, but that they make no demands on their listeners, and thus children never
              "feel compelled to act in specific ways" (paragraph 6). The words "explicit" and "never fail"
              make this choice too strong.

      **D:**    **Yes. The passage states that fairy tales "suggest ever so subtly how...conflicts may be**
              **solved" (paragraph 6). This can be inferred to be equivalent to "obstacles faced in life."**


51.   B      This is an Inference/EXCEPT question.
              Note: The credited response will NOT be given in the passage as an important purpose
              of myth.

      A:      No. Paragraph 5 tells us that myths can express and solve inner conflicts.

      **B:**    **Yes. "Natural phenomena" are not mentioned.**

      C:      No. Myths present the hero as superhuman and as a figure to be emulated (paragraphs 4
              and 5).

      D:      No. In the third paragraph, the author elaborates on the role of myths (and fairy tales) to
              convey a culture's heritage.

52.  A      This is an Inference question.

      A:     **Yes. The author writes that they attain their final form only when written down (paragraph 2).**

      B:     No. The author never claims that one form predates the other. The first sentence of paragraph 3 states that some fairy tales evolved from myths and others were incorporated into them.

      C:     No. While fairy tales today do "personify and illustrate inner conflicts" (paragraph 6), the passage gives no evidence that the written tales change over time to reflect changes in the audience. It was the oral fairy tales, before they were ever written down, that would change from telling to telling based on the audience (paragraph 2).

      D:     No. The author claims that the early tales might have been modified to reflect the special problems of an era; this is not the same as incorporating historical events. This choice takes the information in paragraph 2 too far by interpreting it too literally.

53.  C      This is a Specific Tone/Attitude question.

      A:     No. The only possibly negative thing he says is that the English and French *names* for fairy tales are misleading (paragraph 1).

      B:     No. "Patronizing" means being condescending, while the author is quite respectful and admiring of fairy tales.

      C:     **Yes. See especially paragraph 6.**

      D:     No. The author clearly admires and appreciates fairy tales (paragraphs 6 and 7). Note that the author calls them "love-gifts to a child," which is not a particularly impartial or neutral description. Impartial indicates that the author has no personal opinion.